The Word Processor
and
The Writing Teacher

The Word Processor
and
The Writing Teacher

Linda Roehrig Knapp

A Reston Book
Prentice-Hall, Inc.
Englewood Cliffs, New Jersey 07632

Library of Congress Cataloging in Publication Data

Knapp, Linda Roehrig.
  The word processor and the writing teacher.

  1. English language—Rhetoric—Study and teaching—
Data processing. 2. English language—Composition and
exercises—Study and teaching—Data processing. 3. Word
processing. 4. Computer-assisted instruction. I. Title.
PE1404.K57 1986   808'.042'02854   85-2178
ISBN 0-8359-8828-7

©1986 by Prentice-Hall, Inc.
Englewood Cliffs, New Jersey

A Reston Book
Published by Prentice-Hall, Inc.
A Division of Simon & Schuster, Inc.
·Englewood Cliffs, New Jersey

Printed in the United States of America

Apple® IIc is a registered trademark of Apple Computer, Inc.

AppleWorks™ is a trademark of Apple Computer, Inc.

AppleWriter™ is a trademark of Apple Computer, Inc.

Bank Street Writer™ is a trademark of Broderbund Software, Inc.

Homeword™ is a trademark of Sierra OnLine

KIDWRITER™ is a trademark of Spinnaker Software Corporation

Kidtalk™ is a registered trademark of First Byte

MacPaint™ and MousePaint™ are trademarks of Apple Computer, Inc.

Magic Slate™ is a trademark of Sunburst Communications, Inc.

Master Type™ is a trademark of Scarborough Systems

MaxThink™ is a trademark of Neil Larsen

MicroType, The Wonderful World of PAWS™ is a trademark of Southwestern Publishing Co.

Micrographix Series™ is a trademark of Jostens Yearbook Publishing Company

Microzine™ is a registered trademark of Scholastic, Inc.

QUILL™ is a trademark of DCH Educational Software

SmoothTalker™ is a trademark of First Byte

Story Maker: A Fact and Fiction Tool Kit™ is a trademark of Scholastic, Inc.

Story Tree™ is a trademark of Scholastic, Inc.

The Milliken Word Processor™ is a trademark of Milliken Publishing Company

The Writing Workshop™ is a trademark of Milliken Publishing Company

ThinkTank™ is a trademark of Living Videotext

Twistaplot™ is a registered trademark of Scholastic, Inc.

Type Attack™ is a trademark of Sirius Software

Typing Tutor™ is a trademark of Texas Instruments, Inc.

Unix™ is a trademark of AT&T Bell Laboratories

VersaBraille™ is a trademark of Telesensory Systems, Inc.

Visualtek® is a registered trademark of Visualtek, Inc.

WizType™ is a registered trademark of Sierra On Line

WordStar® is a registered trademark of MicroPro International

Writer's Workbench™ is a trademark of AT&T Bell Laboratories

Zork™ is a trademark of Infocom, Inc.

To Michael
Justin and Molly . . .

who have sometimes had to
tickle
me away
from working on
this book.

CONTENTS

Chapter 5

WRITING ACTIVITIES FOR SECONDARY AND JUNIOR COLLEGE STUDENTS

PREFACE

This is a book for writing teachers. In a sense, any teacher who consistently puts effort into helping students improve their writing is a writing teacher. *The Word Processor and the Writing Teacher* addresses teachers at the elementary through junior college level and focuses on helping them acquire practical information, skills, and techniques concerning the teaching of writing with word processing.

Chapters 1, 2, and 3, for instance, introduce arguments regarding the value of using word processing to teach writing; the equipment and skills needed to begin teaching with word processing; and a variety of teaching techniques that can be effectively used with word processing. Chapters 4 and 5 offer a number of specific classroom activities for teaching composition with word processing. Chapters 6 and 7 cover more specialized areas, including using word processing to produce student publications (Chapter 6) and to help students with special needs (Chapter 7). Chapter 8 presents a panoramic view of other types of writing software that's available, and concludes with a glimpse of current and continuing trends concerning computers and the teaching of writing.

The Word Processor and the Writing Teacher is written for teachers who have never even seen a word processing program, as well as seasoned computer users who have already begun teaching with word processing. Since the book begins with the most rudimentary information, readers are encouraged to skim or skip over sections that present material they already know.

Theories and Assumptions About Teaching Writing

After studying theories of education at college or graduate school, and then wrestling with those theories in the classroom, teachers often develop a more pragmatic set of principles and techniques concerning how they can best help kids learn to write. Well, so have I. Graduate school and at least a dozen years of experimenting with various teaching techniques and curricula have led me to form some basic assumptions about the teaching of writing. These assumptions are gradually revealed in the words and between the lines throughout this book. However, for readers who prefer to have the author's pedagogical principles stated at the beginning, so they can peruse the book with these biases in mind, the rest of the preface lays out this author's particular assumptions about the teaching of writing.

Writing Skills

Two distinct kinds of skills need to be learned in order to become a good writer: composition skills and editing skills. Although writers sometimes use them simultaneously, the skills are nevertheless quite different.

Composition skills are the skills writers need to draft a meaningful and coherent piece of writing. In order to learn these skills students need to practice composing paragraphs and longer written assignments, often. They also need to receive frequent and consistent responses to their writing from other readers, and this feedback should focus primarily on improving the writing rather than criticizing it. In addition, writers need to be permitted and encouraged to write about topics that are important to them personally.

Editing skills include the ability to identify problems in a piece of writing and the ability to propose ways to improve it. Effective editors can detect problems on all levels of writing from grammar and mechanics to general organization and style. In order to edit one's own and others' writing successfully, students need to acquire a working knowledge of basic language skills such as spelling, grammar, and mechanics. These skills are explained in the many grammar and style books that are found in most language arts classrooms. Students also need frequent practice editing their own and others' papers in order to become proficient.

In the traditional method of teaching writing, students typically are introduced to one or two basic skills in a lesson and are then asked to perform short exercises to practice the skills. These exercises are isolated from any meaningful piece of writing composed by the student. Later, when students do write complete reports, essays, and compositions, they usually make very little connection between the basic skills that they studied as a separate activity, and the composition process. In addition, when students compose longer writing assignments, the teacher is typically the person who reviews and edits them; thus, the teacher is the only one who is likely to develop good editing skills.

The method of teaching writing presented in this book focuses on students composing meaningful pieces of writing often, and learning to locate and remedy all levels of problems in their writing. This method treats the act of writing as a multi-step "process" which includes plan-

ning, composing, and revising. The revising process is often the most important, and it typically involves editing and rewriting two or more
drafts.

Constructive Criticism

Writers need regular feedback from others about their writing—feedback
that is constructive and encouraging, and that goes below the surface
level of grammar and mechanics. Classmates can provide this kind of
help for one another in peer editing groups. In small groups of two to
four individuals, students can effectively critique each member's work
and offer suggestions for revisions. Besides receiving useful comments
and suggestions concerning their work, students can also strengthen
their basic skills and pick up new skills from classmates in this kind of
workshop environment. Such groups can quite successfully supplement
the teacher's role as writing critic and tutor.

Audience

Writers need an audience for their writing in order to keep them motivated. Class and/or school publications are one good way to inspire students to produce their best work, strive to perfect it even further, and
then feel a sense of accomplishment when their writing is published.

Other ways to provide an audience for student writers include reading papers out loud to the class and posting them in the classroom,
sharing papers informally among classmates in peer editing groups, and
presenting students' writing as models to follow when doing particular
writing assignments.

How These Assumptions Relate
to Word Processing

The real challenge for writing teachers is to figure out ways to use word
processing to improve the teaching of writing. It is not enough simply to
rearrange the classroom furniture and modify teaching methods to accommodate computers in the classroom. What's much more important is
to rethink, replan, and rewrite the course curriculum to make the best
possible use of what word processing offers writers and writing teachers.
For instance, teachers traditionally treat writing as a single-draft process—students pass in papers, teachers read and grade them, pass them
back, and that's it until the next paper is assigned. Few teachers regularly require students to revise and rewrite second and third drafts of
their papers, largely because recopying or retyping revised drafts is a
long and boring task—certainly too time-consuming to use up precious

class time. As a result, the whole editing and revising phase of writing that professional writers claim is so vital, has received little attention or value in school. In fact, kids often feel insulted when they're asked to revise, recopy, and resubmit a paper, as if it were a punishment put upon them by a malevolent dictator.

Now, with word processing available, the task of recopying revised drafts is as simple as entering the program's print command. With this advantage, teachers can place legitimate emphasis on the editing and revising phase of the writing process, without having to sacrifice other important objectives or activities in the writing curriculum. What remains for teachers to do is to de-emphasize one-draft writing and place a much stronger emphasis on teaching revising and rewriting skills. If teachers can do this successfully, students' attitudes toward revising their writing, as well as their writing skills, will improve.

But . . . the problem of student access to word processors must be resolved before teachers can be expected to fully integrate the new tool into the writing curriculum. How can a word processor be a writing tool if there aren't enough computers available for students to use one often? The solution involves two stages. First, if there aren't a sufficient number of computers, students can use the word processor primarily as an editing tool. It is still worth the effort to use the tool in this way. Even if students don't have enough time to compose on it, they can enter their handwritten drafts and enjoy the benefits of peer editing help, easy revising, and instant printing of as many drafts as they can revise. The second stage will come later, when the school acquires more computers, or more students obtain home computers. Then, students will also be able to compose on the word processor, and at that point the word processor will be the ultimate writing tool.

Linda Roehrig Knapp
Palo Alto, California

The Word Processor
and
The Writing Teacher

Chapter 1

THE WHAT, WHY, AND WHICH
OF WORD PROCESSING

What is Word Processing?

Special machines called *word processors* have been around for a "long" time, at least a couple of decades, anyway. Most of us didn't hear much about them in the 1970s because the early ones were too expensive for most individuals or schools to buy. Nevertheless, word processing systems were used in many corporate offices years before microcomputers with word processing programs captured the public spotlight in the early 1980s.

The original word processors such as Wang and Lanier were designed to do one thing—word processing. In business, the common practice was to place individual units in different offices that were all linked to a central word processing system. These specialized machines were, and still are, very powerful and efficient—quite capable of handling the rivers of text produced by big corporations.

The word processor that's the hero of this book, however, is just a floppy disk that goes into a microcomputer. The software program on that disk directs the microcomputer to function as a word processor. It's easy to use once you learn how. It's efficient. It's even affordable. Although word processing programs are not as powerful as the specialized giants, they are certainly as muscular as most of us will ever need. Microcomputers with word processing software are the kind of word processing systems that are now widely used by individuals, schools, and small businesses.

One reason a microcomputer system with word processing software approaches the affordable for schools and even individuals is that it's so practical. Spending a couple thousand dollars for a single-purpose tool is extravagant for most of us, but the microcomputer can be used for many other functions besides word processing. Just remove the word processing disk and load (insert) another program. An enormous variety of educational programs, applications or tool programs, and games, as

1

well as programming languages such as Logo, Pascal, and BASIC, are available on disk and are commonly used in schools.

When a word processing program is loaded in the microcomputer, the user (a person who is operating the system) enters text, almost like typing on a typewriter. Once text has been entered, the user can employ the word processor's text editing capability to manipulate the text in a variety of ways. The text and the changes the user is making are constantly visible on the computer screen. For example, by using the program's text editor a user can:

- Erase characters and blocks of text
- Insert characters and blocks of text
- Switch the order of characters
- Move around whole blocks of text
- Change the spelling of a word, or change the whole word, and direct the editor to make that change throughout the text
- Save the text
- Save the revised text by overwriting the original draft or by storing it separately (which saves both drafts)
- Direct the printer to print out the text

Let's suppose, for example, that you drafted a letter with pencil and paper and are now entering it onto a word processing system. One thing you'll notice right away is that when you get to the end of a line, you don't have to push a carriage return key; the text automatically jumps down to the next line. This feature, called *word wrap*, is quite a surprise the first time you see it happening on the screen.

As you type along, you may make a few typing errors. Instead of getting out the whiteout liquid or tape, with many word processing programs you simply back up the cursor (the flashing marker that points out where you are in the text) to the spot, erase the error with a keystroke, and type in the correct letter. If the whole word needs alteration, you delete it electronically and enter the new. If you add several words, pushing the text over so that it exceeds the right margin, in most word processing programs the paragraph readjusts automatically.

You've finished typing the letter and discover that the content of the third paragraph is important and really belongs at the beginning. With many word processing programs you simply mark the beginning and end of the paragraph and move the cursor to the spot where you wish to place the paragraph. There, with a keystroke or two, you make it instantly appear. In fact, you can make it appear in as many places as you wish, so maybe you'll decide to try it in several spots before making a final decision.

At this point you're beginning to grow attached to the letter and decide to send it to one or two other people besides Donna Dandy. With the search and replace feature, you can direct the computer to replace *Donna* with *Susan*, for example, everywhere it occurs in the letter. You can add or subtract parts of the letter to personalize it and then print out another letter specifically for Susan.

But, before you print anything, you may choose to use a spelling checker program if you have one that's compatible with your word processing program. A spelling checker will check every word in your letter with its internal dictionary. All the words that it doesn't recognize, including misspelled words, typos, proper names, slang, etc., can then be presented to you one by one. You direct it to ignore the words you want to leave unchanged, correct the ones that are misspelled (you have to enter the correct spelling), and add to the internal dictionary any unrecognized words you want it to remember. Some spelling checkers will also help you correct the misspelled words; when the program displays a misspelled word, you direct it to search its dictionary for words that look similar to the incorrect one, and the program will offer a few choices. Frequently the correct word is one of those choices.

Now you're almost ready to print. Do you want the letter to have normal typewriter style ragged right margins, or right and left justified (straight) margins? You choose. Do you want single spaced lines, double, triple? How about page numbers at the bottom of the page? Once all the format commands (which determine how the printed text will look) are entered, press the keys that instruct the system to begin printing.

These are just a few of the feats that a person can accomplish with a word processing program. Its biggest boon for writers is that it's possible to revise drafts over and over without having to retype the whole thing. A writer can even complete several drafts of a piece before printing it. Then, finally, when he's satisfied that the text reads well and has been adequately proofread, the printing begins. If he enters all the instructions correctly and the system is working properly, the final printout will look just fine.

Why Use Word Processing to Help Teach Writing?

The Arguments

"So what if a word processor can make writing easier," someone protests, "I'm not so sure that's an asset for students anyway. Will using that machine really make kids' writing BETTER? That's what I want to know."

Popular Arguments For Using Word Processing

Teachers who use word processing in the classroom say *yes*. They say their students make more corrections and general improvements than they did before. They say kids take more care in writing and revising their work when they don't have to recopy or retype each draft.

When writing with pen and paper, students have to choose between making corrections and handing in a messy paper with things crossed out, over-written, and inserted, or making minimal corrections and handing in a paper that is unrevised, but clean and readable. Few kids take the time to recopy corrected papers. If, however, they write one draft on a word processor, they can easily make all kinds of revisions before printing out a polished, final copy.

An added bonus for students is seeing their final papers look so professional. This alone is an ego boost that spurs them to work hard and be prolific with the word processor.

When writers use the word processor to compose first drafts, they have an even more powerful writing tool. They can let thoughts and words flow freely without having to worry about neatness, accuracy, or general organization. This, plus the added advantage of being free to start writing in the middle or anywhere they please, provides excellent relief from the "fear of the blank page" syndrome that some writers experience. With a word processor writers can get their ideas down first, then go back to organize, clarify, and refine sentence structure.

Okay, these are indeed arguments that could indicate to many doubters that the word processor is an extremely efficient writing tool which makes revising and reworking much easier, and probably more fun—but what about *better*? A few critics are still not convinced that after using a word processor for a year, Johnny will write *better* essays.

It's true, of course, that no tool can magically make a person's writing better, but it can help. In this case the word processor helps young writers make the improvements that they've learned how to make. Poor writing is often a result of not practicing what's been learned—kids don't have enough time or incentive to practice. The word processor, however, enables writers to practice what they've learned without the boring "busywork" of recopying. And it provides incentive to keep practicing when students see embarrassing mistakes and sloppy first drafts vanish, replaced by a tidy, printed page.

Teachers still have to teach *how* to write, and students still have to *try* to improve their writing. The word processing tool simply gives them both a much better chance to be successful.

Popular Arguments Against Using Word Processing

It's too expensive. You can't possibly teach writing with word processing if there aren't enough computers to go around, and what school can afford enough of them? It's too complicated for teachers to learn to use, let alone teach their students. Even after everyone learns the basic procedures, they're still faced with the hassles of losing text, damaging disks, and being confronted by endless equipment problems that constantly interfere with teaching and learning to write.

Microcomputers in schools are just a fad, a few critics still persist. They're a waste of money and will eventually land in a storage room along with broken projectors and neglected TV sets.

Critics argue that word processing won't improve students' writing skills, and worse, that it can deter the learning of certain skills. For example, children who write using a keyboard instead of pencil and paper will not get enough practice in developing legible handwriting. Critics fear that poor spelling will become an even greater problem than it is now because students will rely on spelling checker programs. (It's typically the critics who mistakenly believe that these programs will automatically correct students' spelling errors.)

Some of the most fiery arguments against word processing come from people who have the least amount of understanding about how microcomputers work. They fear that computers might replace teachers in the classroom, and that computers are too smart and will do too much for the student. For example, one computer center director reported the following experience:

> One afternoon an English teacher stormed into the center waving a student's paper done on a word processor. She threw it on the desk saying, "How am I supposed to grade this?"
> "What's the problem?" asked the somewhat confused center director, as she glanced over the computer-printed essay.
> The teacher, shaking her finger at the paper, retorted, "How can I tell how much the student did, and how much the computer did?"

Arguments Stronger Than Opinion

Even those teachers who are convinced that the word processor is a valuable tool for teaching writing sometimes face obstacles that can block the way to effective teaching with this new tool. Inadequate equipment is one. Trying to use word processing on computers with little memory (less than 48K) or with tape-based storage, often results in such problems as lost text, limited storage for files, and slow processing. Students' lack of typing skills is another problem. Not enough computers for students to be able to use one when they need it, is still another. The rigidity of schedules in secondary schools, where class periods are short and the computer center has to be shared by the entire faculty, can present obstacles so difficult to overcome that many teachers who would love to use word processing throw up their hands in frustration and give up.

What This Writing Tool Can Do

Using word processing in the classroom is still quite new so there is little comprehensive research data to *prove* its effectiveness as a teaching and learning tool. The pioneer research that has been done, however, indicates that students write differently and teachers teach differently when word processing is added to the curriculum.

The Word Processor as a Writing Tool

Seventh and eighth grade students involved in a recent research study at Stanford University reportedly made three times more changes in their written work when using a word processor than when writing with pencil and paper.* The changes were mostly at the word level, but even those were seldom made with pencil and paper, according to the study. Time wasn't a factor in the number of revisions students made, either. In both the handwritten and word processed writing assignments, students had more than enough time to complete and revise their papers. They actually chose to revise more with a word processing program.

What's particularly interesting in this study is that students composing on a word processor made 91 percent of their revisions as they were composing, compared to 75 percent when using pencil and paper. This indicates that with a word processor, student writers are more likely to play around with the wording of their sentences and watch the meaning evolve as they write. In this way they begin to see language as malleable, and composing and revising become more closely integrated within the writing process, rather than always isolated into separate stages. Nevertheless, writers who choose to compose a first draft without stopping, and then return to revise it later, can complete the whole process much more efficiently with word processing.

Another notable finding of the Butler-Nalin study is that 78 percent of the junior high school students involved said they preferred composing on the keyboard to using pencil and paper. This is directly opposed to what some older students and adults have said. Perhaps the more a person gets accustomed to writing with pencil and paper, the more difficult it becomes to change that habit. The reverse is probably true, too.

One nationally known educator/writer, Henry F. Olds, Jr., has said this about his experience with using word processing:

> After a little more than a year of using a text processor for almost everything I write, I no longer write or think about things I write about in the same way. I truly do word process in my head. An example—we are familiar with the feeling of tak-

*Kay Butler-Nalin, "Process and Product: How Research Methodologies and Composing Using a Computer Influence Writing," Unpublished Doctoral Dissertation (Stanford, CA: Stanford University, 1985).

ing out a fresh, clean piece of paper and sitting down to write something. "How do I begin?" we think. Four hours later we may still be thinking about how to begin. The sense that writing is a linear process is so deeply embedded in our consciousness that we are almost totally convinced that the writing of something must start with a beginning. A year of text processing has completely changed my writing consciousness—I no longer start with beginnings because I have become aware that I rarely know what the formal structure of what I want to say should be before I have tried to say it. With the text processor, I can easily merge form and content once my vision is clear. So, freed from premature concerns for the form of things, I can proceed with setting down whatever I want to say.

Writing now, as never before, has become a mode of discovery. I see no reason why my experience, which seems not to be uncommon among other users I have talked with, would not be shared by students who have the opportunity to use a text processor for their written work. Might it not be the case that a large number of students would find writing with a text processor far easier and more pleasurable than either longhand or typing? Might it be that a large number of writing problems would disappear when much of the pain was removed from the task?

As a professional writer, I know that excellence in writing requires hard work. It is a craft—sometimes an art—that demands great energy and attention. But hard work comes only after the joy of it has been discovered. If in the beginning there is only hard work and no joy—the current status of most writing instruction—there will be very little writing of any reasonable quality. I believe that putting text editors in the hands of students can start the writing process in the appropriate place—with the joy of creation and the wonder of discovery.*

Research done at the Bank Street Writing Project, Center for Children and Technology at the Bank Street College of Education in New York, indicates that kids enjoy doing their work on a word processor. The novelty of it entices them to produce more and longer compositions. But, over time, old problems resurface as the excitement wears off. A fair number of students do retain their enthusiasm, however, and those students do make considerable progress.

What all this means is that even without the direct supervision of a teacher, students who have learned to use a word processor can make some improvements in their writing with this tool. Because it eliminates the time-consuming work of recopying, writers are more willing to correct errors and attempt all levels of revisions. Aided by word processing, many also write more often and at greater length because they find it easier and more fun. Add to this the incentive of an attractive printed page, and the motivation increases even more to apply what they've learned about good writing and produce a better product independently.

The Word Processor as a Teaching Tool

Teachers who use word processing in the classroom gradually discover a variety of ways to employ it as a handy teaching tool. One of the greatest

---

*from "CCN Forum: Word Processing How Will It Shape the Student as a Writer?" *Classroom Computer News*, Nov/Dec 1982. Reprinted by permission from Pitman Learning, Inc., and Henry F. Olds, Jr.

Figure 1.1 Teacher using a large-screen projection system as an electronic blackboard. *(Courtesy of VIVID Systems, Inc.)*

advantages of having word processing equipment in the classroom is being able to use the video screen as an "electronic blackboard." With this teaching tool, it's possible to demonstrate all stages of writing from creating an outline to making final revisions before printing. For example, let's say a teacher enters the first paragraph of a student essay that's already been drafted. Students can all participate in the critiquing and editing process. As the class works on expanding and revising parts of the text, the teacher enters their suggestions. In this way they can all immediately observe how well their suggestions work. Teachers can normally type faster than they can write with chalk, and on this electronic blackboard all kinds of changes can be made and observed instantly. It's much more effective than using a chalkboard, ditto sheets, workbooks, or the overhead projector.

If your school can obtain a large screen projection system such as the one pictured in Figure 1.1, the entire class can view one screen. Alternatively, two (or more) video monitors can be connected to a computer, enabling students to view the screen that is located closest to them in the classroom.

Almost any method of teaching writing can be improved with the help of word processing. When, for example, the teacher is teaching writing as a building process, she may begin with a key idea or topic sentence and then add supportive information. This method is particularly effective with word processing because it's possible to demonstrate the building process in action; on the electronic blackboard students can watch the entire writing process develop. After participating in this kind of teacher-directed writing experience, students understand better how to approach their own writing.

Here's another example. If you teach brainstorming as a preliminary activity in the process of writing, the word processor enhances this method too. You can use the word processor to store all the spontaneous ideas that come forth during a classroom brainstorming session about a particular topic. Ask students to organize the ideas in logical patterns and use the word processor to rearrange the original entries into their suggested groups and order of presentation. The result will be an informal outline for a coherently structured theme. Practice this process with the whole class a few times and then let them try it.

Teachers can also use the word processor for student writing conferences (see Fig. 1.2). Together student and teacher sit at the computer screen and review a recent assignment. As they discuss its problems the teacher may, for example, explain certain writing skills and offer suggestions. At the same time the writer can make corrections, indicating whether she's understood the teacher's explanations. When this kind of conference is over, the writer goes away with a final draft that has been

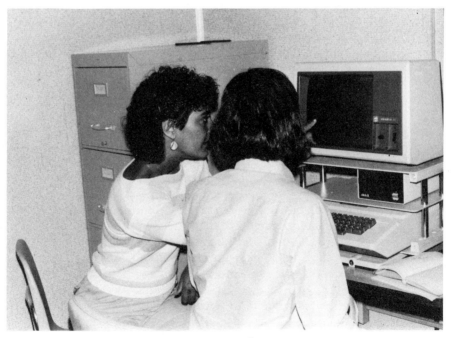

Figure 1.2 A writing conference in progress.

revised by the writer and approved by the teacher, instead of a paper full of red-penciled remarks that must be attended to at a later time. (Chapter 3 presents many more possible methods of teaching with word processing.)

Most teachers discover rather quickly that they can expect better quality written work when their students use word processors. It takes a significant amount of time for students to recopy or retype their papers, so sympathetic teachers often try to minimize the editing and revising steps of the writing process. But with word processing, teachers can give these steps a legitimate emphasis, helping students learn revision skills and the importance of perfecting their work.

An added bonus for teachers is the joy of facing an armful of very readable computer-printed papers as opposed to a pile of handwritten ones. No matter how much a teacher may deny having any bias against poor handwriting when dealing with written content, students will clearly get a fair deal when the printing looks the same.

What Kind of Word Processing Program is Best for Student Writers?

Should kids learn on a powerful "adult" word processor, such as Word-Star® and AppleWriter™ or on one developed specifically for young people, such as Bank Street Writer™ and The Milliken Word Processor™. The advocates on both sides are adamant.

Adult Word Processing Programs

Those who favor an adult word processor say it's important that a full, powerful word processing program be used in school settings because it avoids the problem of having some groups of students using one word processor, other groups of older students using another, and staff using still another. If a school chooses one word processor that's capable enough for students, teachers, and administrative staff to use, everyone will ultimately benefit from the school-wide compatibility of writing equipment. Students will benefit by learning to use an adult writing tool because it will also be useful to them outside the school environment.

Schools that use word processing to help create school newspapers, literary magazines, or yearbooks certainly will need some of the features that are only available in powerful word processing programs. However, students don't *have* to use all of these extra features, and teachers don't have to teach anything more than the simple text editing and printing commands until the students need them. The plus is that the features are there when they're needed, without buying a new word processing program and spending the extra hours learning how to use it.

Educators who advocate the use of adult word processing programs in school argue that by "hiding" the more advanced, fancier capabilities, teachers can simplify the word processor and make it easy for kids to learn. Teachers can also make learning easier by inventing little mnemonics to help kids remember the commands. For example, in the AppleWriter keystroke *Control-B* ("Beginning") makes the cursor jump to the beginning of the document, and *Control-E* ("End") makes the cursor jump to the end of the document. If young people with learning disabilities can learn it (and they have in many classrooms), then certainly children with normal learning ability can. In fact, in at least one school district, seventh and eighth graders earned money for their school by teaching an adult word processing system—WordStar—to adults.

Word Processing Programs for Young Writers

Educators on the other side argue that adult word processing programs have capabilities that most young writers will never need to use (e.g., indexing, footnoting, split screen editing), so why pay more for those extras and the added complexity of operation? They argue that a word processor designed for young writers more successfully deals with their particular concerns. For example, a student writer should be able to learn about using the word processing program from the software itself—not from its manual. The word processing program should also help prevent students from accidentally erasing text by asking them if they're sure they want to erase. In addition, if the WRITE and EDIT modes (methods of operation) are separate so that a writer has to intentionally switch from one mode to another, it minimizes the chance of erasing text by a slip of the finger. The advocates of children's word processing programs say that commands should be continually visible on the screen, and they should be simple, one-keystroke commands. Word processing programs designed specifically for young users offer at least some of these special aids.

A few word processing programs, such as Magic Slate™ and The Writer's Assistant offer three different levels of use so that students can grow into the program's more advanced features. Versatile programs like these can provide young writers with a simple word processor and older students, faculty, and staff with a compatible, adult word processor, thus satisfying many of the requirements of educators on both sides of the debate.

A Few Words About Limited Systems

TELEVISION SCREENS: Television screens generally don't have sharp enough resolution to produce clear, easily readable characters. They are acceptable for displaying graphics and tolerable for use with software that displays little text. But, when the user has to read large amounts of text on the screen, as with word processing, a television screen is definitely a disadvantage. The displayed text is often hazy and difficult to read, so reading it quickly becomes tiring and can even cause eye strain. It's rather like trying to read a very fuzzy copy from a ditto machine. Video screens that are specifically designed for computer use commonly produce sharper, more readable text.

CASSETTE AND CARTRIDGE STORAGE: Some schools have computers that store text and information on cassettes or cartridges instead of disks. Saving and retrieving text on these devices is far more time-consuming than using disks for text storage. In school environments where computer time is almost always limited, wasting precious minutes waiting for the cassette recorder to load or save students' work is extremely frustrating for everyone. It only takes a few seconds to do the same tasks with disk-based storage. The difference between minutes and seconds of waiting time adds up when dealing with thirty students working on thirty compositions.

Features to Consider when Choosing a Word Processing Program

The following characteristics are important to examine and consider carefully when shopping for word processing software.

Single Write-Edit Mode: It is much easier to write with a word processor that allows you to edit while you write. However, a few word processing programs separate these two functions, forcing the writer to purposely switch back and forth between WRITE and EDIT modes, which is frustrating and unnatural.

Text Display: Some weak word processing programs display all the text in upper-case letters, highlighting or otherwise indicating the letters that will be printed in upper case.

Some programs display edited paragraphs without reformatting them on screen, so that what the user sees is a tacky array of lines with gaps where words have been deleted and extended margins where text has been inserted.

Stronger programs reformat paragraphs immediately after insertions and deletions are made; some even indicate where each printed page will end. Some display the page just as it will look when printed ("what you see is what you get"). Most programs offer something in between.

Revising Text: Word processing programs enable you to revise text by overwriting existing characters, deleting as you go, or by inserting text and then deleting the unwanted characters. The *overwrite* method saves some time by automatically deleting as you revise. But the *insert* method enables you to compose a revision before you destroy the original, providing a safe back-up until the new version is in place. Some programs provide both overwrite and insert cursors, leaving the choice up to the user.

The *search and replace* feature, which replaces a word or phrase with another word or phrase throughout a file, is useful for professionals who have to keep numerous records and produce a continuous stream of similar reports and memos. It may not, however, be essential for student writers.

Deleting Text: A strong word processing program provides the means to delete by character, by word, by sentence, by paragraph, and by complete file, using one or two keystrokes. The weakest word processors only delete characters one at a time.

Moving Blocks of Text: Moving sentences, paragraphs, and larger areas of text to different parts of the document is a standard feature of most word processors. But some force you to split up large portions of text into smaller blocks and move each of them separately to the new location. The most powerful word processing programs allow you to transfer blocks of text (of almost any length) from one file to another easily and even to a file on another disk.

Cursor Movement: A user should be able to move the cursor easily over characters, back and forth across a line, and up and down the screen. You should also be able to skip over words, sentences, and paragraphs, hop to the beginning of a document, and to the end. Some word processors scroll horizontally to enable you to view text as it will be printed when the printed line is wider than the screen display.

Formatting Commands: Powerful word processing programs permit the user to make formatting choices both during the writing process (using embedded format commands) and just before printing (using format commands from a menu). *Embedded commands* enable you to change things such as line spacing and margins, anywhere within the document. But if, for example, you want to double-space a whole report, the *print* or *format menu* enables you to instruct the printer to double-space the entire document.

Formatting features such as variable line spacing, adjustable margins, page numbering, headers and footers, boldfacing, underlining, subscripts and superscripts, should all be available. Italics and foreign language symbols are even available on some.

Good quality printers can print boldface, subscripts, superscripts, and even italics and some foreign language symbols. However, a capable word processor is needed to be able to direct the printer to use them.

Printing Commands: A strong word processing program permits the user to stop and start the printing process mid-document, as well as print only a section from the middle.

HELP—Menus, Manual, Reference Card, Tutorial: Help menus should be easily available. The program manual should explain all aspects of using the word processor in clear, comprehensible detail. The information should be logically orgainzed and indexed for quick reference.

A separate, quick reference card that lists the commonly used commands is particularly helpful, especially for word processing programs that don't have help menus. (Teachers might even duplicate reference cards for each student, and laminate a few for classroom use.)

A *tutorial*, or "getting started" chapter, is essential for those who are new to word processing. Some packages even include a complete tutorial on a separate disk and/or audio tutorial on cassette.

If you purchase a package designed for school use, there are probably additional materials included (specifically designed for young people) that carefully explain how to use the word processor.

Safety and Convenience: It should not be easy for the user to lose text by accident. Some programs help prevent this by asking for a *yes* or *no* verification before executing any fatal *delete* commands. A yankback feature (retrieves text just deleted) can also prevent complete disaster.

For convenience, the most commonly used functions should be the simplest to execute, using one or two strokes on easy-to-reach keys.

Additional Features: A complete mail merge program is essential to many school administrative offices, but probably not for students, unless they are doing projects that involve mass mailing.

A compatible spelling checker program (which also points out typos) is a precious tool for teachers, administrators, and anyone else who doesn't have time for careful proofreading. You can, after all, own a spelling checker and still maintain control over who uses it and when. Keep in mind that today's spelling checker programs don't automatically correct spelling errors.

Information in this final section was taken from an article written by the author and published in *Electronic Learning*, March 1984.

Chapter 2

LEARNING TO USE THE TOOL:
TEACHERS AND STUDENTS

Teachers

Learning to use a word processor is as enchanting as beginning an exotic vacation . . . or as wrenching as facing the most arduous examination. You choose.

We'll imagine a word processor has been at the top of your wish list all year. Holiday season arrives, and someone is good to you! You open it up, plug it in, and it's the first day of your life in the Computer Age.

Before you electrocute yourself, however, better begin this adventure one step at a time. The first step is to pull the directions out of the carton and read how to connect the components (parts of the system) in order to create a functioning microcomputer system. With most personal computer systems these days it's not difficult, but it is important to plug the various cables into their proper places. The system package should (but don't assume that it does) come with all the paraphernalia needed to get started, and perhaps a tutorial disk that can help you figure out how to operate the system.

The basic system includes several components. The *Central Processing Unit (CPU)* is the guts of the computer. This essential unit executes instructions and controls the other computer operations. The *keyboard* is an input device, which means it receives information from a user and sends it to the CPU. One or two *disk drives* house and control the disks that are used to store programs, text, and so forth. The system's *video display screen* shows what's happening, or at least what the user needs to know.

The *printer* is an extra component that also plugs into the central computer. In school environments it's common for a class, or even a whole school, to share one printer. Be aware of the fact that printers need to be compatible with the computers to which they are attached; printers are not built to link up with any kind of computer. In addition, you'll need a cable and possibly other equipment to interface the computer to the printer. (Maybe you'll decide to save the printer installation for another time.)

Once the computer's cables are all connected and properly plugged, follow the directions in the manual to start up the system. If you're lucky, the procedure will be as simple as this example: Insert the tutorial disk that introduces you to the system. Turn on the master switch and close the disk drive door. The software will then teach you how to operate the microcomputer.

After you've progressed through the introductory disk, you're ready to begin word processing. Most microcomputers do not come with word processing software as part of the system package, so we'll assume that your generous benefactor purchased a word processing program, too! Word processing software comes with its own manual and start-up instructions, so better dig out this information now.

If there's a tutorial disk included in the software package, that's an easy way to get you acquainted with using the system as a word processor. If not, the manual probably has a tutorial section that will also take you step-by-step through all the word processing procedures. If the software package doesn't have either, complain to the company that puts out the product. However, that won't help you now. Spend today's energy fiddling with whatever you can glean from the manual. You probably can piece together enough to get started and perhaps tomorrow you can locate a self-teaching tutorial for this specific word processor in a computer store or bookstore. If not, ask at the store where you bought the software for the name of a satisfied customer.

Most word processing packages do come with self-teaching materials, however, so let's assume that you've spent some time systematically learning to use the program. A few hours of intimate interaction with the system will probably be enough to establish the basis for a lifelong relationship between you and the word processor.

Following is an example of one adult's somewhat frustrating initiation into computing and word processing. He describes his (and his family's) experience in a personal letter:

You can't imagine how long it has taken to write this letter.

First there was a dinner at Cathy and Rob's last fall when the talk turned to the possibility of using word processing to help kids learn to write.

Then there was your Christmas letter . . . same message . . . heightened interest.

Then there was Christmas. Unexpectedly, Lee's brother rendered his surplus Commodore 64 and disk drive. So home we came from Detroit with a computer.

Then came "Word Invaders" and "ZORK."™ After that we told Nathan no games until he learned to type. That went pretty quickly with the help of "Typing Tutor."™

Meanwhile, I began to get enthusiastic about the notion that maybe a word processor could actually lead me to write a letter—who knows how many friends there are out there to reestablish communication with.

Then came "Cut and Paste". A disaster. Every time we went to PRINT we got all the capital letters as italics and all the lower-case letters as capitals. Utter exasperation. (My opinion of computer manuals and instructions—every one I've ever seen—would automatically expletively delete on this computer.) So after a while we returned that program and got our money back. (Either the program was defective or the manual was, and I didn't need to decide which.) Then after a couple of weeks, "Homeword."™ Lee and I spent one long Saturday evening working on it. This time all the capital letters printed as lower-case and all the lower-case letters printed as capitals. Lee to the rescue, and hours later she had sorted out something to do with secondary access codes and lo-and-behold, it seemed to work!

This is my first letter. Since it's been six months in coming as an answer to your Christmas letter, the first thing is to say that we were sufficiently inspired by your account of your own initiation to computers to give it a try ourselves. More on a later occasion about what the addition of a computer and word processing actually means to us. In a nutshell, some disappointment in the seemingly low quality and high cost of most of what appears to be available in software for the kids; some encouragement from Nathan's receptivity to doing compositions for school (fourth grade level) and some letter writing . . .

Now, however, comes the challenge I dread. Can I figure out how to get this to FILE? Will it PRINT? Will the page breaks work? What if I need to get into EDIT? Then there is LAYOUT. Will this ever see the light of day? If you read this letter, that will be the only way to tell you that what needs to happen next will, in fact, be transcended. Here goes . . .

[It printed—in fact, the writer tried several format options and sent them all!]

You could—if that's all the time you can spare, and you're a bit of a daredevil—face the class with a rudimentary level of skill at word processing and begin teaching students. You'll develop the more advanced skills together and share the beginner's frustrations of losing text, or feeling like idiots because you can't get the program to underline or insert page numbers, or puzzling over error messages that may flash on the screen as the computer monster gobbles up somebody's precious work. Agonizing experiences such as these are an almost unavoidable part of the learning process. If a teacher goes through them before introducing a class to word processing, she might be able to reduce the disaster rate. But accidents will happen.

Learning to use a word processor is, in some ways, like learning to make a pie crust or bake bread. At first, no matter how precisely you follow the directions, things go wrong. The pie dough keeps cracking while you roll it out; the baked bread loaf slowly deflates as it cools, and you can't figure out why. But later, after time and practice, the crust rolls smooth and the bread domes elegantly. You practically can do no wrong, even with a little careless handling. Word processing is rather like cooking; anyone can learn—it just takes practice and time to become a master.

The recommended method is to develop your own cooking skill with this new appliance before you introduce it to a room full of student chefs. Spend a summer playing with it, a few months during the semester, or at least a couple of full weekends. Find other teachers (or non-teaching friends) who use the same type of computer and word processing program, and ask them for help and advice when you get stuck. Ask the local dealer. Find out if there's a toll-free phone number to call for help with your brand of computer system or word processing software.

Another route that numerous teachers take to enter the world of computers and word processing is to sign up for an introductory computing course. Computer dealers offer them; school districts offer them; communities offer them. If you prefer to learn with a group of other beginners, such a course might be the best answer. You can also join a computer club or user's group. There's bound to be one within reach that focuses on the brand of computer you're using. Ask at the local computer store for information on clubs in your area.

Once a teacher has learned the basic word processing procedures and has had a chance to practice and become comfortable using this tool, the next step is to bring the same skills to students in the classroom.

Teaching Your Students

Writing students will also have to spend a fair number of hours just learning word processing skills and becoming comfortable with the tool. Most kids enjoy using the word processor. Comments such as these are not unusual: "You can fix things right away and you don't get bored." "It's fun, and it's definitely changing my writing for the better." "I'm not sure my writing is any better, but I like it a lot because you can go back and change something without scribbling."

However, problems do occur when students are asked to learn to use the tool *at the same time* that they're expected to learn new writing skills. Some students complain mightily when faced with both pressures at once. Arguments like this are common: "In this class we're trying to learn word processing *and* how to write. It's too hard to learn both at once. I do want to learn word processing, though, because I think it will be very helpful. . . . Maybe having a specific time to learn without having to worry about a writing assignment would be good."

Attempting to teach new writing skills and new word processing skills simultaneously can be disastrous because the two sets of skills (writing skills and word processing skills) and the two sets of objectives (learning to write and learning to use a word processor) are set against each other, competing for class time and students' attention. Don't do it. While students are learning to use the new writing tool, keep the pressure off writing skills that will be part of the course grade. Kids are often so grade-conscious that they're likely to spend a lot of energy worrying about whether they'll be graded on machine skills or writing skills at the end of the term. If you keep the task of learning to use the word processing tool separate from learning to write, students are more likely to have a relaxed and friendly attitude toward learning. As soon as they're accustomed to using the tool, then incorporate it as a fundamental part of the writing curriculum.

A teaching strategy is important. Writing teachers need to plan beforehand how to introduce word processing so it doesn't occur haphazardly and botch up both objectives—teaching writing and teaching word processing. However, to accomplish the second objective, students have to learn the basic skills of operating a word processor. How do teachers introduce word processing successfully, without frustrating students by competing priorities? There are a variety of possible strategies; following are a few of them.

If Your Classroom Has One or More Computers

First, teach students who are unfamiliar with computers the basics of how to operate one. (Microcomputers used in schools today commonly have self-teaching tutorial disks that lead students through the basics of operating the system.) When students are comfortable with rudimentary skills such as loading disks and entering keyboard commands, progress into teaching word processing skills. Don't introduce new writing lessons during the time students are getting comfortable with the equipment and learning how to use the word processing software. Let writers use this time to practice what they already know about writing while concentrating on learning to use a new machine.

Second, when the classroom word processor has become practically a familiar friend to your students, then begin shifting the focus over to using it as a tool for helping them write better. This is the time to start teaching new lessons in writing.

If the Available Computers Are Located in a Computer Lab

Try to persuade the authorities at the school's computer center (lab) to lend you a computer for classroom use, just for two or three weeks. This should be enough time to teach students fundamental word processing skills and get them started doing writing assignments on the computer. When the system has to be returned to the lab, the class can refocus on learning new writing skills. At that point students (at least at the secondary level) should be comfortable enough with word processing to be able to go to the lab to complete assignments.

If it's not possible to bring a computer into the classroom for the initial learning process, perhaps your school's computer center is equipped with self-teaching tutorials on word processing that are designed for students, or perhaps there are tutors available who can teach those skills to your students. If either of these options exists, you can send writing students to learn how to use the computer center's word processors on their own. For example, you might help your students schedule a half-dozen or so sessions in the lab with an assigned tutor, or self-teaching tutorial. Then you inform them that at the end of a specified period of time, you'll begin to give assignments that must be completed on a word processor. In the meantime you can continue spending class time teaching only writing skills.

This technique is more likely to be successful with high school and college students who are generally expected to take on more independent responsibility and are better able to seek assistance from peers or other teachers who happen to be in the computer center. The advantages of this approach are that students who already know word processing skills won't be bored while the others learn, and a teacher doesn't lose time teaching skills that are essentially outside the core writing curriculum. To many teachers and academic department heads, this latter advantage is significant.

Another technique you could use, if you're willing to put in the extra time, involves inviting small groups of students to afternoon workshops. Schedule a regular time in the computer center when you and students can meet. During these small group sessions, demonstrate how to operate a computer and teach the basic skills of word processing. Then have students practice these skills on the lab computers, individually or in pairs. In order to teach word processing to everyone in the class, however, a teacher will have to repeat the workshops continually until all students have participated, or else arrange for students who attend the early workshops to serve as tutors in the remaining ones.

No Matter Where Your Computers Are Located

Whether you have computers in your classroom or down the hall in a special computer room, you can use student tutors to help teach others in the class the basics of word processing. Here's one way to do it. Ask for a few student volunteers (or select individuals you think will be most successful) to learn word processing skills after school. Spend several afternoons training them in the basics and helping them develop procedures for tutoring other students. Those students who already use word processing programs at home, or who have learned the skills elsewhere, are prime candidates to tutor classmates. When the tutors are comfortable using the school's word processing software, organize the class into small groups so tutors can teach the new skills to classmates. If the school's computers are located in a lab, you'll also have to schedule lab time for these groups.

After the tutors have finished their job, it's time for the teacher to move on with new writing lessons. This is also a good time to examine how well the individual groups function and do some rearranging where necessary to establish good working teams. If you can, it's helpful to arrange groups so that there is at least one computer "expert" per group. If this person is not the group's writing ace, that's even better for group morale, as it establishes a fair balance of skills. More information will be shared in the following chapter concerning how to use these peer groups as part of the ongoing structure for a writing class that uses word processing.

A Generic Lesson Plan for Teaching Word Processing Skills

When students have learned how to load disks and enter commands and information into the computer via the keyboard, they're ready to begin to learn word processing.

Discuss with the class at length the difference between entering text on the computer and typing on a typewriter, including such topics as viewing text while you type, the use of the return key, and making corrections and revisions.

Demonstrate on the computer step-by-step how to start up the specific word processing program and begin a new text file.

Have students dictate a paragraph or two while you, or a student, enters it on the computer keyboard. During this exercise, show them how to make capital letters (if there's no shift key on the computer you're using); then begin teaching some simple editing procedures such as how to delete and insert words, and how to move the cursor around the text. If the program you're using requires writers to switch back and forth between WRITE and EDIT modes for these procedures, teach that now, too.

Each word processing program has its own set of labels (single letters, abbreviated words, or graphic images, called *icons*) that are used to represent the various functions it performs. Each word processing program also has its own set of commands that a user enters to direct the computer to perform the various functions. It would be advantageous for each of your students to have a quick reference card listing all the labels and specific word processing commands that they're likely to use. If such a card is not available (and reproduceable) as part of the purchased software package, you can easily create one yourself and duplicate it for everyone in the class.

Once students have observed and practiced entering text, deleting, and inserting it, as well as moving the cursor freely around the written document, it's time to try moving blocks of text. Again, each program has different commands for these procedures, but essentially you're teaching students to mark the text to be moved, copy it into a *buffer* (temporary storage area), and insert it at a new location.

Just before you're ready to end the first lesson is a logical time to teach students how to save the text they've entered and edited. Spend a few minutes explaining the computer's two types of memory: *internal memory,* which holds text and information only until the computer's power supply is cut off; and *external memory,* which holds text and information more permanently in external storage media such as disks. Ask them where they think the text they've written is now, before they've saved it, and what would happen if someone turned off the computer. Discuss the importance of frequently transferring their work from the computer's internal memory to the safer external memory of the disk. Then teach them the specific commands necessary to save their work on to a disk.

Begin the next lesson with how to retrieve a file from the disk and get it back into the computer's internal memory (and back up on the screen), so you can continue working on it. In this lesson and in lessons that follow you'll cover other word processing operations such as the following: searching for a particular word or phrase and replacing it with another word or phrase; calling up special "Help" displays that remind the user which keyboard commands are used to perform various operations; deleting large sections of text and deleting an entire file; copying files on to another disk; renaming files; and any other operations your particular word processor offers that you feel the kids should be introduced to at this point. On the other hand, you may choose not to teach some of these functions until after students have become more familiar with the very basic operations.

After students in the class have had opportunities to practice entering, editing, and manipulating blocks of text, it's time to introduce them to the formatting and printing procedures. If you're using a very limited word processing program this lesson may be as simple as telling students to enter the keyboard command that prints their text. If your word processing program has a large variety of format and print options you may initially pick just the basic ones to teach students. Then later, when they need to print right and left justified columns or use boldface letters, for instance, they can learn more sophisticated formatting. For now, at least show them how to get the format options displayed on the screen and help them pick the ones they'll need for printing. Commands such as single/double spacing of lines, numbering pages, and stopping the printer mid-document, may be of use to them right away.

Please don't assume from the lesson plan outlined above that this is all there is to teaching word processing to students. It's not quite so simple. Every word processing program has its own quirks that will probably cause your students some frustration while they're learning. For example, a few of the older programs don't display capital letters, indented lines, or reformatted paragraphs. Some require the user to go through elaborate formatting procedures before printing out text. Others require the user to type complicated, multi-stroke key commands in order to complete each operation. And students have their own quirks, too. For example, moving blocks of text may appear totally unfathomable to some kids, and it's likely they'll lose many precious sentences in the process of learning. Some will accidentally copy the rough draft onto their revised draft, instead of the reverse. Others will forget to save their work before turning off the computer and a ten-page paper might tragically vanish in an instant, along with the student's chance to get an A.

As their teacher, you may have to give some individuals considerable encouragement during the learning process. Yet, with support and sympathy, practically any student can learn to use word processing and thus enjoy its multiple advantages over writing with a pencil or typewriter.

PRACTICE: No matter which strategy you choose to introduce word processing skills, lots of practice is essential to become comfortable. Here's one way to ensure ample practice: when students have learned the rudimentary word processing skills, devise a few exercises (if none are already available) to give them practice in using these skills.

Enter the exercises on a disk for students to begin using as soon as they're ready. These exercises could include practice in some simple writing skills which were covered in class long ago. Here's one example of this type of exercise:

> Rewrite the following sentences in the PRESENT tense. Feel free to rewrite as much as you wish in order to keep the sentences meaningful.
>
> 1. Dad will go to Safeway this afternoon to get some hamburger and potato chips for the party tonight.
> 2. Mike passed his math test with a score of 85.
> 3. Susan rode her bicycle to school this morning and it took her only ten minutes.

You can fill many disks with similar exercises drawn from the English department files or from any grammar textbook. There are also many other ways to practice using the program's text editor. For example, you can take nursery rhymes, popular advertising jingles, or familiar expressions and then alter them noticeably.

Here's one:

> Mary had a little pig
> whose fur was gray as dust
> and everywhere that Johnny went
> the goose was sure to come.

Ask kids to restore the rhyme to its original form so Mary once again takes her pet lamb to school. Or, you may discover that starting with the original rhyme and inviting kids to make amusing, imaginative alterations, works better.

Follow up this activity by asking students each to draft a short letter with pencil and paper (or you could pass back a recent handwritten assignment) and enter it onto a word processor. Then, individually or in small groups, they can make corrections and revisions with the text editor. This exercise provides additional practice with word processing skills, yet it also begins the shift toward focusing on using word processing to revise their own writing.

It's fairly easy to devise creative ways to practice each of the word processing skills, even the more advanced ones. Students can practice the search and replace feature, for instance, by writing letters. Let's say they write holiday greeting letters or thank-you notes. They can personalize the same letter for different individuals by using search and replace to alter names, gifts, and other details of the original letter.

The class can practice transferring files onto different disks in an activity such as the following: Divide the class into small groups. Ask group members to write separate paragraphs about a common topic, and enter their individual paragraphs on separate disks. The group's task, then, is to combine all the paragraphs into one essay, on one disk. To do this, they will have to transfer their individual paragraphs onto the common essay disk.

At this point, the class should be ready to shift focus from learning to use this tool, to learning to improve their writing with the help of the tool.

At some point during the course of your experience with teaching writing using word processing, you'll wrestle with the issue of whether or not writers who use word processors should learn proper ten-finger keyboarding skills. The further you get with using word processing in the classroom, the more you'll discover that the issue isn't really whether kids should learn keyboarding, but *when.*

Keyboarding Skills

Keyboarding Skills: "Learning to use the alphabetic, numeric, symbol, and function keys on a computer and/or typewriter-type keyboard."

Typewriting Skills: "The development of speed and accuracy at the keyboard as well as the application of those skills in a production mode."*

---

*Truman H. Jackson, Specialist for Business Education, State Department of Education, St. Paul, Minnesota.

The Theories

There's a school of thought which professes that the learning process requires (or is at least reinforced by) the hand-to-brain coordination that occurs when you write thoughts out by hand. When learning letters, for instance, young children memorize the shape of a letter by writing it over and over, and thus imprint a tactile and visual image of the letter in their minds.

A few elementary school teachers have reportedly encouraged kids to use the word processor's power to edit and revise written work, but then required students to recopy the final draft by hand, before turning it in. These teachers believe that children learn the material more completely if they write out the assignments by hand.

This theory seems a bit extreme when applied to students who have already learned basic reading and handwriting skills. Many people who are respected as intelligent scholars use the keyboard to compose and revise practically all their written communication. If there is, in fact, an enduring need to coordinate hand and brain in the writing process, doesn't using the fingers on a keyboard provide sufficient hand/brain coordination to accomplish that need?

Few would argue that young children should omit the initial process of learning to write letters and words by hand, but once they have mastered the craft, it seems reasonable that they could also begin to use a keyboard. Let's suppose then, that children do learn to write by hand, and then later in elementary school begin using the keyboard for writing more often than they use pencil and paper. Will their handwriting deteriorate so much that they'll feel compelled to type everything in order not to subject their readers to illegible penmanship? Maybe.

Already there is evidence that people grow dependent on such practical tools as they become more available. Take the calculator, for example. Surely people's skill in doing simple mathematical computations atrophies when they have a pocket calculator at hand. The same is true for handwriting skills. As adults use the keyboard for increasingly more written work, their handwriting is likely to deteriorate. It's already happening to some of us. If young children spend more time practicing keyboarding skills and less time practicing penmanship, the same result will probably occur.

When the computer revolution first made an impact on the schools, microcomputers were used primarily for computer literacy courses and for running courseware that didn't require much typing. But in 1983 and 1984 word processing programs designed specifically for young people became very popular, and soon elementary school children began writing compostions on the computer keyboard.

However, students who struggle over the keyboard, pecking out words at an agonizing rate, often tend to write less than they do with pencil and paper, or than they would if they knew how to type. Some get so frustrated that they develop a loathing for word processing (and writing) in general. On the other hand, those who have great difficulty with handwriting find word processing a terrific boon to their writing and prefer it even if they have to poke with two fingers. Think what they could do with better keyboarding skills!

The Realities

The fact is, using a computer keyboard will very likely become the standard method for writing text in schools, homes, and businesses. Consequently, learning keyboarding skills will soon be recognized as a necessary basic skill in education. The sooner we accept this, the better our kids will fare.

Schools that already realize the importance of teaching keyboarding, and are beginning to think seriously about how to fit the skills into the K-12 curriculum, are still debating these questions: Should we teach keyboarding as part of the regular curriculum, and if so, when? Should we wait until third or fourth grade, after most kids' handwriting is satisfactory, or teach these skills simultaneously in first or second grade?

The debate is especially hot in districts that are introducing computers and word processing in the lower elementary grades. Some of these schools discourage students from using a word processor until they've learned the correct fingering. In some cases teachers enter the text for the children. A few even arrange for parent volunteers to enter the kids' work onto a word processing system. This is supposed to minimize development of bad habits caused by using the "hunt and peck" method of typing. Beginning writers then use the keyboard only to edit and revise their papers. Schools that feel this strongly about keyboarding skills usually have initiated, or are about to initiate, some kind of classroom keyboarding instruction at the elementary school level.

Young children, at least by the fifth or sixth grade, are increasingly using the computer keyboard in school, at home, in their parents' offices, and at their friends' houses. Are we going to let them pick up haphazard finger techniques for some four or five years before offering the traditional typing elective course in tenth grade? Let's begin teaching keyboarding as soon as we introduce kids to word processing.

There's still another question being debated by keyboard enthusiasts that complicates the issue for educators who are committed to teaching the ten-finger technique now. Which keyboard should we teach: the standard QWERTY layout (designed ages ago to slow down fast typists so they wouldn't jam the old manual typewriter keys), or the newer Dvorak layout, designed for users to enter text easily and rapidly on modern electronic keyboards? On the Dvorak keyboard the most frequently used letters and letter combinations are conveniently arranged as the home row keys. (The *home row* keys are the keys where the fingers rest. On the QWERTY keyboard they are ASDFJKL; and on the Dvorak keyboard they are AOEUTHNS.) The Dvorak keyboard configuration has become popular enough for the computer industry to sit up and take notice. Apple Computer, Inc., for example, designed the Apple®IIC keyboard with both the QWERTY and Dvorak configurations. All the writer has to do is push a button to switch modes.

For whatever reasons, the majority of schools around the country are not yet actively taking the responsibility to teach keyboarding as a fundamental skill. Many adults and students have learned to use helter skelter two-finger techniques, and since word processing has only become widely used in the last year or two, no real pressure has (until now) been put on schools to include ten-finger keyboarding in the regular curriculum. Secondary schools typically do offer elective courses in typing, but this sort of arrangement doesn't work as well in elementary schools because students in the lower grades don't usually have individual schedules and a choice of subjects.

The computer industry is characteristically quick to move and so when the need to help computer users learn keyboarding skills became apparent in 1983, software publishers rushed to fill the gap. As a result, there are currently numerous teach-yourself-to-type disk tutorials on the market. (A few even offer a version that teaches the Dvorak keyboard.) Many teachers who have been left to cope with students' poor keyboarding skills as best they can, are giving kids these tutorials to help them learn ten-finger techniques.

Software Tutorials for Keyboarding

Software tutorials can be extremely effective in helping motivated individuals (of any age) teach themselves where the fingers go on the keyboard, or for typing teachers to use as aids in the classroom. Frankly, however, several of the packages now on the market have serious drawbacks that make them fairly ineffective for teaching keyboarding skills.

Game-format tutorials, such as Type Attack™ and MasterType™, typically omit, or present very skimpy explanations of correct finger positions on the keyboard. They focus on increasing the user's speed in typing single characters and character combinations. Very few of the exercises provide practice in typing meaningful sentences or paragraphs.

Games are pretty enticing, however, and can be useful in a regular typing course as supplementary practice material or in conjunction with disk tutorials that teach ten-finger skills more effectively. But keep in mind that speed games are not likely to encourage correct finger placement on the keyboard; when beginners type single letters instead of key combinations, and practice while under the pressure of attack, the index fingers reach for the keys most naturally. As one twelve-year-old put it, "You should already know how to type to use these programs. They just make you try to type faster."

Comprehensive tutorials, such as Alphabetic Keyboarding and MicroType, The Wonderful World of PAWS™, are far more helpful in teaching proper keyboarding skills. They include complete instructions for correct finger movements from pressing the home row keys to reaching for others further away.

They also provide appropriate practice exercises and frequent timed drills. Appropriate exercises, typing experts say, are ones that present gradually expanding character sequences that help the learner gain speed and reduce errors. In addition, the exercises must also consist of meaningful groups of letters, words, and sentences. This is because skilled typists type familiar words and phrases as single units, not as separate letter-by-letter strokes. (Learning to type is rather like learning to read—we learn to recognize groups of letters as meaningful words, and then we no longer have to read [type] those words letter-by-letter.)

Shorter, single-disk tutorials, such as Typing Tutor and WizType™ provide minimum basic instruction about proper finger positions on the keyboard, with practice drills that focus on the newly introduced keys. Exercises present single characters and character combinations, and each section typically concludes with a timed sequence to test the learner's speed. After the timed drill, a report of the number of errors and keyboarding speed is generally displayed on the screen.

A major disadvantage of a few of these short tutorials is that they don't provide adequate practice in typing meaningful sentences and paragraphs. Some offer practice exercises that are no longer than a single sentence, and some combine characters randomly to create paragraphs of nonsense words and sentences. A few of the short tutorials, however, do provide sufficient instruction and meaningful practice in keyboarding to get a student properly oriented to the keyboard.

Students who are motivated to learn keyboarding and teachers motivated to teach it can do so successfully with or without software tutorials. Carefully chosen tutorials, however, can be effectively used in schools, either as a supplement for a teacher-taught keyboarding unit or as an independent self-taught mini-course. The tutorials can certainly take the pressure off overworked teachers and definitely aid in classroom situations where half the kids have already learned the skills and the other half have not. No matter where you stand concerning how elaborately ten-finger keyboarding needs to be taught, or if it should be taught differently at different levels, the underlying principle is the same—kids do need to learn where to put their fingers on the keyboard, and they need lots of practice.

Features to Look for in A Keyboarding Tutorial

Following are some features to look for when shopping for keyboarding tutorial software.*

ESSENTIAL

- Home keys should be introduced first, followed by the others. Illustrations of the correct technique for striking home keys and reaching for others are also valuable.
- Meaningful letter and word combinations should be used to practice keys soon after they are introduced.
- Frequent feedback should be given about the learner's accuracy and speed.

IMPORTANT

- The program should display upper- and lower-case letters and recognize the difference when they are entered by a user.
- Error correction should be possible while typing exercises.
- Users should be able to escape a lesson at any time and return to the previous menu without rebooting the system.

VERY HANDY

- The program should provide space for teacher-created exercises and timed tests.
- If speed goals are set as part of a timed drill, the user should be able to establish the words-per-minute goal.
- Letters, numbers, and punctuation marks should be clearly visible on the screen.

WOULDN'T IT BE NICE IF THE PROGRAM ALSO INCLUDED . . .

- A choice between practicing microcomputer keyboarding techniques (e.g., use of wrap-around lines, delete key) and typewriter keyboarding

---

*Information in this section is from an article written by the author and published in *Classroom Computer Learning*, September 1984.

techniques (e.g., use of carriage return). Unfortunately, some good programs teach only typewriter keyboarding skills.

- A management system to keep track of students' progress.
- Provision for the user to select exercises that focus on speed (number of errors not important), accuracy (speed not important), or both.
- Separate versions with vocabularies appropriate for different educational levels, such as elementary, secondary, and adult.
- A pricetag that's less than $50!

Chapter 3
TEACHING TECHNIQUES
WITH WORD PROCESSING

Teachers are almost always able to assume that the customary writing tools—pencil and paper—are readily available to everyone in the class. Consequently, our traditional methods of writing instruction are based on the assumption that students are equipped to write any time during class, and that, by the time they reach junior high, whatever written work isn't completed in school can be finished at home overnight.

When we're introduced to a new and complicated writing tool—the word processor—and told to include it as an integrated part of the classroom curriculum, many teachers resist. Obviously there are not enough of these expensive machines to go around. How can we possibly expect students to use a writing tool effectively if they have to share it with twenty or thirty classmates, or trek down the hall to a computer lab?

When teachers begin using word processing as a classroom teaching tool they generally have to make significant changes in the way they teach. First of all, they need to change their method of organizing the classroom, which also means altering teaching techniques. With one or a few computers available and a classroom full of students, teachers must devise ways of sharing the computers and structuring class time so students can complete their work at the word processor without missing other lessons. Even if they have access to a computer lab, teachers still have to plan on- and off-computer activities, small group activities, and whole class activities, centered around the use of word processing. Underlying these immediate tasks is the teacher's ongoing struggle to acquire more word processing equipment for students to use. If we expect students to use the word processor as a writing and editing tool, they certainly have to be able to get their hands on one often.

Some of these problems will be eased as schools buy more computer equipment, and as the number of students who have computers at home continues to grow. The more writers who learn to use word processing at home, the easier it will be for teachers and students to adopt the word processor as a regular classroom writing tool. In addition, as more students begin using home computers to complete school assignments, the less competition there will be for individual computer time in school.

Until there are enough computers available for students to use one whenever they need to, however, they'll have to take turns. This undoubtedly means that students usually won't be able to use the word processor as a tool for composing school papers; they will, however, be able to enter handwritten drafts and use the word processor to edit and revise their work before printing it out and passing it in. The next two sections of this chapter suggest a few teaching techniques for teaching writing with this new electronic writing tool.

Computers in Individual Classrooms

Elementary school decision-makers often choose to place computers in individual classrooms, while secondary school authorities typically opt to house most of their computing equipment in a computer lab. Schools that own just one or very few computers commonly make them available to teachers by some kind of sign-up procedure, or arrange to rotate transportable computers from classroom to classroom on a regular schedule.

A computers-in-the-classroom arrangement is especially convenient for elementary schools because students generally spend most of their time in one room with one or two teachers, rather than moving to a different place for every subject. Placing computers in this classroom setting works well because scheduling student time on the equipment can be spread out over the whole day, not just one class period. In addition, because children in the lower grades don't usually produce as much writing as do older, more prolific students, they normally don't need quite as much individual computer time.

Even in schools that have computer centers, teachers can sometimes arrange to borrow a computer for temporary classroom use. With one computer in the classroom for a couple of weeks, it's possible to teach students how to use the word processing software and get them started working with it as a writing and editing tool. When the system must be returned to the center, students at least will know the basics of using the text editor and be able to complete writing assignments. Any time teachers can arrange to get a computer into the classroom it's certainly an asset; just having the machine sit in familiar "home territory" helps students (and teachers) become more comfortable using it.

One Computer in the Classroom

Clearly, when there is only one computer in a classroom, word processing cannot replace pencil and paper as the most common writing tool for students to use in composing first drafts. Instead, it's used more effectively as an editing tool to help simplify the process of editing and reprinting revised drafts.

There are also many other uses for a word processing computer in the writing classroom that can help students learn about writing. Let's suppose that you have one microcomputer with word processing software in the classroom for the whole year. How do you organize teaching methods and classroom logistics to teach writing most effectively with this machine? Following are a few possible techniques.

TEACHER AS DEMONSTRATOR: Initially, you'll use one computer to demonstrate for the class how to operate the computer system and how to use the word processing software (Fig. 3.1). Then students can practice the procedures individually or in groups before attempting to use the equipment for assignments on their own.

One rather effective way of teaching the pre-writing, composing, and editing stages of writing is to use the word processor as an electronic blackboard, as mentioned in Chapter 1. Use it to teach writing skills by demonstrating for students how to brainstorm, organize ideas, draft sentences, and then revise and edit them—on the spot. If there isn't a screen available that's large enough for everyone to see, you can connect two monitors to a computer with a Y cord. The same technique also works

Figure 3.1 Teacher as demonstrator.

for smaller groups of four to six students clustered about an average twelve-inch screen.

TEACHER AS SCRIBE: This technique involves a teacher typing at the computer keyboard while students compose stories and paragraphs orally. It works particularly well in classes of very young students who can't yet write, or are just learning. In this kind of situation children have the opportunity to tell well-developed stories with detailed explanations that they'll see later, looking splendid in print. This technique may be used to generate stories as a group activity, or in pairs with one student typing and the other telling.

Having a teacher write "for" the students is not intended to be a substitute for the children learning to do it. Instead, it is a supplementary activity to remind very young writers that they can actually express much more than they might otherwise be willing to when faced with having to write the words themselves. It is also particularly effective with writers of all ages who have physical difficulty with handwriting.

The teacher can also serve as a scribe by entering a paragraph or composition on the word processor that has some obvious need for revision. The class then goes over the piece sentence-by-sentence, stopping to discuss what improvements are needed. The teacher enters the changes and the class immediately sees the effect of their revisions. In this way, students begin to understand how to use the word processor as an editing tool.

STUDENTS AS EDITORS: In this technique, students first write drafts with pencil and paper, and then enter them onto the word processor for editing, revising, and printing. The arrangement enables a teacher to have students compose the first draft at their desks during class or for homework and then enter their work later, when it's their turn at the computer. In a class of thirty writers, for instance, who are at school for six hours, each would have about ten minutes a day of computer time. Probably twenty minutes every two days, or a half hour every three is preferable.

Some elementary schools arrange for parent and older student volunteers to enter the handwritten drafts onto the word processor after school. This enables young writers to spend all their computer time editing and rewriting their work. However, using volunteers to type the original paper is certainly more difficult to arrange in the upper grades where students usually write considerably more.

After the papers have been entered onto the word processor, students work individually or in small groups to correct their work using the program's text editor (see Fig. 3.2). Kids do this kind of editing and revising much more happily when they can use a word processor; all

Figure 3.2 Student editors working in small groups. *(Courtesy of Nancy Bingamon, Richardson Independent School District, Richardson, TX)*

writers want to improve their writing, but many won't bother if it entails the drudgery of copying it over.

STUDENTS AS TEAM MEMBERS: Teachers who already use some kind of small group instruction in the classroom will find the transition to teaching with word processing considerably easier. If the small group method is new, then this is a good time to explore its particular features. When a classroom has only one or a few computers, organizing students into small groups becomes a must. Unless, of course, there's a computer available for every student.

The amount of learning accomplished by two to four students working together depends on how well the system is organized and how effectively a teacher can inspire a spirit of efficiency and teamwork. A little practice helps; both students and teachers need to get used to working in this fashion. Groups of two are ideal because students can usually manage to get both their papers edited and revised comfortably in one sitting. Three and four writers per group can also work successfully, and a group that size won't fall apart when one member is absent. It also enables more students to work at the word processor during the same period of time, though only one at a time can type on the keyboard. It's helpful to experiment a bit with the size of groups to see what works

Figure 3.3   Students as team members. *(Courtesy of The Intercultural Learning Network, UCSD, San Diego, CA)*

best for the class (see Fig. 3.3). Editing groups that grow larger than four, however, are likely to create havoc, garbled text, and a disrupted classroom.

When everyone's settled and accustomed to working in this kind of environment, the advantages of the small group system become more and more obvious. Kids work faster, develop a supportive team spirit, and learn a lot from each other. They practice their writing skills among peers who can help them improve, and they practice editing skills by critiquing and editing their own and others' papers, as a regular group activity. Working in peer groups provides student writers with a supportive, yet also critical audience. Many students who exert very little effort when writing for a teacher suddenly become ardent perfectionists when writing for their classmates. Teachers who use peer groups regularly, say it's a superb way to organize a writing class, with or without word processing.

There are lots of ways to get a class started working in groups. One common way is to begin class with everyone sitting as a large group. The teacher may spend a fair amount of class time explaining and demonstrating specific writing skills selected for attention and practice that day. Then the class breaks up into small writing groups to begin working on assigned activities. They may edit one another's papers, draft new writing assignments as a team, complete exercises, and so on. Alternatively, members may work independently for part of the time and then later join in groups to share and critique what they've each done.

Students who are not working at a word processor can be reading and marking printed drafts for revision, drafting assignments with pencil and paper, brainstorming new composition topics, or doing any other routine desk activities.

STUDENTS AS TUTORS: Small groups established specifically for tutoring work a little differently. This type of learning environment can work successfully if there are tutors available who have already learned the writing skills to be taught. These tutors may be classmates, older students, or adults. Tutors work with one or a few students at a time, helping them learn specific writing skills, draft new papers, or revise completed ones.

Even very young tutors can help members of the class detect spelling errors and problems with basic grammar and punctuation. Tutors with more advanced writing skills can help classmates with all levels of writing, from basic mechanics to general organization and style.

In peer tutoring situations where students tutor their own classmates, the difference in their writing levels may be small. In this situation the participants can still help one another quite a bit, because just having another person read and discuss a piece of writing helps the writer identify areas that need revision. Tutoring groups made up of students with fairly equal writing skills actually operate more like regular peer groups—everybody teaches and everybody learns writing skills from each other (Fig. 3.4).

TEACHER AS TUTOR: At a later stage of the writing process, the teacher may read revised drafts and make suggestions for further improvements. Students are often able to help each other correct spelling, grammar, and punctuation errors, but frequently (especially at the elementary level) teachers are needed to help students with higher level composition skills such as word choice, sentence development, and general organization. Following a teacher's suggestions, student writers then have another go at editing and perfecting their papers.

During this stage of writing the teacher might choose to join a group while peer editors are at work on a member's paper. The teacher can become the temporary facilitator of the group, leading them to recognize problems that they may have missed, and helping them figure out how to make changes. Or, the teacher may choose to demonstrate how to critique a paper, focusing on the particular writing skills the class is currently studying.

Another method is to arrange to meet privately with individual students at the computer. This kind of tutoring session works like the teacher-student writing conference introduced in Chapter 1. The teacher and student read a recent writing assignment on the screen together, and

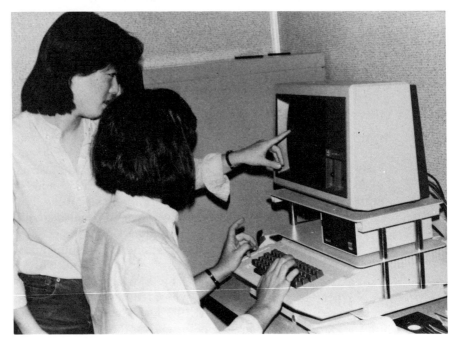

Figure 3.4 One student tutoring a classmate.

as they discuss the areas where it needs improvement, the writer makes changes that can be observed instantly. Using this method, the student gets the editing practice and the teacher learns how well the student has understood the suggestions and explanations.

COMPUTER AS PUBLISHER: After one, two, or more revisions, the final draft is finally printed. Seeing this polished, professional-looking copy almost invariably makes kids feel proud and prompts them to begin the writing process all over again.

If there's a printer in your classroom . . . terrific. You'll have printouts whenever you desire. If one printer must be shared by everyone in the school, then you print once a day, or whenever you can. Some teachers make a weekly trek to the district office to print student papers. However you have to do it, don't hesitate; the reward is a room full of beaming faces and a warm surge of new energy. It's electric.

More Than One Computer in the Classroom

Techniques for teaching writing with a computer in the classroom are the same if you manage to get several computers in the room. An obvious advantage to having multiple computers is that each writer can have more time at the keyboard. If there are several computers available, then there is probably enough time for individuals to try composing right on the word processor.

Another advantage to having multiple computers is that the teacher can be working with students at one computer while others work at the remaining ones. Once a draft is on the word processor, writers work in editing groups to help one another revise before handing their papers in, either on disk or as a printout. If, for example, four computers are available to groups of three editors each, it means that twelve students can be simultaneously helping one another improve their writing (Fig. 3.5).

All steps of the writing process are easier and quicker when there are more writing tools available. If we believe the word processor is a more powerful and effective tool in helping people write better, it's worth any effort to keep trying to get more computers in the classroom, until there's one for every writer.

Computers in the Computer Center

Junior high and high school students usually travel to a different classroom for each subject. Conversely, the computers in these schools typ-

Figure 3.5 Writers working in editing groups. *(Courtesy of Apple Computer, Inc.)*

ically remain in a single room, the school's computer center. This means that everybody—teachers as well as students—must arrange to go there in order to use a computer. The problem with this set-up, of course, is that it means our writing tools—the word processors—are not available when we're teaching writing in the classroom. How can a teacher get around this problem?

TEACHER AS MANIPULATOR: First, try pushing your way onto the computer center's master schedule and reserve as much class time in the center as possible. If you can schedule any or all of your classes there for the entire semester, you're lucky. If you can manage to bring your students there every day for a week, that will at least enable you to teach the basics of how to use the word processor and get them comfortable with the equipment in the center. After that, students will go there more freely on their own time to do assignments and work with peer editing groups. If you arrange to reserve a few computers in the lab during class time every day, then rotating groups of students can leave the regular classroom to get computer time for writing and editing assignments. Even if it's impossible to arrange enough computer time for them during class, you can help them schedule extra time in the lab during some other part of the day. Many schools have computer centers that remain open, and lively, long after the school day is officially over. A few even have enthusiastic parent volunteers who keep the doors open evenings and weekends.

Second, if it's not possible to teach in the computer center, try borrowing one of the center's computers to bring into your classroom for a few weeks (Fig. 3.6). With one system in the classroom you can teach students how to use the word processing program and get them started working with it as a writing tool. (See Chapter 1 for more about teaching word processing skills to students.) When the computer has to be returned to the center, students will at least know the basics of using the text editor and be able to complete writing assignments.

Third, if you're blocked in attempting the first two approaches, don't give up. Math and science departments often get top priority in scheduling computer center time. Keep fighting for your rights and maybe next term you'll get an equal share. In the meantime, you can assume that if the computer center has functional computers and word processing software, students can learn to use it and complete writing assignments with it. Some word processing programs come with self-teaching tutorials. If none are available try arranging tutoring sessions so that students who don't know how to use word processing can learn from those who do.

If these methods don't work, go to the lab and teach students yourself—after school, before school, or even during lunch if the computer center is free. After you help students learn the basic skills of word pro-

Figure 3.6 Try borrowing one of the computers from the lab.

cessing you probably won't have to push them to go to the center on their own to write with this powerful tool. Some schools have computer centers that are noted for their friendly, helpful ambiance; if you're in one of those schools, your writers can easily get assistance with operating the equipment from others in the lab.

TEACHER AS CLASSROOM MANAGER: Once the class learns the basics of word processing, teachers can assign papers and direct students to schedule their own time in the computer center. However, allowing some flexibility of assignment deadlines is often the most sensible approach, unless you don't mind keeping track of the daily changes in the computer center's schedule and the hourly state of (dis)repair of every computer in the room. It is inevitable that the rhythm of a writing process that depends on computer center word processors will be occasionally interrupted. If your standards call for excellence in the product received and permit a little flexibility in the timing, you're much more likely to survive this new teaching-with-word-processing approach (Fig. 3.7).

Figure 3.7 Allowing for some flexibility is often the most sensible approach.

TEACHER AS COACH (or, Word Processing in the Computerless Classroom): Trying to teach writing with a word processor when there isn't even one in the classroom is rather like coaching the soccer team in the locker room before and after they play. You discuss tactics, strategies, and methods; you make suggestions and give encouragement; you point out errors made by team members and offer advice for improvement; you establish specific goals, plan, and make new assignments. Then you send them out to the field, hoping that they'll try hard and do even better this time (Fig. 3.8).

In the computerless classroom, a teacher must help writers learn to critique one another's papers so they can go to the computer center in editing teams and work on revising assigments. Help them arrange regular times in their school schedules to go to the computer lab, in groups and individually, so they can complete their assignments on time.

Spend as much time as possible yourself in the computer center helping students with their writing while they're composing or revising. Schedule student writing conferences in the lab so you can go over their work right at the word processor. On these occasions, do your coaching "in the field" by helping students revise and improve their writing while working at the word processor.

TEACHER AS EFFECTIVE TEACHER (or, Word Processing in the Computer Lab): Let's suppose that you successfully arrange to teach writing students in the

Figure 3.8 Teaching writing with a word processor when there isn't one in the classroom, is like coaching the soccer team in the locker room before and after they play.

computer lab during classtime. This probably means that there is a computer for every one to three students, and that every group can work on a word processor at the same time.

With this supreme advantage, writers can compose on the keyboard individually, and then work in groups to edit, revise, and perfect final drafts (Fig. 3.9). In a powerful workshop environment such as this, the teacher can move around helping each editing group while they work independently. Alternatively, a teacher can orchestrate the class so that all groups are working on the same activity.

If you're teaching in a computer center where each computer is linked into a local network system, it's possible to do much more. (A local network system is created when computers are cabled together; it enables users to share software and display the same text on all the computer screens, or to work independently with different software.) For example, perhaps you choose to have the whole class work on an editing activity together. You put an example of a student's work on the master system, and presto, all the other terminals display it as well. The class discusses how to edit and revise the piece, and the changes that are typed in are immediately visible on everybody's screen (Fig. 3.10). This is like the electronic blackboard technique discussed earlier, only with linked computers the text is displayed on many screens, and everyone may actively participate in the editing process.

Now let's say you want students to work independently or in small groups. Each computer in the network system can also operate as a separate unit, so writers are able to compose their own drafts and save them

Figure 3.9 Writers can compose on the keyboard individually and then work in groups to edit, revise, and perfect final drafts. *(Courtesy of Apple Computer, Inc.)*

in personal files on the master system. At the same time, if you want one or two students to work on specific activities of your choosing, that's possible, too. Simply take the master disks containing the exercises or other materials you want to make available to students and place them into the network system. Now, all of the computers have access to those materials. In this way, assignments, classwork, quizzes, and so on can be "passed out" electronically to individual computers. The teacher is able to "tune in" any screen and watch a student's progress. In addition, teacher and student can send messages back and forth with the computers. Students do the written work and then "pass it in" by saving it on the master disk.

A well-designed and properly installed network system of word processors permits teachers to teach the whole class together, or in groups, with everyone interactively participating. It cuts out the hassle of students handling disks because they can store and retrieve their work on the master system. It also enables students to keep in closer electronic communication with teachers and other writers in the class. Once a teacher masters the particular complexities of the school's system, networked computers can be an extremely effective and efficient way to use word processing for teaching and learning to write (Fig. 3.11).

Figure 3.10 With networked computers, text can be displayed on many screens, and everyone may actively participate in the editing process. *(Courtesy of Corvus Systems, Inc.)*

Figure 3.11 There are many ways to create a computer lab. *(Courtesy of Judi Heckel, Mattoon, IL).*

INTRODUCTION TO THE WRITING ACTIVITIES IN CHAPTER 4 AND CHAPTER 5

The following two chapters include classroom writing activities for elementary and middle school students (Chapter 4) through high school and junior college level students (Chapter 5). All of the activities share the underlying assumption that teachers, and in most cases, students, have learned how to use the word processing program they'll be using for these activities.

It's possible to complete most of the activities without the aid of word processing, but having it available makes both the teaching and the learning of writing through the activities much more effective. For example: students can work more efficiently in peer editing groups; they can revise their work more easily; and they can print as many drafts as they rewrite and as many copies as they need.

Many of the activities involve teachers in making multiple copies of example compositions and using the chalkboard for various classroom exercises. If there is a large screen projection system, or enough computers (or connected monitors) available so every student can see a screen, then it's possible to use a video display to replace the chalkboard for many exercises. It's also possible to use a printer to replace the photocopy machine when providing students with copies of classmates' papers.

Teaching Basic Skills

Most of the activities in Chapters 4 and 5 involve students in composing complete paragraphs and compositions, rather than writing short exercises that focus on particular basic skills. One effective way of teaching basic writing skills, such as spelling, grammar, mechanics, and usage, is to address a few of these specific skills *after* a first (or second) draft of a writing assignment has been completed. While reading a set of papers, for example, a teacher may identify one or two basic skills problems that are evident in several of the papers. She can then duplicate excerpts from the papers that contain the problems and pass them out to students when they next meet. The class then reads the excerpts, locates the problems, and discusses how to correct them in the context of the paper. The teacher carefully explains the specific writing skill(s) being spotlighted, and concludes the lesson with some additional exercises that provide further practice in these skills. It's fairly easy to locate explanations of basic writing skills that are accompanied by exercises appropriate for the level of the class, in any number of grammar textbooks. (There is an example of this process in the "Describing a Face" activity in Chapter 5.)

Another practical approach to the teaching and learning of basic writing skills (which also works well with the approach described above), is to teach students to help each other learn these skills in peer editing groups. When students learn how to critique one another's writing so that they can identify problems and make suggestions for improvements, they can be extremely effective in helping themselves and others improve all levels of writing skills.

Granted, elementary level students cannot be expected to develop highly sophisticated critiquing skills, but they can become quite proficient at recognizing what "makes sense" or doesn't, and what "sounds right" or does not. Learning to make these distinctions in a piece of writing, and learning to figure out what to do to improve it, will help students improve their fundamental skills such as spelling and punctuation, as well as higher level skills such as organization and style.

Advanced writing students also can benefit from having peers critique their work. No matter how skillful a person is at writing, it's always useful to have someone else read an early draft and provide constructive criticism. This is because most writers cannot effectively be their own objective audience. Most writers need a second reader to provide perspective and feedback about how another person perceives the piece of writing.

Teaching Students to be Effective Writing Critics

Finishing a draft does not mean writing is over. The writer needs to both edit and revise. This is the time to change to more specific language, to adjust the organization, to add necessary information, to delete irrelevant details, and to correct spelling and punctuation errors. Using the computer, the revisions are integrated instantly, and therefore, no separate draft exists.

Editing and revision make up the third stage of the writing process. Often reading the story aloud, either to oneself, another student, or a teacher, helps a student identify needed changes. The questions that come from this reading can lead the writer to seeing and hearing his or her work through the eyes and ears of an audience. Questions such as "Did I use enough supporting details to clarify my position?" or "Can I move sentences or paragraphs around to be more persuasive?" encourage students to revise and rethink their writing. The writer may also use a checklist or series of reminders such as "Did I begin each sentence with a capital letter and end with a period, question mark, or exclamation point?" At the computer, revision never means copying over what has been written. . . . Revision becomes a process recurring throughout the larger writing and rewriting process.*

One of the most important skills all writers need to acquire in order to improve their own writing, is the facility to recognize what's wrong with it now, so that they can attempt to make it better. The ability to critique a piece of writing constructively is a skill that doesn't come automatically to most people, however. Writers have to learn it and practice it in order to help themselves and others become better writers.

One way to help students learn critiquing skills is by arranging them in small peer groups of two to four students, and having them regularly critique one another's writing assignments. If the teacher puts considerable effort into teaching students critiquing skills, they can soon begin working fairly independently in these groups, reading each other's papers, critiquing them, and making suggestions for improvements.

The following procedures may be useful for teaching students to critique classmates' papers in peer editing groups. The same process should be repeated several times in the beginning while students are learning the procedures themselves, and then periodically throughout the course.

Begin the process by demonstrating to the whole class how to critique a paper. To prepare for this demonstration, select a student-written paper that lies somewhere within the class's normal range of writing competency and duplicate copies for everyone, or bring the disk to class for display on the video screen.

(*Note:* Initially, students will be uncomfortable with sharing their papers among peers, and especially with having their papers critiqued in front of the class. Explain that every writer's work can be improved, and that while writers may feel uncomfortable while their papers are being discussed, the long-range benefits of the experience are well worth the brief discomfort. The teachers should also make sure that occasionally even the best writers in the class have their papers critiqued in the same manner. Conversely, it's also important to frequently read and praise successful papers written by all students.)

When you are ready to begin the demonstration, pass out copies of the paper to be critiqued (or get the essay up on the screen) and follow these steps:

---

*From the *Quill Teacher's Guide* (Lexington, MA: D.C. Heath and Company), p. 7. Reprinted by permission.

1. Review with students what the assignment was, and write on the chalkboard a list of the specific suggestions or advice you made when the assignment was given (e.g., "Use concrete details when describing the person's face," "Don't use words that contain a direct opinion.").

2. Read the paper aloud to the class. Explain that reading a paper out loud is an important step because it helps the writer (and others) hear how it "sounds". Many common writing problems, such as awkward sentences, weak transitions, and poor organization, can be detected simply by reading a paper aloud. Teachers should also advise students to go through this simple process themselves, just before completing any draft they write.

3. Ask students to comment on the positive aspects of the paper (e.g., "The transitions between ideas are smooth"; "The general organization is logical"; "The ending is effective"). Then point out a few general areas that are less successful (e.g., "The paper is a bit too general—it needs more specific examples"; "The tense keeps switching between past and present").

4. Then go back and re-read the first paragraph, sentence by sentence, asking students if each sentence "works" in context. Guide them to recognize where the problems occur and discuss what's wrong. Ask for suggestions on how to reword the sentences to make them work better.

5. Continue critiquing the paper in this manner until the end. Students probably won't remedy all the problems during the critique, but it's likely they can identify the most important ones and make suggestions to the writer about how the weak areas could be improved in the next draft. When critiquing papers longer than two or three pages, students won't have time to go into as much depth as when critiquing short, one- or two-page papers.

   Tell students that when they go through this process in editing groups the writer of the paper being critiqued should take notes and make corrections whenever possible. Writers can either make notes in the margins of a printed copy of the paper, or embed bracketed notes in the text while it's on the screen.

6. Conclude the critique with a summary of the areas which need the most revision. If there are an overwhelming number of problems, pick out a few important ones for the writer to work on improving for the next draft.

   After two or three such demonstrations of the critiquing process, students can meet in small editing groups and begin critiquing one another's papers, following the six steps listed above. The teacher should continue working closely with the groups—especially in the beginning—

helping them focus on working together to identify problems and offering suggestions for improvements.

When the critiquing session is over, writers can then take the suggestions made about their papers and use them to write second drafts. If the critiquing of the first draft is left up to student editing groups, then the teacher may choose to read the second drafts and make further suggestions for revisions in the final draft.

A pleasant way to end the cycle is to share some of the particularly successful final drafts with the class, so that students may enjoy praise and feel a sense of accomplishment at least as often as they are directed to focus on the unsuccessful aspects of their work. It also helps if teachers save some of these final papers to present as models for students in future classes when they attempt a similar assignment for the first time.

Learning to critique and revise a piece of writing is a skill that's different from learning to compose. Yet it has not been widely taught in school, mostly because teachers generally have chosen not to require students to recopy or retype second and third drafts of their papers. With word processing, however, the time-consuming and boring job of recopying disappears. What's left is the more thought-provoking work of identifying problems in one's writing and devising solutions to improve it, similar to debugging computer programs or problem-solving in math and science. It's difficult work, but it's often captivating, and certainly the benefits for students—significantly improved writing—makes it well worth the effort.

Chapters 4 and 5 were strengthened by daily communication and assistance from writing students at Horace Mann Elementary School, Day and Meadowbrook Junior High Schools in Newton, MA; Hingham High School in Hingham, MA; Masongola High School in Malawi, Africa; Andover Junior College in Andover, MA; Menlo College in Menlo Park, CA; and San Mateo Community College in San Mateo, CA.

Chapter 4

WRITING ACTIVITIES

FOR ELEMENTARY AND

MIDDLE SCHOOL STUDENTS

The writing activities that follow are designed primarily for elementary and middle school students. Many of the activities, however, are appropriate for intermediate level writers and can be adapted for older students. Conversely, numerous activities presented in Chapter 5 can be successfully used with elementary school students.

The activities in this chapter have been developed for classrooms with one or more computers and word processing software available, yet most of them can be easily modified for use in situations where students need to go to a computer lab to use word processing equipment.

Group Story

PURPOSE: Inventing stories in a group environment offers the teacher an ideal opportunity to introduce the basic structure of a story and teach writing skills in an informal and nonthreatening manner. Inviting students to create stories with their classmates is not intimidating because the narratives are fashioned in the spirit of entertainment, and no single child is expected to produce a complete story the first time.

In this activity a teacher prompts and assists in the creation of a coherent and grammatically correct narrative that, when printed out, can serve as a model for students as they write their own stories. In addition, students generally feel more confident in attempting to write a story independently after first participating in the story-making process with their classmates.

THE FIRST ACTIVITY: Begin with a class discussion about what kinds of things even the simplest story has to include: A *beginning* (Once upon a time, Mary . . .), a *middle* (something has to happen involving Mary), and an *ending* (. . . and Mary lived happily ever after). At least one character has to do something, or something has to happen to the character.

Ask students, for example, to think about what happened this morning while they were eating breakfast, on their way to school, or outside during recess. Any one of these experiences could become a tiny story, and you might offer one as an example:

> . . . . Sunday morning, when everybody over ten years old was still asleep, Mary decided to get her own breakfast. She climbed up on the kitchen counter and reached high for the cereal box. But, as she tried to pull it off the top shelf, out fell boxes of pretzels, Hershey bars, and marshmallows, instead.
> Now, Mary, being a very well-behaved girl who naturally didn't want to cause a mess in the kitchen by pulling down any more boxes, decided to make do with what she had. Wearing a grin that made her ears wiggle, Mary munched a bowl of pretzels with chocolate chips and marshmallows on top. . . .

You could suggest that inventing a story might be more interesting than describing what actually did happen this morning, but that some of the real life experiences we have are indeed good story material.

Next explain that the class is going to write a group story on the word processor with everyone making contributions to the plot. Since everybody will be adding something different, the story will naturally be fiction, but it may include things that have actually happened to them and their classmates.

As you move over to the word processor and start a new file for this story, you might inquire, "What name shall we give our major character?" *Enter:* ONCE UPON A TIME THERE WAS A YOUNG BOY NAMED JONAS. "Okay, Sara, what shall we say next?"

From here on, you shouldn't have any trouble getting a lot of action in the story. The tricky job for you as facilitator is to help the storytellers see that they need to provide descriptive information about the characters, setting, and so forth, and to help them see the importance of building a climax and designing an appropriate conclusion.

The particular advantage of using a word processor in this activity is that you can enter and revise the storytellers' contributions quickly and easily. As the story progresses, the class may decide to alter certain facts, incidents, or other elements, and individual students will surely want to change the wording of their segments as they compose them orally. When the first draft is completed, the whole class can also participate in making further additions and revisions.

When the story is just the way they want it, print it out and duplicate enough copies for everyone. Ask students to save the completed text to use as a model for the stories they will each write the next day. You may also invite students to illustrate their printed copies and share them with classmates.

THE SECOND ACTIVITY: During class on the second day, individual students might dictate stories for you to enter onto the word processor, while the rest of the class begins drafting stories with pencil and paper. Or you may ask them to compose on the word processor during their scheduled computer time.

After their first drafts have been entered onto a word processor, have them review the stories in groups of two or three. They can help one another correct errors in spelling, punctuation, and other fundamental skills, as well as offer suggestions for improving higher-level skills such as word choice and paragraph organization. After this peer editing process is finished, go over the stories yourself, or with the student editing groups, and make further suggestions for improving the final draft.

In situations where there are several computers available, the class can do both the composing and revising in small groups. One group member enters the text on the keyboard while they all work together in developing the story.

At the conclusion of this activity students will each have their own printed story. These could then be illustrated by the authors, duplicated, and bound together into anthologies for every child in the class.

Spontaneous Writing

PURPOSE: Improvised personal writing that is neither corrected nor graded by a teacher helps writers become fluent and comfortable with writing in general. When kids don't have to worry about grammar or mechanics and when they write about themselves—a subject on which they are indeed experts—they begin to overcome a variety of fears concerning writing. In addition, spontaneous writing that's done directly on the word processor helps writers become more comfortable with composing on the keyboard.

THE ACTIVITY: Introduce the class to this activity in a whole group session, without a word processor. Ask students to choose an imaginary friend to "talk" to on paper. Advise them to invent one they would feel completely comfortable with while discussing personal thoughts and feelings. Explain that starting tomorrow they will spend a few minutes every day writing on a word processor to their "friend" about the suggested topic for the day and anything else they may wish to write about.

To get started, ask everyone to take out a pencil and paper and make a list of their five most prized possessions. (A few students may need to be reminded that people are not possessions.) Then ask them to write a sentence or two to their imaginary friend about the most cherished possession. They might write about why it's special, what it's for, or whatever seems appropriate. For example, say Tim chooses his bicycle. He might write:

> Dear Iggy,
>   My bicycle is the most special thing I own. You might not think that a bicycle could be so very special, but this bicycle is. You know why? Because it takes me far far away from my older sister. She's always yelling at me to pick up my stuff, or be quiet while she's talking on the phone, or something else. What a grouch! But, when I jump on my bicycle and ride far away, I don't have to hear her yelling.
>
> > Your friend,
> > Tim

Follow this exercise with an informal discussion in which students share what they've written with classmates.

If you wish, choose another topic from the list of suggestions that follow and go through this exercise again. After students have written a few notes to their imaginary friends, explain that the letters they write from now on will be done on a word processor, when it's their turn to use one.

FOLLOW-UP ACTIVITIES: Each day that you plan to do this activity post a suggested topic for students to write about (see list). They can begin with this topic and then write about anything else they wish. At the end of their turn at a word processor, ask them to save that day's letter on a disk. Students should each have a personal disk for this continuing activity, and every time they write they'll add a new letter to the disk file.

Let the letters accumulate over weeks and months, and then toward the end of the year ask students to re-read them. They're usually surprised by this experience, finding that thoughts and emotions they once felt so intensely often seem ridiculously remote and insignificant a few months later. They will also notice other changes, such as more fluid sentences, more coherent paragraphs, and a variety of other improvements in their basic writing skills.

A Few Suggested Topics*

Tell your imaginary friend about:

- Your favorite sport and why you like it
- Your favorite game or hobby and why you like it
- Three things you like about school and why
- Three things you wish you could change at school, and how you would change them
- Two things you wish you could change about yourself and why

*(These topics, as well as topics suggested in two activities in Chapter 5, are influenced by Values Clarification ideas fostered by Sidney Simon.)

- Your favorite relative and why he or she is your favorite
- Two things you are good at and why
- Two things you are not good at and why
- An embarrassing thing that happened to you this week
- The nicest thing that's happened to you this week
- Your favorite TV character
- What kinds of things make you cry (give examples)
- What kinds of things make you angry (give examples)
- What you're most proud about
- How you are feeling right now
- What you would do with a million dollars (or a hundred dollars)
- Your favorite subject in school and why you like it best
- Your least favorite subject in school and why you like it least
- Three things you've done this week that you feel good about
- Your favorite food
- Three things you've learned this week
- What you like to do most after school
- What you like to do most on weekends
- List three of your father's or mother's favorite expressions and explain what they mean
- List three of your favorite expressions and explain what they mean

Finishing Paragraphs

PURPOSE: This activity helps students learn the function of a topic sentence as the key element for organizing a paragraph. It also helps them learn to write sentences that provide further information and support the topic sentence.

PREPARATION: Locate some well-written paragraphs with effective topic sentences and duplicate them for students to use as models. If possible, use student-written paragraphs. Also locate some paragraphs that are poorly organized with weak topic sentences or none at all. Duplicate these for students, too. (You may decide to make a demonstration disk of the examples rather than duplicate them.)

Following is an example of a well-organized paragraph:

When Dad went food shopping today he brought home five bunches of asparagus. He didn't buy any other vegetable, so you can imagine what we'll be having for dinner every night until Sunday. I figure we'll have boiled asparagus tonight, creamed asparagus on Wednesday, asparagus souffle on Thursday, asparagus nut muffins on Friday, and asparagus soup on Saturday. And, if there's any left over, you can guess what's for breakfast on Sunday—asparagus pancakes. Next week I think I will go and help Dad with the shopping.

Next is an example of a poorly organized paragraph.

Dad likes asparagus. He even bought five bunches of it today at the market. Next week I guess I'll go along with him and help him out with the shopping. This week we'll probably have to eat asparagus every night for supper—would you believe boiled asparagus, creamed asparagus, asparagus soup, and asparagus souffle? We'll probably even get asparagus pancakes on the last day, if we're unlucky. I wish Dad didn't like asparagus so much.

THE ACTIVITY: Begin by asking students to define *topic sentence*. Assist them, if necessary, by explaining that its function is to state the main idea of a paragraph, and that it often presents an attitude or opinion about the main idea. Explain that a good topic sentence makes a meaningful generalization that is broad enough to cover all the supportive information presented in the paragraph, and specific enough to be interesting. You might write a few example topic sentences on the chalkboard or word processor, and ask students to propose some as well.

Next, hand out the duplicated examples of well-written paragraphs with effective topic sentences (or display them on the video screen). Discuss how the rest of the paragraph supports the topic sentence with details such as additional facts and/or examples. Then pass out or display the example paragraphs that are not so well organized, with weak topic sentences, or none at all. Help the class revise these paragraphs by strengthening the structure; devise an appropriate topic sentence, rearrange the order of sentences, and add supportive information wherever necessary.

Write a few weak topic sentences on the chalkboard or word processor, and ask volunteers to help improve them. For example:

Weak	*Strong*
Dad likes asparagus.	When Dad went shopping today, he brought home five bunches of asparagus.
Sometimes it gets very hot in the summertime.	There's Aunt Betsy over on the porch; today she's just sitting, sweating, and sipping lemonade.
Doing strenuous exercise is a great way to let off steam when you're angry or upset.	Next time you feel like smashing someone in the face, try running a mile instead.

Finally, ask students to compose a paragraph using one of the revised topic sentences. They could do this at their desks and enter the paragraph on a word processor when it's their turn, or if there are enough computers available, they could compose it directly on a word processor.

After students have entered their paragraphs, have them meet in peer editing groups for help in revising and editing their work.

Writing Letters

PURPOSE: The following four activities introduce formal and informal letter writing styles and help students learn to choose the one that's appropriate for the audience being addressed. The activities also help students learn to compose letters that express their personal opinions in a manner that is logical and convincing.

PREPARATION: Prepare two example letters as described below. Make printed copies for students to use in a group discussion, or bring to class a disk containing the example letters and plan to display them on a video screen.

Letter 1 is an informal letter to a friend or relative, using an informal writing style and personal letter format. *Letter 2* is a formal letter to an adult, using a formal writing style and business letter format. Following are two examples.

Informal, Personal Letter

(DATE:) April 11, 1985

(GREETING:)
Dear Steve,   **(MAIN BODY:)**
My mom told me that you're going to be in a play next month. Is it really true? She said you're going to be Captain Hook in the play, "Peter Pan." Boy, are you lucky! Captain Hook is my favorite character of all.

My mom also said that she would take me to see the play at your school and that I should find out from you how to get tickets. How much are the tickets and where can we buy them?

I can't wait until I see you in that play. Maybe you can come and stay overnight at my house afterwards. My mom says it's all right with her, so ask your mom, okay?

Write back soon.

(CLOSING:) Your cousin,
(SIGNATURE:)

John

Formal, Business Letter

(HEADING:) 111 Diamond Place
Scenic, CA 94043
September 25, 1985

(INSIDE ADDRESS:)
Ms. Josephine Barry
Mayor of Scenic
City Hall

006 Main Street
Scenic, CA 94043

(GREEETING:)

Dear Mayor Barry: **(MAIN BODY:)**

An article in this morning's *Town Tribune* stated that you support the recent proposal made by a realty company to close Baker Park and build a city office building there.

I can't understand why. The article says that a report made by the same realty company claims that Baker Park isn't used very much. Well, the people who wrote that report must be blind, or they've never been to the park. There are lots of kids (including myself) who play there every day after school.

If you close the park, where can we go after school? Should we play baseball in the City Hall parking area, or the vacant lot next to Luke's Lunch? Who knows, maybe we'll turn out to be juvenile delinquents if you take away our park.

Even though I'm not old enough to vote, I hope you will pay attention to these arguments. Besides, both my father and mother want you to keep the park too, and they are old enough to vote.

Please answer this letter.

(CLOSING:) Sincerely yours,

(SIGNATURE:) *Glenn Rudnick*

THE FIRST ACTIVITY—A Positive Informal Letter: Ask members of the class to explain how they think their writing would differ when writing to a friend or close relative, compared to writing to an adult they've never met. Hand out, or display on a video screen, the previously prepared example letters, and read them aloud. Compare the language used in both, the structure, and the overall appearance.

Next, discuss the reasons why people write letters to friends, and to strangers. If they don't mention it, suggest that we often write to friends to express our feelings about issues that concern us, and sometimes we also write to adults to express our personal opinions about important issues.

Ask students to think of a friend or close relative who has recently done something the student thinks is terrific (besides something done specifically for the student such as giving a gift). Then have students compose a letter to that person using an appropriate writing style and letter format. Encourage them to express as specifically as possible what the person has done and why the writer thinks it's so remarkable.

Students may compose letters on a word processor or with pencil and paper, depending on how many computers are available. If there is not enough computer time for students to compose at the keyboard, they can at least enter their drafts after they've been written by hand.

When first drafts are completed, editing groups can meet to critique members' work. Encourage editors in these sessions to focus their comments on how successfully writers have stated their reasons for supporting the friend or relative's recent action. Also advise them to determine if the writer used appropriate language and a suitable writing style for the person addressed.

Student writers can then revise and print out second drafts, and hand them in to the teacher. The teacher may suggest further revisions and request a third draft, or go on to the next activity.

THE SECOND ACTIVITY—A Positive, Formal Letter: In this activity, students compose another letter that expresses positive support for something the recipient has done. This time, however, the recipient is an adult that the writer does not know well, or has never met—for example, the director of a sports program, the designer of a favorite game, the author of a cherished book, a local or national politician, or a TV or movie personality.

Review with the class how this letter would differ in language, writing style, and format, from the informal letter to a friend. (Refer to the example letter used in the previous activity.)

Brainstorm with the class some possible actions worthy of praise and support, such as altering the swimming schedule at the community pool so that children ages six to twelve can swim on Saturday mornings, or writing an article in a popular young people's magazine proposing that schools hire students to mow lawns, serve meals, work in the office, and do other jobs around the school. Ask them to choose a particular action they support and write a formal letter to the person responsible for the action.

Once again, editing groups will meet after the letters have been drafted. Specifically, they will help writers revise their language and style to make it more appropriate for the audience, and also offer suggestions for improving the writers' methods of expressing opinions. Students can then refine and polish their work in second and third drafts.

THE THIRD ACTIVITY—A Critical, Informal Letter: This activity involves writing a letter in which the writer strongly disapproves of something done by a friend or close relative. Briefly review the appropriate language and writing style used in informal letters, and the need to state specifically what the person has done and why it's so terrible.

Ask students to think of a recent action of a friend or relative that they feel truly angry about, such as a parent's new rule that places restrictions on watching television, a sister's refusal to lend her new dress, or a best friend's decision to invite someone else to the ball game. Have them compose informal letters to the offenders that express what the person did wrong and why the writer feels it was intolerable. Follow-up activities are the same as for the previous letter-writing assignments.

THE FOURTH ACTIVITY—A Critical, Formal Letter: In this activity students write a formal letter of complaint to an adult they don't know well, or have never met. Briefly review the kind of language and writing style appropriate to a formal business letter, and the need to be specific and unemotional in the criticism.

Ask students to suggest the kinds of acts they feel would be worthy of reproach, such as discontinuing a favorite television program, or receiving a mail-order package that contained a pink blouse with puffy sleeves and yellow bows instead of the navy blue shirt with a pointed collar and epaulettes that was ordered.

Then ask writers to compose formal letters of complaint that clearly state what they object to and why. Follow-up activities are the same as for the previous letter-writing assignments.

Describing an Object

PURPOSE: Writing a description of a single object that successfully transmits its essence to the reader, requires the writer to examine the object carefully and then use specific details to describe it. Such exercises help sharpen a writer's observation skills, and provide the opportunity to practice the use of precise, factual language while attempting to convey a complete "picture" of an object.

PREPARATION: Collect a number of small, familiar objects such as a wrist watch, baby rattle, scissors, egg beater, banana, and so forth. (The number of objects should be equal to or greater than the number of students in the class.) Place these items in a box and bring them to class on the day you plan to do the activity. Don't show students the objects before you're ready to pass them out.

THE ACTIVITY: Begin by discussing how we experience the objects around us with all five of our senses. Pick a few example objects in the classroom, such as a chalkboard eraser, a shoe, a notebook, and write them on the chalkboard or word processor. Then develop a list of specific words that describe each of them. Try to get students to think of words that depict how all of our senses experience the object. For example:

> *Chalkboard eraser:* dusty, powdery, stuffy, firm, squeezable, charcoal grey, dry, etc.
> *New shoe:* glossy, pointed, stiff, red, rigid, bright, leathery, clop-clop-clop, fresh, etc.

Peach: pinkish-orange-yellow, soft, fruity, squishy, gushy, juicy, sweet, wet, drippy, sticky, etc.

Notebook: scribble marks, dog-eared, half-filled, bendable, open, worn, messy, whitish-beige, spiral-bound, cool, smooth, etc.

Next, give each child one of the objects from the box you brought to class. Ask them to list as many words as they can think of that describe how their particular object looks, feels, smells, tastes, and sounds.

After sharing and expanding these lists with classmates, have students choose a few of the words from their lists that they wish to use in a written description about their object. Ask them to arrange the descriptive words in a logical order of presentation (e.g., general to specific, specific to general, or sight to taste). Then ask them to compose one or two paragraphs that describe the object, so that readers can recreate a complete image of the object in their minds.

Here's an example description of a new brown shoe:

> A new brown shoe with no foot wearing it is like a chocolate bar with no kid eating it. It's stiff and shiny, without a smudge of human contact. . . . You can even read the label. When you pick it up and bend it in the middle, a long dark wrinkle alters the shape permanently, making it look a bit older. It still smells like its ingredients, however, the shoe a little like leather, a little like glue, and a little like the box that contained it on the shelf.
>
> The brand new object feels slick and slightly soft as fingers trace the sides, from top to bottom and right to left. Fluorescent light reflects off the polished surface and sharply distinguishes the rich, brown outer surface from the creamy beige inside. If you grasp it with a hand and tap the end on a wooden surface, the noise echoes softly in the classroom. Then, gently lick the smooth, chocolate-colored coating with your tongue, and you'll discover how silly it is to compare a shoe to a chocolate candy bar.

When the first drafts have been entered onto a word processor read some of them aloud, inviting comments about the successful aspects of the description as well as the areas that need revision. Students can then continue to critique one another's descriptions in peer editing groups, complete second drafts, and pass them in.

Describing a Place

PURPOSE: This activity provides writers with practice in examining their surroundings carefully, and then reporting their experiences while seeing, feeling, smelling, tasting, and hearing a particular environment.

PREPARATION: Locate and duplicate for students a model of a place description that includes specific details and rich, sensory imagery. The following is one example written by an older student:

The air conditioner is always on. Business goes on all year round, but the summer weather brings crowds of people every day. A bell rings each time the door swings open and closed. White, spotless round tables rest in front of a long counter and a pink menu lies on each table. Four pink chairs patiently surround each one, waiting for a customer to sit down. On each side of the counter one can look through glass windows into icy freezers that hold 36 flavors of cool, creamy, and colorful ice cream. Nearby, dark brown hot fudge warms itself next to the golden butterscotch. A ladle stands in each container waiting to dribble its contents onto the flavor chosen by the eager eater. Chocolate, strawberry, and vanilla syrups sit until needed for shakes, sodas, and sundaes. Bananas, marshmallows, nuts, bits of pineapple, and cherries wait to be added to somebody's banana split.

The salesperson, dressed in white pants, pink shirt, and white smock, prepares whatever the customer desires. A few feet away, two children press their noses against the glass at the candy counter. Inside, jelly beans of all colors and flavors are lined up in little plastic bags with handwritten labels and pricetags on each one. Chocolates fill each beige paper dish, but the bright red and gold foil under the chocolate cherries gives them a special, classy look.

Just feasting my eyes on the creamy chocolates and the gooey caramel fudge ice cream makes me feel five pounds heavier.

THE ACTIVITY: Pass out the place description you have duplicated and read it aloud. Then discuss what sensory words and phrases the writer used in the description and how the details were organized into a structured whole. For example, in the previous description the writer used the words *rings, cool, creamy, warm, icy, dribble,* and so on, and organized the piece according to how a viewer might look around the store.

Next, tell students to imagine that they're going to write a description of the classroom and ask them to suggest some words, phrases, or sentences they might use in describing it. List these on the chalkboard or word processor. The language should help the reader see, hear, taste, smell, and touch certain elements of the classroom. Here are a few examples:

- I can hear the muttering of twenty-five ten-year-old voices.
- Yesterday's lessons are smudged yellow on the chalkboard.
- A faint smell of tuna fish and mayonnaise slips out of Jennie's lunchbox.

Discuss how a descriptive piece about the classroom might be organized (e.g., a guest walks into the room and takes a look around. . .).

Finally, ask students to choose a special place that they would like to describe, such as their bedroom at home, the lunch room at school, a favorite restaurant, or a scary ski trail. Have them brainstorm lists of descriptive words, phrases, and sentences, arrange them in a logical order for presentation, and compose a first draft. When first drafts have been entered onto a word processor, editing groups can meet to share and critique the papers before students revise and print out their work to pass in to the teacher.

Describing a Person

PURPOSE: This activity draws on the same skills used in describing a place—keen observation and precise reporting of concrete details. A description of a person, however, also offers a glimpse of the character that lives beneath the physical description.

PREPARATION: Cut out thirty or more pictures of individual people from old magazines. Try to collect pictures that represent a variety of ages, types of clothing, facial and body expressions. Number each picture on the back in order to keep track of them later.

A day or two before you plan to begin the activity, select one of the large magazine pictures that you feel is most interesting. Tape it up on a wall where students will be sure to notice it, and leave it up for a couple of days without commenting on it.

THE FIRST ACTIVITY: Begin the activity with a discussion about the picture on display. Ask students what impressions or opinions they have about the person in the picture, and then ask them how they made those judgments. Discuss how things such as clothing, facial expressions, body posture, age, and setting have a powerful influence on people when they form initial impressions of others.

Next, help students see how this process of forming opinions based only on appearance works from a writer's point of view. Writers can very effectively guide readers into forming impressions about people by carefully crafting physical descriptions that indirectly convey particular personality traits.

At this time, pass around the magazine pictures of individuals, asking students to choose one they would like to write about. Explain that they will write a physical description that should include details about the dress, hair style, expression, and so on, that they see in the picture. This description should not include anything they cannot see, however, such as clothing that's not evident in the picture, an imaginary conversation, or overt description of the person's character. The writer should, instead, attempt to guide the reader into forming an impression of the individual pictured by carefully choosing which details to describe; this will subtly lead the reader to make certain inferences about the person's character.

When students are finished, ask them to write the number of the picture on top of their paper, collect the pictures and papers, and save them for the next activity.

THE SECOND ACTIVITY: This time the teacher passes out the same pictures that were used the day before, but to different students. Try to distribute them so that girls receive the pictures chosen by boys the first day and boys receive the ones first selected by girls, or at least give each picture to a student who is in some way different from the one who wrote the first description. Remind students to keep to the specifics of what they can observe in the picture, yet still try to entice readers to form impressions about the character of the person pictured.

When students have finished writing, ask them to write the number of the picture on their paper, collect the papers, and match them with the numbered descriptions written the day before. Read some of the pairs aloud and discuss the similarities and differences in the two observers' impressions of the same person. Are there significant differences between the impressions conveyed by the two observers? After reading several of these pairs, can the class come up with any generalizations about making first impressions? Do the girls in the class typically form different kinds of impressions than the boys do when observing the same pictures? What does this information about first impressions mean for writers?

THE THIRD ACTIVITY: Ask students to pick one of the pictures they have already written about (hopefully you won't have to settle disputes that may arise if two students want the same picture), and return the description that goes with it.

Have students write another description of the same person, but this time ask them to take it one giant step further. Encourage them to imagine they know the person quite well. They may like the person a lot, or they may intensely dislike the person. In this description writers should invent specifics about the character's behavior, such as things the person says or does, or how other people treat the character.

The writer must never directly say that the person is good or evil; the final judgment must be left up to the reader. The writer's job is to describe the looks and actions of the character so effectively that the reader will form an opinion about the character that is identical to the writer's. But, readers must be allowed to form their own opinions based on the facts the writer delivers.

At this point you might read some examples of this type of character sketch. Following is an excerpt of one written by an older student:

> I walk into the old farmhouse and see a ninety-four-year-old German lady sitting in a broken-down rocking chair in her dining room. She sits next to a table piled high with old newspapers and *Reader's Digests*. There are men's oxford brown shoes on her feet and heavy nylon stockings rolled to just under her knees. My grandmother has worn the exact same dress style for as long as I can remember. This one is a faded, wildly patterned print, and over it she wears a ratty, cream-colored, dress jacket. My family gives her new dresses and pretty sweaters and nightgowns, but they all reside in her dresser drawers, "too good to wear."
>
> Her face has the vacant look of someone who is far away, and when I walk in her door, it takes several seconds for her to remember who I am, the oldest of

seven grandchildren. Her hair is fluffed around her head, thin and soft as thistle-down. A face full of memories, and so many years of living, looks at me with a kind of absent-minded pleasure. Lines cobweb her worn face and masculine, bushy eyebrows bristle over her faded blue eyes. . . .

When they have finished this assignment, ask students to choose the best one of the three descriptions they wrote and enter it onto a word processor. Editing groups can then critique the selected descriptions, making suggestions about how to improve them in the second draft, which will be handed in to the teacher. Ask each editing group to pick one or two of the most successful ones to share with the class. Read these aloud and/or post them in the classroom.

Short Biography

PURPOSE: This activity introduces students to several fairly sophisticated composition skills, including the following: interviewing; taking notes and organizing them into suitable composition material; discarding information that doesn't support the main ideas; choosing a method of development; and coordinating all these skills to complete a short biography successfully.

PREPARATION: Arrange for another teacher or guest to come into the classroom for a short interview on the day you plan to do the activity.

THE ACTIVITY: Discuss with the class the purpose of an interview—why writers use interviews to collect information, and what types of writing make use of the interview process most often (e.g., news articles, editorials, biographies). Talk about what sorts of questions interviewers ask their subjects.

One effective way to approach the topic of giving interviews is to hold a personal interview in the classroom. Ask a student volunteer, or invite a guest to come into the classroom for a short interview. Let's say a sixth grade teacher, Mr. Lucas, agrees to come for a fifteen-minute interview concerning his life as a middle-school teacher.

Before the guest arrives, however, discuss with students what questions they think they should ask Mr. Lucas to find out more about his teaching career, and tell them to write down a few of them. Help students devise direct questions such as, "What do you like best about teaching?" and "What do you dislike most about teaching?" rather than "How do you like teaching?" Encourage them to pursue vague answers that they might get with follow-up questions. For example, if an interviewer asks, "How is Smith Elementary School different from the school you taught at last year?" and the subject answers, "Well, the school schedule is different and they have a larger sports program," the interviewer should come back with follow-up questions such as, "Would you please describe what's different about their school schedule?" or "What specific sports and activities are included in their sports program?"

Suggest that they conduct the interview like a press conference with a variety of students posing questions to the guest, one at a time. Ask students to take careful notes during the interview.

When the interview is over and the guest has left, discuss with the class what things the person said that were most useful in helping others get to know him as a teacher and as an individual. Ask them to read specifics from their notes that they would use in a paper describing the guest. This exercise should make it very clear that detailed interview notes are important when it comes time to write about the individual.

Next, explain that the class interview was a practice exercise for the activity they will begin now. Explain that they will each interview a classmate (and be interviewed by that classmate) and write a short biography about the person interviewed. Discuss what kinds of questions they could ask that might provide interesting information for a short biographical sketch.

Divide the class into pairs of students (who don't know each other very well) and then ask them to spend a few minutes thinking about and writing down questions for the interview. Explain that these questions will serve as guidelines for the interview, but that they will probably think of many other questions as the interview continues.

Allow thirty to forty minutes for pairs to complete the first interview and finish taking notes. You may decide to save the second interview (in which the student who first interviewed becomes the person being interviewed) until the next day.

When all interviews are completed, discuss possible ways to approach writing a short biography (e.g., chronological development, or development that focuses on major interests, accomplishments, or strong beliefs). Suggest that the type of developmental structure they choose will depend largely on the specific information collected from an interview. Go through a couple of possible developmental plans with them, using one student's interview notes.

Ask students to compose a draft of the biography and enter it onto a word processor. After that, classmates are invited to read and critique the biography that was written about them. In fact, the same pairs that worked together for the interviews could work together again as editing pairs. Or, if you place two sets of pairs together in groups of four, then at least two of the four critics will not be personally involved in each biography that's critiqued.

Following these critiquing sessions, ask students to revise their papers and hand in the second drafts. After reading these, a teacher may select some to read to the class, and/or make further suggestions for third draft revisions.

Personal Story

PURPOSE: This activity helps increase students' understanding of the basic structure of a story, including the following elements: an introduction of the setting and major character, a plot that involves a series of events leading up the climax, a climax, and a resolution. Writing a short narrative about a personal experience that happened in one's own life is an effective way to begin learning story writing skills because the writer knows the plot and major character very well, and because the method of organizing such a story is simply chronological.

PREPARATION: Find and duplicate a few examples of well-written personal narratives to use as models for the writing assignment. The following example was written by an older student:

THE BABYSITTER

While my parents were on a two-day vacation, a sixty-three-year-old crinkly-faced lady by the name of Mrs. Hunt stayed with my brother and me. Mrs. Hunt is not your everyday, run-of-the-mill babysitter, and this occasion was, in many ways, out of the ordinary.

We all went to the airport to send my parents off and Mrs. Hunt drove my brother and me home. She literally crawled along the highway at 20 mph in a 55 mph zone. Other drivers kept honking and screaming obscenities as they zoomed by. One man even pulled alongside of us and shouted, "Hey, lady, is your gas pedal broken?" I just hid myself from view until we got home.

For dinner that night, Mrs. Hunt prepared baked salmon, peas, brussel sprouts, and broccoli. Yeecccccchhh!! Obviously, the lady was big on green vegetables, and she sat down at the table making sure my brother and I ate every last bit. I pleaded with her not to make me eat them, but she was adamant. I even tried to squish the vegetables in my napkin when she turned her head, but she caught me, and I was forced to consume them until my plate was bare. As I rose from the table, a wave of nausea hit me and I threw up all over the place, including my brother and Mrs. Hunt. After I finished retching, she said coarsely, "You probably have the flu."

The next day, which was Sunday, I was feeling much better, and not waiting for Mrs. Hunt's permission, I snuck out of the house and headed for a carnival down the street, where I won a goldfish by throwing a ping-pong ball into its bowl. Winning the goldfish made me very happy because I'd been wanting to have pet fish for a long time. When I got home, I strolled into the kitchen with my goldfish and bowl, and there Mrs. Hunt stood, cooking more frozen vegetables, and giving me disapproving looks for sneaking out of the house while I was supposedly sick. After placing the bowl next to the sink, I raided the refrigerator for lunch, ignoring Mrs. Hunt's comments about children with poor manners.

Suddenly, I noticed that Mrs. Hunt was emptying the fish bowl into the sink. I was horrified! I raced over to her and screamed, "Stop!! What are you doing?!"

I'm cleaning out your fish bowl," she calmly replied. By then I was speechless because the fish had fallen into the garbage disposal, which was off, thank goodness. At that point, I decided to pull out the fish with the aid of two spoons, but before I could even get the spoons, Mrs. Hunt attempted to turn on a light, and instead, accidentally turned on the garbage disposal.

I cried—for about a day, and fortunately for me *and* Mrs. Hunt, my parents were only gone for two days. I can't imagine what would have happened had she stayed any longer.

THE ACTIVITY: Discuss with the class the elements involved in relating a specific personal experience to an audience. Take, for example, the experience of going to a Chinese restaurant with parents and using chopsticks for the first time. Would the storyteller begin by explaining; "As we left the restaurant I noticed the slippery noodles had formed unique decorations on the furniture," or, "In the midst of a battle with some mushrooms, I nicknamed the two sticks 'King Arthur' and 'Sir Lancelot' "?

Ask students what information they would present first and how they would develop the story after that. Ask them to invent a climax for the Chinese restaurant experience, such as: "Just when King Arthur and Sir Lancelot finally managed to spear the sweet and sour pork, snow peas, and mustard greens that slid around the plate, the waiter arrived with a bowl of Lotus seed pudding."

Then work on a resolution, such as this example:"The next time my parents took me out to dinner we went to The Country Western Steak House." By this time, the class has created a practically complete narrative, with each part of its structure identified in the context of the story.

Pass out the duplicated example of a personal narrative and read it aloud. Then ask students to identify the introduction, specific incidents that help develop the plot, the climax, and the resolution. Introduce the first-person point of view and discuss how the writer includes his or her personal feelings about the experience. Talk about how the narrative might be different if told by a different person, using the third-person point of view.

At this point, ask students to suggest some of their own personal experiences that could make interesting story material and write their ideas on the chalkboard or word processor. Help them think of experiences that are likely to have a definite series of events leading up to a specific climax. Here are a few examples:

- The time I got lost at Yankee Stadium
- The biggest surprise of my life
- The funniest thing that's ever happened to me
- The first time I rode on a motorcycle
- The last time I'll ever go on a picnic with Sue
- The hardest thing I've ever done
- The scariest thing I've ever done

Ask students to choose an experience in their lives that they'd like to write about. Have them note the following information: the place where the event occurred; specific events that lead to the most exciting part; the most exciting part or turning point (climax); and the resolution. Then ask them to list other ideas and details they want to include in the narrative. After they've written these notes and rearranged the ideas in the order they will appear in the story, students can begin composing.

If they write out first drafts by hand, they should enter them onto a word processor before meeting in editing groups for the critique. Later, when the second drafts are completed, they may be handed in to the teacher for further comments and suggestions before a final draft is printed. At the conclusion of this activity, read some of the more interesting ones aloud for the whole class to enjoy.

Communicating Via Computer

PURPOSE: To help students understand the power (and limits) of the written word when it is the sole means of communication.

TIMING: This activity involves one computer and no more than six or eight students. If your class is larger than eight students, and most are, save the activity for a time when you happen to have just a small group. Ten or fifteen minutes is all the time required, although the session could continue for as long as you and the other participants wish.

THE ACTIVITY: When an occasion arises where you and a few students are left in the classroom alone, head for the computer and load the word processing software, if it's not up and running already. Indicate, by placing an index finger to your lips, that silence is necessary for the mysterious activity that will follow.

Begin by typing a brief message that will appear on the screen, such as: "My favorite dessert is cottage cheese with blueberries." All the students present should be able to see the screen message. Get up, maintaining absolute silence, and indicate that it's someone else's turn to sit down and write a message. The next person may respond with a curt remark such as, "Yuck," or a more chatty comment such as, "Really? I can't stand cottage cheese, but I sure do love chocolate chip ice cream with strawberries on top and french fries on the side. A Coke would be nice, too."

This kind of silent, but highly interactive, personal communication could continue among participants for quite a while. If the "conversation" gets stuck on any one subject for an overly long time, you can take another turn at the keyboard and switch topics. You might introduce topics that invite students to discuss their feelings and opinions about personal matters (such as the topics suggested for the Spontaneous Writing activity) or about more academic issues such as their opinions of a book the class just read, or what they learned during a recent field trip to the local newspaper office.

There are three implicit rules of this game; hopefully you will never have to state them overtly in a screen message. First, topics introduced must be familiar to most of the participants. Second, all communication is accomplished through written messages only. Third, messages are brief and everybody takes turns at the keyboard.

Writing Conversation

PURPOSE: This activity helps students begin to listen more carefully to what people say, and to understand that what a person says provides a lot of information about his or her character. In addition, inventing a dialogue gives student writers the special experience of relating thoughts and events through conversation only.

PREPARATION: Locate and duplicate one or two short dialogues between two people that successfully convey an idea or event and also give the audience a glimpse of the speakers' personalities. The following is an example dialogue written by an older student. It's longer than students at this level would be expected to write in an assignment, but shows how dialogue can effectively present an event and also characterize the speakers.

THE KINGDOM

An old woman walked up to the park bench closest to the pond and plopped down with a sigh. Out from under her sweater she pulled a paper bag. With the rustle of the bag, fat pigeons flocked to her feet. The birds cooed while she threw crumbs to them.

From across the pond a young school girl rushed toward the woman. She threw her books on the end of the bench and glided shyly over to the old woman.

"Hi!"

"Oh, well hi there sweet thing."

"Whatcha doin?"

"Why, I'm feeding the birds, honey."

"Can I try?"

"Of course you can. Here."

The old woman handed the bag of crumbs to the anxious girl.

"Do you come to the park often?" asked the little girl.

"Oh, yes. I have a lot of friends here."

"Ya do? Who?"

"Well, the squirrels, the ducks, and of course these birds here."

"The animals are your friends?"

"Yes they are."

"Ah come on, you're foolin' me, huh?"

"No I am not fooling you."

"Yea, I bet they talk to ya too."

"Why, yes they do!"

"Ah, come on. Well, if they talk, tell me what they say."

"These birds tell me about their kingdom."

"Kingdom! No birds have a kingdom. Do they?"

"These birds have a kingdom. See that circle of trees over there?"

"Yea, what about it?"

"That's their kingdom. Inside the circle is a tall white porcelain castle where the birds live, and in the middle of that, there is a nice blue pool for the birds to bathe in."

"Have you been there?"

"Oh no, the birds just tell me about it. See that fat bird over there on top of that statue's head?"

"Yea."

"That is the king, King Charles. He changed his name a few years back, it was Bernie before."

"He still looks like a Bernie!"

"Yes, but don't tell him that, it would hurt his feelings. See that skinny bird hopping around below the statue? Well, that's the court jester. The king always makes him entertain, with hardly ever a rest, not even to eat. That is why he is so skinny and why the king is so fat."

"What's the mark on the king's chest?"

"Oh that, that's an old battle wound from the War of the Pelicans. It's just a simple peck wound, but he proudly flaunts it."

"What a brat!"

"Look at that beautiful white bird sitting quietly at the edge of the pond. See her? Her name is Lily."

"She looks sad, or somethin'."

"Yes, she is very sad. You see, the king's son is very much in love with her and she with him. But the king disapproves of this, because she is the daughter of a beak cleaner, which the king considers to be very low, too low to be in love with his son anyway. There are plans for the marriage of the king's son with another bird from the kingdom across the pond."

"Oh no, that's awful. We should do somethin'."

"Yes we should, do you have any ideas?"

"Well, we could hmm . . . , well I guess we could, hmm . . ."

"We could switch brides at the wedding. Does that sound good?" the lady suggested.

"Yea, we could do that. But what do you mean?"

"The wedding is tomorrow afternoon. What we will do is kidnap the bride-to-be from the other kingdom and replace her with Lily. Then we can think of some way to get the bride and groom away from here after the wedding."

"Yea, that sounds good. We'll teach that old king!"

"All right, let's meet here at about this time tomorrow. That should give us enough time."

"Okay, I'll see you then."

As the little girl ran off across the park the old woman yelled out, "Bring some rice!"

THE FIRST ACTIVITY: Pass out and read aloud example dialogue(s). Talk about how the dialogue manages to convey something about the individual characters as well as the topic they are discussing in the conversation.

One way to demonstrate the potential vitality of dialogue is to stage a few impromptu dialogues in the classroom. In these mini-dramas, students are placed in hypothetical situations that force them to invent dialogue that befits the assigned character and situation in which they are immersed. Here are some example situations that may lead to rather spirited dialogues:

- *Characters:* two sisters and a parent
  Situation: One sister has a new dress that she has worn only once. The other sister, who does not have a new dress, has just been invited to a party. She asks her sister if she can borrow the new dress. Her sister refuses.
- *Characters:* three friends
  Situation: The three friends are going to a ball game all by themselves. They take a bus to the ball park and when they get off, one friend notices that there is a drugstore nearby. He suggests to the others that they go in the store and steal some candy to eat during the game.
- *Characters:* two parents and their ten- and 11-year-old children
  Situation: The parents have always established regular bedtimes for the children. Only a few months ago they changed the 9:00 bedtime rule to 9:30 on weekdays and 10:00 on weekends. The children want to stay up until 10:00 on weekdays, too. They approach their parents with this request.

Ask the students to spend a half an hour sometime during the afternoon or evening listening to, and writing down a conversation between, two people. If they wish, they may tape-record the conversation first, and then transcribe it from the recording.

Explain that there is a standard format to use when writing a dialogue (i.e., start a new paragraph whenever a different person begins speaking, put quotation marks around the direct speech, etc.). Refer them to the example dialogue handed out and suggest they use it as a model for style and format. The next day students may wish to share dialogues they think are particularly entertaining.

THE SECOND ACTIVITY: Now students are ready to try inventing a dialogue. Ask them to think of situations that would involve a conversation between two people. Situations that contain some kind of conflict, like the ones used for the classroom improvisations, often produce effective dialogues. Have students share a few of their suggestions with the class and then ask them to tell you what situation they've chosen, before they begin. This early check will help them avoid attempting dialogues that are likely to be unsuccessful because they are too complex (such as conversations that involve more than two people) or too boring (such as conversations about how the local football team is doing).

Have them enter first drafts onto a word processor, and then meet in editing groups to critique them. Editing groups may wish to pick out one or two of the most effective dialogues, print the "scripts," and "perform" them in front of the class.

News Articles

PURPOSE: Writing news stories helps students learn to distinguish fact from opinion when relating events. In this activity students will be introduced to the traditional style of journalistic writing—the inverted pyramid—which requires information to be structured so that the vital *who, what, when,* and *where* facts are included in the first paragraph.

PREPARATION: Pick a few recent news articles from a local newspaper that exemplify clear, inverted-pyramid style writing. Try to find articles from both a city newspaper and a school newspaper. Duplicate these for students.

THE FIRST ACTIVITY: Hand out the example newspaper articles and read the first paragraph of each, asking students to pay attention to the information presented in both first paragraphs. Discuss why news articles typically present the results and the most exciting part of a news story in the beginning, instead of saving it until the middle or end, as in a narrative. Make sure to include explanations such as the following: (1) readers are often in a hurry when they read newspapers so they want the facts first; (2) splashing the dramatic information in the more visible beginning paragraphs sells papers; (3) editors frequently cut final paragraphs off news stories just before publication to make room for more important news.

Explain that news stories are supposed to report only the facts surrounding an event. They are not supposed to include the writer's opinions. If any opinions are included at all they must be opinions stated by someone who was involved in the experience being reported, or related to it in some way. Explain that reporters typically do interview such people, soliciting their opinions concerning the event, and quoting them in the news story.

Ask students to suggest newsworthy events that recently happened at school, such as:

- A smashing victory for the girls' soccer team
- A guest speaker who spoke at a school assembly about smoking

- An incident in the lunch room that involved vandalism
- A llama that came to school with Mrs. Brown last Friday

Have them pick a topic for a news article and then note the vital *who, what, when,* and *where* information surrounding the incident or event. Ask them to compose a first sentence, or "lead," for the story that includes that specific information. Have them read these aloud so that classmates can help each other develop powerful leads for their stories.

Have students list the other points they want to include in the article and arrange them in order from most important to least important. Then ask them to finish writing the story.

THE SECOND ACTIVITY: Ask students to pick an event that they know will be happening at school, such as a sports event, a committee or club meeting, or a special activity planned for a class. Ask them to attend it, take notes during the event, and interview one or two people present at the event. Remind them to prepare some interview questions beforehand (see the previous Biography activity for further details on giving an interview), and that their own opinions must not be included in the article. Then send the reporters off to do their job.

When first drafts are completed and entered onto a word processor, students can meet in editing groups to critique and revise their work. Ask them to print out and hand in second drafts.

Writing Instructions

PURPOSE: Learning to write clear and complete instructions is a fundamental step in the process of learning to write with accuracy and clarity in any form of writing. This activity helps students understand the significance of writing clearly and accurately because if they don't, readers will not be able to follow the directions to a successful end.

PREPARATION: Find and duplicate a few examples of clearly written instructions for students to use as models for the writing assignment. You could use recipes from cookbooks, program instructions from user's manuals, sewing directions from pattern packets, instructions that come with model cars, planes, boats, and so on.

THE ACTIVITY: Begin this activity by talking with students about their experiences with following directions in order to complete some unfamiliar task, such as baking popovers, putting together a model airplane, or running a new software program. Did they find it easy, or difficult, to follow the written instructions? How clear were the directions? How detailed does a written set of directions have to be for the reader to be able to complete the task successfully?

Pick a simple task familiar to most students, such as brushing one's teeth. (Getting dressed, riding a bicycle, or jumping rope are other such examples.) Ask a volunteer from the class to explain step-by-step how she brushes her teeth. Ask the rest of the class to write down each step as she explains it. When the directions are finished, discuss whether any steps were left out, or if any of the explanations were unclear. Make the necessary amendments so that everyone has a set of directions that clearly explains how to brush one's teeth. A more engaging alternative to this would be to bring a toothbrush and toothpaste to class and demonstrate the procedure while students write down the steps, one after the other.

Ask students to explain how an essay that gives instructions is organized (i.e., step-by-step, in the order the steps are performed for successful completion of the task). Brainstorm with the class other possible topics for this kind of essay and write a list on the chalkboard or word processor. The list might include topics such as the following:

- How to play hop scotch
- How to do the elementary back stroke (side stroke, crawl, etc.)
- How to plant a garden
- How to climb a tree
- How to change a diaper
- How to make a tape recording of a record
- How to bathe a dog

Have each student choose a process that's familiar to him or her and begin the assignment by making a list of the materials needed to perform the task, and then a list of the steps in the order they must be done. (At this point it would be a good idea to check their topic choices, making sure they don't choose a process that is too complex to explain in this short assignment.) When they're finished with this exercise they can take the specific steps and expand them into complete sentences and paragraphs that clearly explain all the necessary steps to complete the job.

After these first drafts are finished, read a few aloud and discuss whether a person could realistically follow the instructions—as written—and finish successfully. This critiquing session with the whole class will provide a model for how editing groups should approach the next task—reading the essays and evaluating their clarity, accuracy, and completeness, and also making suggestions for improvements. After editing groups have critiqued the papers, the writers can complete second drafts and hand them in to the teacher.

Writing a Definition

PURPOSE: Thinking out and writing clear and complete definitions of terms are basic skills that are important for all students to acquire. This activity gives students the opportunity to examine how in-depth definitions are written and to practice writing some.

PREPARATION: Locate an example of an essay that clearly defines a topic that's simple enough for everyone in the class to be able to understand. Duplicate this as a model for the class. Following is a typical example of a student-written definition essay:

A MOTORHOME

A motorhome is a vehicle that has all the necessities of a house built into the interior. Most motorhomes are two-axle motor vehicles that require a normal driver's license to operate. They are usually powered by big, V-8 engines, but sometimes smaller engines are installed to achieve better gas mileage. Ranging from 18 to 38 feet long, 10 to 13 feet high, and 8 to 9 feet in width, most motorhomes have hot and cold running water, electricity, ovens and cook tops with three or four burners, air conditioners, heaters, a separate toilet and shower, dining table, cupboards for storage, and a multitude of concealed beds. The motorhome is set apart from a camper or a trailer because the driver sits inside the living section—no walls separate the driver from the rest of the vehicle. They can travel anywhere a car or bus can go and are especially good for camping and long cross-country trips.

The motorhome first appeared in the mid-sixties. People needed a cheap, economical way to travel long distances on land. The first prototypes were rustic, oblong bodies, that looked like giant sausages. As the idea spread, more companies started building them. The shape became more aerodynamic and the prices dropped due to competition. When the oil shortages of the seventies appeared, people couldn't afford to pay for gas. The end seemed near, but now gas prices have dropped, and travelers are using the motorhomes more and more. It looks like the motorhome has moved into the lives of many Americans and is here to stay for a while.

THE ACTIVITY: Begin this activity by passing out and reading the example essay to the class. Ask them what the purpose of the essay is (i.e., to define and tell the reader a bit about motorhomes), and how successfully it accomplishes the purpose. Discuss the writer's method of organization. (First he describes motorhomes by presenting facts and specific descriptive information. Then he presents its functional qualities by placing it in historical perspective.)

Discuss with students other questions such as the following: Was the writer reasonably objective, or were there biased words and strong opinions presented? Was the definition complete enough? Clear enough? How could it be improved?

Next, brainstorm with students at the chalkboard or word processor, other possible topics for definition essays. For example:

- *Objects*: a bicycle, clothing, a violin
- *Animals*: a cocker spaniel, a morgan horse, a hummingbird
- *People*: a policeman, a parent, a lawyer
- *Ideas or attributes*: intelligence, wealth, honesty

Have the class select one of these topics and brainstorm about what they feel would be important to include in a definition essay about that topic. Write their suggestions on the chalkboard or word processor. With the class, arrange the items in the order of proposed presentation and compose a topic sentence. Continue composing the essay as a class, or leave it at this stage, if you think they understand how to compose the rest of the essay.

Ask students to choose a topic for their own essays, brainstorm ideas, arrange them in the order of presentation, and compose a topic sentence. Check these steps before directing them to continue writing the assignment. Students can then compose the first draft at their desks or at a word processor. When the first drafts have been entered on a word processor, students can meet in editing groups to critique their papers and plan a revised draft. Have them print out and hand in the revised second drafts.

Writing a Comparison

PURPOSE: Comparing two items that are similar enough to be comparable and yet still notably different, is a technique that writers use fairly often. This activity helps students understand how the technique is used, and provides an opportunity to practice it.

THE ACTIVITY: Divide the chalkboard in half and label one side CATS and the other side DOGS. Then ask students to think about the positive characteristics of having a cat for a pet, compared to the positive characteristics of having a dog for a pet. For example, they might offer the following:

CATS

- Keep themselves clean
- Don't bark
- Are small enough to cuddle up in your lap
- Don't have to be let out of the house to go to the bathroom
- Don't jump up on you and knock you over
- Don't constantly beg you to throw a stick for them to chase.
- Purr softly when you pat them

- Are fun to watch when they play with balls and string and other cat toys

DOGS

- Are more openly friendly and affectionate
- Can learn to do tricks
- Can learn to stay off the furniture
- Warn you when someone's at the door or in the yard
- Are openly happy to see you when you get home
- Come along when you go to a friend's house
- Go to the bathroom outside, instead of inside in a special litter box

Discuss how a writer could organize an essay that compares, for example, cats and dogs. One might compare them point-by-point, or divide the paper into two parts and discuss each pet separately. Have the class choose a method of comparison for this essay and rearrange the list items into groups and order of presentation in the essay.

Try composing such an essay collaboratively on a word processor. Start by having students create a topic sentence such as this: Cats and dogs are both popular pets, but there are several things you should keep in mind before choosing which one you want to own.

Ask them to dictate what should be written next, and then continue the essay in this manner to the end. Revise and rewrite the essay as a class, print out the final draft, and make copies for everyone. They can use this as a model for writing their own comparison essays.

Ask students to suggest other topics for comparison and write them on the chalkboard or word processor. Here are a few examples:

- Your room and your sister's (or brother's) room
- Two superheroes (e.g., Superman and Spiderman, or Wonderwoman and Spiderwoman)
- Two other popular television heroes
- Two recently read books
- Writing letters to friends far away as compared to calling them on the telephone
- Sailboats and motorboats
- Ping-pong and tennis
- Football and soccer
- Mothers and fathers
- Sisters and brothers

Students can then select a topic and begin listing comparable characteristics. Before composing the essay, have them choose a method of comparison, arrange the list in the order of presentation, and write a topic sentence. Students may continue composing the essay after these preliminary steps have been checked by a teacher.

Students may need help at different points in the process; sometimes it's difficult to develop a complete list of comparable information, or to plan a method of organization. Either the teacher or members of the students' editing groups should be available for consultation.

When the first drafts are completed and entered on a word processor, students can get feedback and suggestions for improvements from their editing groups. After the essays have been critiqued and revised, students can print out and pass in their second drafts to the teacher.

Persuasive Essay

PURPOSE: Being able to persuade people to adopt a particular point of view on a topic is a very powerful skill; many people never acquire the technique of effective persuasion. The key to success in persuasion is to develop logical arguments that are supported by factual information, evidence, and examples. Persuasive essays that use emotional arguments laced with biased words and personal opinions are rarely as convincing to an intelligent audience.

PREPARATION: Locate an example of a persuasive essay that uses logical arguments supported by factual information to make a stand on an issue that's familiar to most students. Duplicate it for students, or bring it to class to read aloud on the day you plan to begin the activity. Following is an example persuasive essay written by an older student. (It may provoke some students to write an essay that takes a positive stand about the increased use of computers.)

WHAT'S WRONG WITH THE COMPUTER?

The Technological Revolution introduced computers to the civilized world and computers have introduced us to the Information Age. Since this has happened, the need for computer knowledge has become vital. However, there are many disadvantages of the computer, and the trend towards total dependency on the computer is frightening. Before we advance one step further towards computer dependency, we need to look closely at some of the nonbeneficial effects of computers.

As computers continue to replace humans in the work force, unemployment will also continue to rise. Computers and computer-operated robots are now doing a number of jobs. In the auto industry they paint and assemble cars. In the clothing industry they do the jobs of tailors. In business, the accountants are being replaced. In airplanes, the flight navigator is now a computer. In libraries, the computer catalogs and keeps track of books. In classrooms, teachers' aides are being replaced by computers. In the medical field, symptoms are entered into a computer which calculates diagnosis, thus replacing the physician as diagnostician. In hotels, making reservations and many of the other services are being done by computers. The goal of these "advances" is to get more work done by fewer people. The final outcome is fewer people working and greater unemployment.

With computers taking over jobs previously done by people, the problem of de-humanization grows. As businesses and schools replace people with computers, it becomes apparent that there is a disregard for the large group of people who need the gratification received from work. Human qualities are exchanged for machine performance; for example, when a teacher's aide is replaced by a machine, the student will not experience humanness—facial expression, eye contact, and the effects of voice inflection. In this situation, the students don't receive the human interaction that is vital to wholesome learning.

Loss of human interaction is probably one of the most detrimental long-range disadvantages of the computer. Those who work alone with their computers will lose the opportunity for social stimulation. Children who organize their lives around computers for play and learning will fail to learn how to socialize. One well-known psychologist at Stanford University, Dr. Zimbaro, has already seen this de-velopment and calls it "hacker syndrome." These kids would prefer to communi-cate to the person sitting next to them via computer terminal. Some fear that their vast experience of computer games and simulations, and their limited experience interacting with other human beings will greatly distort their view of reality.

Purchasing and maintaining a computer requires a sizable amount of money. Thus, there is a concern that computers can widen the gap between the rich and the poor. It is already evident that white, middle class children are by far the ma-jority of young personal computer users. It's becoming evident that those who don't learn computer skills will face an obstacle to future employment, and schools in poor areas cannot afford computers and teacher training.

Even when businesses or individuals purchase computers and become depen-dent on them, they face problems. If the computer is accidentally unplugged, or the electricity goes off for even an instant, everything that was in the computer's internal memory is lost. In addition, if the operator makes any mistake when giving an instruction, such as typing a dash instead of a comma, the program won't work. For example, several years ago all long distance telephone service was cut off to Greece because of such an error. It took months to correct the program and restore the phone service.

A new area of crime is also emerging with the increased use of computers. Tam-pering with data is easy once a person gets access to the program, and embezzle-ment is rising.

The tremendous amount of knowledge that computers can store and rapidly dis-play makes information about every citizen in the country accessible to the govern-ment. Financial records, personal records, school and job records—there may be no escape from the past. How far this invasion of privacy will go, remains to be seen.

In conclusion, there is no doubt that the computer is the machine of the present and future. It will create more spare time for the worker *who has a job*. In some ways it will do a better job than the people it replaces, but at what cost to human qualities and the human race? The wise will keep in mind the dangers of growing computer dependency and will work to avert the social and economic difficulties that the computer age will bring.

THE ACTIVITY: Pass out the duplicated persuasive essay (if you made copies for students) and read it aloud. Then encourage students to ana-lyze what specific arguments the writer makes and why the arguments are or are not convincing. Which arguments are least convincing? Most convincing? Suggest some other arguments the writer could have used.

Brainstorm with students some topics that they have strong opinions about and that fall within their realm of experience. For example:

- The school should have Coke and candy vending machines.
- Kids should be allowed to decide for themselves when to go to bed.
- Teachers should not give homework over weekends and vacations.
- Kids should be allowed to borrow computer disks from school to take home overnight.
- Kids should get paid for doing extra chores at home.

As a class activity, pick one of the suggested topics, choose a side, and ask students to help make a list of possible arguments. Write these on the chalkboard or word processor. Help them develop arguments that are logical and substantiated with facts and examples. For example, if the class selects the topic "Kids should be allowed to decide for themselves when to go to bed," they might list the following arguments:

- Some kids need less sleep than others.
- How can young people learn to be responsible for themselves if they aren't given the opportunity? This is an excellent way to learn self-responsibility.
- For example, if a kid stays up late and has to get up early for school the next day, she will probably learn for herself whether she needs to go to bed earlier. If she isn't tired the next day, then it wasn't too late for her and she should be able to stay up late again.
- Kids can promise not to play music or have the TV on too loud, so they won't bother anyone else.
- etc.

Ask students to help compose a thesis statement (topic sentence) that clearly states the topic and the stand that will be supported in the essay. Here's an example: "When children reach the age of nine or ten, they should gradually be allowed to take on more responsibility for themselves, such as deciding what time to go to bed at night."

Go through the list of arguments and decide how to group them for the essay. Establish the order of presentation and plan a strategy that the writer could use that would be clear and convincing.

As students dictate sentences, the teacher can enter the text onto a word processor. Various suggestions and revisions will inevitably be offered, so the teacher should be prepared to make a lot of changes while they draft the essay. When the class essay is finished, the teacher can print it out and make copies for everyone to use as a model for writing their own persuasive essays.

Have students select a topic for their own papers and go through the same preliminary steps indicated above. Check their lists and topic sentences before they get too far along in the drafting process.

When first drafts are completed, they can share them with classmates in their editing groups. At this point, it would be a good idea for the teacher to go around and help editing groups work out a system for critiquing these essays, such as providing them with a list of specific elements to focus on when reviewing the essays. Because students are likely to hold strong and conflicting opinions about the topics being presented in the papers, a little help from a more objective adult might be needed. The following checklist for editors could be helpful:

- What is the topic sentence and how clearly does it introduce the topic and the writer's stand? Give some suggestions for improvement.
- What are the writer's chief arguments and how logically does he or she support the arguments? (Does the writer provide examples, facts, other details?) Give some suggestions for improvement.
- Does the writer successfully avoid using emotional or biased words in the arguments? Give some suggestions for improvement.
- How well organized is the essay? Give some suggestions for improvement.

When the first drafts have been critiqued, students can rewrite and print second drafts to hand in to the teacher.

Writing a Review

PURPOSE: The techniques involved in writing a review of a television show, movie, book, restaurant, software program, etc., are somewhat similar to the techniques used in writing a persuasive essay—the writer critiques the subject of review, presents an opinion, and supports it with evidence and examples. Oftentimes in a review, however, the writing style is more informal and biased, and slang words are commonly included.

In addition to having the ability to persuade, a reviewer needs another skill—the ability to offer the reader a glimpse, or summary of the subject being reviewed, without presenting a detailed account of the entire experience.

This activity will help student writers begin to acquire these difficult, but important skills.

PREPARATION: Locate a well-written review that critiques a movie, book, computer program, etc., that's familiar to most students. Duplicate copies for the classs. Following is an example review of a restaurant written by an older student.

SHABBY ANDY'S ENDS SEARCH FOR LARGER SERVINGS

One of the more irritating things that the restaurant diner experiences is without a doubt the "micro-steak syndrome." The hungry eater transports himself somewhere on the classier side of the restaurant world, only to be dismayed by the steak (or lack thereof) that is placed before him. He has spent up to $30 on a hunk of beef that he has a difficult time locating on the plate.

But, remember, nice restaurants don't necessarily focus on quantity—quality is job one. So the eater gets a tiny portion, but is treated to an elegant environment. "Big deal!" the serious eater would retort. Fortunately for his kind, a restaurant does exist that goes against the grain.

Located in Campton on Campton Avenue just before the Route 221 overpass, one finds Andy's. Upon absorbing your first view of this place, discouragement may overcome the prospective porker. The parking lot is composed of gravel, and by the looks of his establishment, Andy doesn't attach much importance to appearances. But you mustn't be misled by looks—even when you're inside. The door opens up into a semi-sleazy bar inhabited by some varied individuals. It usually isn't too crowded. Another doorway leads into the dining room, which is no spectacular sight either. Very humble table settings are spread around the room with the barbecue in a corner. The barbecue—that's the star of the show.

Andy's barbecue is the site of the creation of a limited number of simple but choice meals. All of the menu items (steak, chicken, and ribs) share one particular quality: they're large and engrossingly tasty. The steaks are unusually hefty, about 24 cubic inches, and call for a relentless jaw and a well-developed slicing motion.

Accompanying the steaks on the grill are Andy's renowned ribs. Basking in luscious barbecue sauce, they too are sizable and are delivered in large quantities to the customer.

Chicken is also a tasty possibility. The diner may choose a half or a whole fowl which is barbecued precisely for maximum flavor.

All dinners come with a baked potato that resembles an oval softball. The potato is smothered in melted American cheese, if the eater so desires, or else just butter. As a special treat, garlic French bread is served after being smoked on the barbecue.

The total meal costs from about $10 to $20. This includes the added attraction of watching the cook prepare the food, deftly wielding a butcher knife and adjusting the barbecues so as to acquire the best possible quality. It's something to do if the table conversation is boring. Service is rather fast—about fifteen minutes—and the servers are polite but informal.

So, if you're sick of being a victim of the "micro-steak syndrome," enjoy a healthy dinner at Andy's. It might not be the most glamorous place around, but it's satisfying and relaxing.

THE ACTIVITY: Begin by discussing with students the purpose of a review, who reads them, and why. Then pass out and read aloud the example review. Begin a discussion of the review with questions such as: What is the reviewer's opinion of the restaurant (or whatever the subject of review is in the example presented)? What are the stated reasons for liking, or disliking it? Do students feel the review is convincing? Why/Why not? How is the review organized?

Ask students to suggest things that they think would be interesting subjects to review. Write their suggestions on the chalkboard or word processor and ask them each to choose one. Ask them to write down the basic, factual information about the object of review; for example, the name of the television show, time and day it is broadcast, channel, type of show, major personalities in the show, and so on. Have them state their opinion about the show and list the reasons why they liked/disliked it. Then ask them to write a few sentences that very briefly summarize the show in order to help the reader picture a little bit of its "flavor."

When these preliminary exercises are completed, writers can begin sorting the information and planning how to organize their reviews. After checking out pre-writing plans with the teacher, or members of an editing group, students may begin composing their first drafts.

Use the follow-up procedures suggested in the Persuasive Writing activity, in which the teacher works with editing groups and provides a list of specific checks for group members to refer to while critiquing papers. Add to the list an item that directs editors to evaluate the brief glimpse of the subject that's presented in the reviews. For example: Does the writer successfully provide a preview of the subject without telling the reader too much about it?

Print out the final drafts and post them in the classroom so that students can read reviews of various shows, restaurants, or books that they might want to enjoy or avoid as a result of reading classmates' reviews.

Chapter 5
WRITING ACTIVITIES
FOR SECONDARY AND
JUNIOR COLLEGE STUDENTS

The writing activities that follow are designed primarily for secondary and junior college level students; however, many are also appropriate for younger writing students. In addition, a number of the activities designed for elementary and middle school students (Chapter 4) may also be effectively used in intermediate level classrooms.

In this chapter it is assumed that secondary and junior college students will have word processing equipment available in a computer lab or classroom in order to complete the writing assignments that accompany the activities.

You will notice in the text that students are regularly directed to bring written assignments to class on a disk, so that editing groups can read and critique them using a word processor. If there is not enough word processing equipment available for this process to work, simply ask students to print out a copy of their written work for each member of their editing group. Writers can then note the group's comments and suggestions concerning their work on a printed copy, rather than on a screen copy.

Journal Writing

PURPOSE: The use of journal writing as a class activity is firmly based in the theory that in order to learn to write better, one must write a lot. Journal writing in this continuing activity is private, informal, uncensored, unedited, and ungraded (except to check it off as completed). Its value is that it helps students overcome fears about writing (e.g., the "fear of the blank page" syndrome); it helps them become more fluent and prolific; and it helps them sort out thoughts and ideas that they may later wish to include in a writing assignment.

THE ACTIVITY: Discuss with students what they think keeping a journal involves. For example, it could mean writing a "Dear Diary" series of personal thoughts and confessions, recording a more formal account of daily activities, or collecting assorted thoughts and creative ideas. Explain that they will be keeping personal journals for the duration of the course (on disk) and that their journals may take any or all of these forms . . . it's up to them. Suggest other possible ways they could view their journals, such as:

- A jewelry box (or treasure chest) for unique quotes, observations, or jokes.
- A scrapbook for ideas to use in later writing assignments
- A "sketch pad" for prose descriptions or poetic images of places, people, dreams, and so on
- A telephone for holding conversations with yourself or with an imaginary person
- A microphone for recording or broadcasting your thoughts, opinions, and ideas to the rest of the world
- A series of letters to a real or imaginary friend, or to yourself

Share with them the stated purpose for keeping a journal as an activity in a writing class and explain that, most of all, it simply gives them practice in writing. Anyone who wants to become a good basketball player must practice dribbling, passing, shooting lay-ups and foul shots. Anyone who wants to become a good musician must practice counting rhythms, fingering, and playing short melodies. Journal writing provides a similar kind of regular practice in writing that's important for anyone who wants to become a good writer.

Explain that everyone will be expected to write a specific number of printout pages per week. (The amount varies depending on the level of the class.) Tell them that they may keep private journals if they wish; they simply need to have the assigned number of pages "checked off" by the teacher. This can be done by printing the journal entries and leafing through the pages with the teacher, or by scrolling through entries on the computer screen while the teacher notes the amount. You may request that students occasionally write entries that a teacher may read, as well as entries that they're willing to share with the class. And, occasionally you may give journal assignments specifically designed for sharing with classmates. Most students actually want the teacher to read their journals. When reading, however, take care to abide by the initial rules—no censorship, no editing, and no suggestions about how they could improve the writing. Comments in students' journals should refer only to the subject matter being discussed, as in a personal conversation.

Ask students to save their journal entries throughout the semester. Suggest they keep printed entries together in a looseleaf notebook arranged chronologically from the original entry to the most recent. Then, when the semester or year is about to end, make the last journal assignment one that requires students to go back and reread all their previous journal entires, then make a final entry that expresses how they think they have changed since the first day they wrote in their journals. The final entry should be one that the teacher may read, too. (See the Final Journal Entry activity.)

To help create a relaxed classroom environment suitable for journal writing, read a few playful journal entries to the class. As examples, here are a few observations:*

- At a football game yesterday at Waldo Stadium a blind man sat next to me listening to the radio.
- A drunk teenager trying to cross West Main at Michigan was being assisted by a little old lady.
- A man returned to his parked car to find its hood and fenders gashed and crumpled. On the dashboard he found a piece of folded paper. Written in a neat feminine hand, the note said: "I have just run into your car. There are people watching me. They think I am writing down my name and address. They are wrong."
- A small boy, obviously lost, walked up to a security guard at Hudson's department store and asked, "Did you see a lady walk by here without me?"
- In the middle of a heated argument with me, my wife goes to the refrigerator, gets a bottle of ginger ale, fills two glasses, gives me one, and continues the argument.

Then, have students write a few short entries of their own. Instead of asking them to write observations such as those just listed, you might present some questions that entice them to observe a few things about themselves. For example:

- When was the last time you got very angry? Explain.
- What are you feeling now? Try to describe your feelings accurately.
- Are you basically a happy person, a nervous person, a complaining person, a generous person? Pick an adjective that best describes you and then explain why.
- What makes you cry?

---

*Ken Macrorie, *Telling Writing*, Third Edition (Upper Montclair, NJ: Boynton/Cook Publishers, Inc., 1970), p. 7. Reprinted by permission.

- If you were not you, but another student in this school, who would you want to be, and why?
- What do you and your parents argue about most often? Explain their point of view first, then yours.
- What habit do you have that you'd like to break? Why?
- Can you remember a joke? Try to tell one now.
- Explain your biggest fault.
- What bores you the most? Explain.
- What do you want to have accomplished by the time you're 30?
- What sort of a person do you want to marry? What chief characteristics should this person have?
- How do you feel about being alone at your house for a whole day, overnight, for several days?
- What have you complained about today?
- List the characteristics of the friend that you like best/least.
- What are you most afraid of? Why?
- What makes you angry?
- What is your favorite time of day? Why?

If the teacher participates in these in-class journal writing activities and shares her responses with students, then students who are reluctant or shy are likely to join in much more readily.

Any time during the semester that there are a few spare minutes of class time, you might ask students to pull out a piece of paper (or get on a word processor) and write a journal entry similar to the ones listed. For a homework assignment, ask students to write a page or two of journal entries on a word processor. Tell them to print out and bring to class one or two that they would be willing to share with classmates the next day.

Journal writing, because it is informal, loosely organized, and unedited, provides students with an ideal opportunity to learn to compose text on the computer keyboard. Composing text on the keyboard eliminates the need to write a draft out by hand and thus saves time and energy that could be put into editing and revising the entered text.

Informal Autobiography

PURPOSE: This activity is a good one to do at the beginning of the year when students don't know each other very well. Sharing autobiographies helps classmates become more comfortable with one another, and helps create a friendly, supportive environment. The writing skills involved in writing a short autobiography are not as simple as they might seem to students at first. Writers must first select a few characteristics about themselves they wish to introduce to others, and then choose specific examples from their lives that convey those characteristics in an interesting way.

PREPARATION: Find an example of a short autobiographical sketch to use as an example for this activity. Duplicate it for the class. The following is a student-written example:

Dear Class,

Has it been three months already? This summer has whizzed by so fast I've hardly had time to do my favorite activity—nothing, nothing but sleeping in the sun, dreaming up poems in my head.

By the way, my name is Debbie Smith. Original, huh? There were three other Debbie Smiths in my high school. The kids called one Debbie, one Deb, and one Deborah. They called me Debbie Smith. The Smith was always attached, just like the Brown in Charlie Brown.

I was born in Hong Kong and spent the first ten years of my life living in various places in the Orient. My father was an American writer in Taiwan and my mother was a young Chinese girl looking for a job as a secretary. Just like in old Susie Wong movies, East met West and here I am. I've lived in Sealand, California, for almost nine years. As a freshman in college I attended U.C. San Diego, but got sick on cafeteria food and dorm living, so I am now a sophomore at Sealand College Business School.

So much for my exciting life. As I was saying, the summer was much too short. I spent most of my time working and playing at Johnson's swim school and club pool. For eight hours a day, five days a week, I lived in a small 95 degree indoor pool teaching kids how to blow bubbles, doggie paddle, and do big arms. My skin dried out like a peach pit and my hair was killed by chlorine poisoning. I had crying kids, screaming kid, kids that splashed, sneezed and spit in my face, and kids that peed in the pool. I'd just smile through it all and think to myself how lovely it would be to punch their little faces in. Then they'd smile back so innocently or bring me crayoned pictures or cookies the next day, and I couldn't help loving the stinkers.

On the weekends, I worked as the Social Director for the swim club, organizing such activities as barbecues, beach parties, overnights, and treasure hunts. Being the kind of person who rarely plans or organizes anything, I found this job to be extremely challenging and a pain in the neck.

I should have been rich by the end of the summer but most of my paychecks went to my parents for school, and the rest went for dozens of swim suits, record albums, parties, crazy hats, and ice cream cones. I've been a spendaholic since I was ten, and collect all kinds of things from wine bottles to apple seeds. I save almost everything except my money

I spent my last summer weekend in Santa Cruz with three friends of mine. For three days we played in the sun like six-year-old kids—making sand-people, throwing frisbees, pretending to be fish. We swam in the cold, chlorine-free ocean, catching rides on the backs of waves. I love the ocean. I could watch it forever, rising and falling, pounding in the bones of my ears and sucking my feet down into the sand. Actually, I was born in the ocean but I climbed out onto the land where my fins grew into arms and legs. If I die, I want to be buried at the bottom of the sea so I can start all over again.

Before we left Santa Cruz we watched the sun sink into the ocean one last time, blew the last of our money on popcorn, cotton candy, souvenir trinkets, and rides at the Boardwalk. We got drunk on Mateus and wandered around the town like gypsies, listening to and singing with the sidewalk musicians.

Then I was back at Sealand, standing in a line to get my name checked off so I could stand in another line. I finally got through the line to see my advisor . . . Computer Science, Business Law, Organizational Theory, Finance I, Managerial Communications, and Creative Writing. I guess it's back to business.

Yours truly,

THE ACTIVITY: Begin this activity by explaining that during the term students will be working closely together in small editing groups. They will regularly share papers with others in their editing group and occasionally with the whole class. Therefore it would be helpful to get acquainted and learn a few things about each other right away.

At this point, rearrange the class so that students are not sitting next to close friends, and ask them all to sit in different seats every day from now on. Hopefully, students will get to know each other, or at least feel comfortable with classmates as they mix with them in the classroom.

Ask students to write a few journal entries that they are willing to share with classmates, on one or two of the following subjects:

- How did you feel during the first day of this class?
- How do you think the teacher felt?
- Have you formed some first impressions about other students in this class whom you don't know? Pick such a student and jot down what you imagine that person to be like. For example, what do you imagine are his or her interests, skills, favorite foods, etc.?
- What two things would you like others to know about you?
- Describe your two greatest skills and your two greatest failings.

Then, ask student volunteers to share their entries. When the discussion has gone on as long as you feel it should, shift it over to the topic of autobiographies. Ask students what they think an autobiography is and explain that they will be writing short autobiographies to be shared with classmates. The autobiographies they will write should be informal, in the form of a friendly letter to the class.

Pass out and read the example autobiographical letter. Discuss what characteristics the writer chose to reveal about herself (e.g., she enjoys relaxing and dreaming up poems; she is part Chinese and part American and lived in the Orient for the first ten years of her life; she's a swimming teacher, a Social Director, a spendaholic, and a collector . . .). Discuss the techniques she uses to convey these characteristics (specific examples, such as experiences while teaching swimming; facts, such as her heritage, where she's lived, and what she's doing now; and descriptive details, such as the Charlie Brown explanation, and her expression of love for the ocean). Ask students what they think makes this autobiographical letter so interesting and entertaining for readers.

When the discussion about the letter is finished, ask students to write a list of a few characteristics they would include in a letter about themselves, and then have them add to the list specific information, incidents, and so on, that demonstrate each characteristic. Suggest that they sort out items that are extraneous, and arrange the remaining items in a logical order of presentation.

Students may compose these letters by hand before entering them onto a word processor, or they may try composing from their detailed notes, directly on the keyboard. Ask them to bring a printout of the letter to the next class.

When the next class begins, ask students to read their letters to classmates and after each is read, encourage them to comment on some of the strong points of each letter. Focusing on the strong points of early writing assignments is a useful way to begin teaching editing skills and get students accustomed to having their work discussed among peers.

Simple Metaphors and Similes

PURPOSE: Using metaphors and similes in writing is an effective way to create interesting and unique images in readers' minds and make unfamiliar objects and ideas more comprehensible. Presenting these poetic comparisons can also make ordinary things suddenly appear fresh and new. Inventing simple metaphors and similes is not a difficult skill to learn, but it can create new problems in students' writing, such as mixed metaphors, clichés, and forced comparisons that simply don't work.

PREPARATION: Locate a few simple metaphors and similes and duplicate them as examples for the class. Include some of your favorite published poems that use metaphor or simile as a major literary device, as well as some of your own, or students' poetic comparisons. Following are a few student-written similes and metaphors:

- His feet are as stiff as a new shoebox.
- The conversation flowed like a desert stream.

- Pencils being held
  like natives with spears
  ready to throw
- Life is a cesspool filled with garbage
  or a whirlpool constantly in motion
  never ending. . . .
- This cafeteria is like a cellar—cold and dirty—until friends enter.
- My heart is empty
  like a fire burnt out.
- Arguing with Tom is like spitting into a hurricane.
- Evergreens . . . long slim green fingers
    bend with the wind like hooded,
      hunched conspiritors.
- Morning . . . . The sky sheds its clothes and walks naked across the world.
- Suds stick in an empty coffee mug
  like the ring around a vacant tub.
- She's got hips like a quarter horse.

THE FIRST ACTIVITY: Write the words *Metaphor* and *Simile* on the chalkboard or word processor and ask students to define them and give examples of each. For instance, they might say that both are figures of speech that involve comparisons between two essentially unlike things. An easy-to-recognize difference between metaphor and simile is that a simile uses *like* or *as* to connect the two things being compared, and a metaphor does not. An example of a simile is: *Her eyes are like saucers.* An example of the same comparison written as a metaphor is: *Her eyes are saucers.*

Her eyes are like saucers is a simile, but it's also a cliché. Explain that one of the reasons for using similes and metaphors in writing is to invent fresh ways of seeing ordinary objects.

Pass out your example metaphors and read them aloud. Discuss what makes them successful and why writers like to use them in their writing.

Writing metaphors and similes can be difficult if attempted cold, without warming up the brain and stimulating the creative juices. Try to encourage a relaxed and supportive environment in the class by sharing the example comparisons and perhaps some of your own. Then ask the class to try inventing a few comparisons, too. You might start, for example, by having them all examine one of their hands very carefully. Ask them to concentrate on the hand and try to think of other familiar things that they are reminded of while studying the hand. Then ask them to write a short metaphor or simile. Give some examples, if you think they need further help.

- Veins on my hand like tiny streams flowing underground.
- Life lines on my palms seem like ancient scars of cuts and scratches.
- Wrist skin curdles, flakes, and is scratched off, like yesterday's milk dried in a coffee cup.

If a teacher participates in this writing exercise it will help the class feel even more relaxed and willing to try, too.

Ask students to share some of their comparisons, and encourage others to comment on the positive features of each. When they have finished this exercise, explain that in the next, longer writing assignment, they will compare themselves to one of the following:

a flower/ plant/ fruit

an animal

a month of the year

a machine

Suggest that they choose one specific flower or animal, etc., and then list all the characteristics they can think of that they share with the chosen object. Next, they will decide how to organize the paper, and rearrange the list into the planned order of presentation.

Read aloud one or two examples of this assignment. The following are two such examples:

Being kicked repeatedly by unsatisfied customers gets very irritating after a while. I break down occasionally; but give me a chance, nothing is perfect! Give me thirty-five cents and I will return your offering with any one of six flavored sodas. But there are certain signals you must read before you proceed. Above all, be friendly, and chances are I will be friendly in return. If all of my lights are on, don't press the issue or you may be sorely disappointed, not to mention that you won't get your money back. If there is a little white piece of paper on my chest that says OUT OF ORDER, just leave me alone, or you will really be sorry. Just remember these little signals and we will get along fine.

I am a chipmunk. I have fluffy red hair which can be spotted from far away. I love to nibble constantly and use my small, sharp teeth to help me gnaw what I eat. My steady diet consists of nuts, nuts, and more nuts. Peanuts, hazelnuts, walnuts, almonds, you name it, I eat it.

When I am not nibbling, I am probably sleeping. I sleep quite often, usually when there is something that needs to be done. Admittedly, I am lazy. I am also incurably curious, constantly sticking my nose in where it doesn't belong. One day I'm going to get it bitten off, I know, but so far I've been lucky.

> I also have a dreadful habit of hoarding things, or so Ma and Pa Chipmunk tell me. Really useless things. . . . Ma and Pa say it's just a phase and hope that I'll grow out of it soon. So do I! Ma and Pa put everything I bring home in my room and some of those tin can lids are darned uncomfortable to sleep on.

Ask students to enter their first drafts on a word processor and bring the disk to class on the date it's due. Tell them that this assignment will be shared among members of their peer editing groups.

THE SECOND ACTIVITY: Arrange students in small peer editing groups and explain that they will be working together in such groups throughout the course. Explain that they will be critiquing one another's papers regularly, before revising and printing a second draft to pass in.

Demonstrate the steps that editing groups should go through when critiquing members' papers. Also give them each a handout listing these steps so they can refer to it if they forget. (See the Introduction to Chapters 4 and 5 and the section, "The Peer Group System" in Chapter 3 for information about arranging the class into editing groups and teaching critiquing skills.)

After you have demonstrated for the class how to critique a student's paper, ask the groups to meet separately and review one another's papers on their own. You'll need to remain available to assist the groups as they go through this process for the first time. In fact, it will take several sessions and lots of coaching before the groups will run smoothly without your help. Even after that it's important for a teacher to continue visiting groups frequently, so that the attitudes of group members will remain serious and focused on the task at hand.

When student papers have been critiqued by peer groups and reviewed by the writers, the second drafts should be printed and passed in. You then can decide if writing a third draft is necessary for this assignment. Be sure to read some of the most successful ones to the class.

Avoiding Clichés

PURPOSE: Recognizing clichés and focusing on them by recalling many that we commonly use, helps us become more aware of how easy it is to fall into using the same worn-out words and phrases. Then, attempting to invent witty ways to express familiar ideas helps sharpen the senses and offers a prime opportunity for writers to practice choosing fresh words. Some clever images, similes, and metaphors—perhaps our clichés of the future—may well arise from this exercise.

THE ACTIVITY: Ask the class for a definition of cliché (e.g., a trite expression or idea), and then give them a few minutes to write down as many clichés as they can remember. It's surprising that out of context, they're often difficult to recall. Have students share theirs with the class while someone writes them on the chalkboard or word processor. If necessary, you might suggest additional clichés so that at least one or two dozen are written for all to see. Can they remember some of their friends' and family members' favorite expressions? Can they recall their own pet words and phrases? Or each other's, perhaps? Here are some examples:

white as a sheet	apple of one's eye
chip off the old block	play with fire
sharp as a tack	dyed in the wool
fast as lightning	head over heels
agree to disagree	stars in her eyes
avoid like the plague	raining cats and dogs
face the music	cute as a button
in the same boat	life is a bowl of cherries
short and sweet	peaches and cream complexion
sell like hotcakes	water over the dam
walking on air	don't count your chickens
swear like a trooper	flat as a pancake
wrong side of the tracks	it was a dream come true
twinkling of an eye	speaking of the devil

Discuss how using clichés affects a piece of writing and why good writers avoid using them. Ask them what kinds of articles and what types of periodicals they think would contain the most clichés.

Next, suggest taking some of the clichés listed on the board or video screen and twisting the words around to give them new life. Or, invent new ones . . .

short and sweaty

wrong kind of slacks

flat as a floppy

faster than a microwave

slow as a granny

bald as a mirror

a look you could pour on a pancake

You'll probably have to offer a few yourself to get the students started; then give them five or ten minutes to try writing some on their own. Sharing these inventions is usually entertaining and helps spread the creative spirit.

In concluding this classroom activity, encourage writers to be continually aware of over-used words and phrases in other people's speech and writing, as well as in their own. Urge them to experiment with more original, lively ways to express themselves.

For a homework assignment, ask students to read through periodicals in which they think they're likely to find clichés. Have them photocopy one selected article and underline the clichés. Ask them to then revise the article, replacing all the stale expressions with more imaginative ones. When they bring the assignment to class, encourage several students to share their newly coined expressions with the rest of the class.

Describing A Face

PURPOSE: Writing a description of a relatively small, but complex item, like a face, is a good exercise in careful observation and precise expression of detail. Describing a face also involves presenting a complete image of the face in a way that conveys some aspects of the character behind the face.

PREPARATION: Locate one or more short facial descriptions that successfully create an image of the subject's face, and also give the reader a glimpse of the subject's character. Duplicate at least one as a model for students. Following are two student-written examples in which the writers describe their own faces as they look in a mirror.

> Traces of age, hours of smiles are like deltas reaching out from sea-green mirrors surrounded by forests of lashes. These rivers run along to feed golden rushes of waterfalls, flowing freely down my cheek and shoulder. My nose becomes a cave, protruding from some porous rock, maybe lava, shimmering with minerals. My vision is like a cliff dweller's as I move down to my lips, wrinkled and full of lines as an old Indian's smile would crinkle his face. There are soft, rolling hills down to the jutting cliff of my chin, and a drop into sheer nothingness. Then I move back to those green eyes . . . the center of life in a face, and begin again.

> There is a face in the mirror in front of me. Do I ever, truly, look at this face, except as a canvas for my make-up? Why is that face so pale and drawn, with lines finely etched around each eye? There is no sparkle today, and each eye is shot through with traceries of blood across the white. Deep within each eye—there is no personality reflected, just colors—blue, green, and amber, melt one into the other. Dark circles are unsuccessfully hidden by make-up under each eye. Eyebrows are brushed up like a collapsed wooden fence in the snow. Wispy, reddish-brown hair surrounds my rounded face, punctuated with a slightly lopsided chin. There are hints of grey at the temples trying to hide under the rest of the hair. Corners of my mouth are drawn down with memories of past laughter carved on each side. One lip is thinner than the other, with even, closely spaced lines running along each lip. Wedge-shaped shadows on each side of my nose draw my face downward. When I look at this face, I see answers to questions I didn't know I needed to ask.

THE FIRST ACTIVITY: Begin the activity with an informal writing exercise in which students brainstorm new descriptive words to replace the ordinary ones we use so often. Write the word *hair* on the chalkboard or word processor and ask students to think of as many words as they can that help describe a person's hair. For example: tangled, rumpled, starched, faded, dull, glossy, polished, radiant, wispy, bouncy, etc.

Write *eyes* on the chalkboard or word processor and ask them for words that describe eyes, such as liquid, azure, vacant, piercing, cutting, dazed, drooping, wet, etc. Continue the exercise with *eyebrows, mouth, nose, ears, complexion,* and so on.

Then move on to brainstorming other words that describe ways that people *laugh, smile, cry, talk, shout.* For example, other words for *laugh* could include chuckle, chortle, titter, cackle, guffaw, hoot, giggle.

Ask students next to describe how a person's face looks when he or she is *angry.* Here's an example: He glared at me with target-eyes that could no longer see. His bowed cheeks drew tight over sharp bones, and his mouth fired words he could no longer hear.

Continue doing the same exercise for other emotions. Remind students that to be most effective, they should describe specifically how the facial features look when expressing the particular emotion.

Try these emotions: *happy, frightened, content, confused, lonely, depressed, excited.* It would help considerably if one or two students (or the teacher) would demonstrate these facial expressions, so that students can closely observe while they are writing.

Explain that the next writing assignment will involve describing someone's face. They will need to choose a person whom they know well for this assignment, and preferably someone whom they can watch closely for a while before writing the description (e.g., a parent, sibling, roommate, close friend, a familiar television personality, or oneself, while looking in the mirror). The description should include precise details of the facial features and it should communicate hints of the person's character—but only through the facial expressions. No abstract words or descriptive words that convey direct opinions or personal judgments are allowed (such as intelligent eyes, evil mouth, gorgeous lips, sinful smile).

Pass out the duplicated, example facial description; discuss the specifics the writer used, and then perhaps read one or two other short facial descriptions. Ask each student to choose a subject for a facial description, study it, and then write a one- or two-paragraph description. They should enter it on a word processor and bring a printout to class.

THE SECOND ACTIVITY: Ask a few volunteers to read their essays aloud and ask the class to offer positive comments after each one is read. Then ask them to make a few suggestions for improvements. If they can't, or don't, then you can help by offering some.

Collect the papers and go on to something else. This activity will be continued in the next class, after you have had a chance to critique the papers.

THE THIRD ACTIVITY:

Preparation: Read the facial description papers and look for a few writing problems that are evident in several of the papers, such as tense switching, lack of a transition between paragraphs, or unclear pronoun reference. These problems will then be addressed during the next class and discussed within the context of the writing assignment.

Another way to teach basic skills in relation to the writing assignments is to make up a list of specific things for the editing groups to look for when they critique a particular assignment. Enter the list on a word processor and print out a copy for each group. Both methods of follow-up help students focus on certain basic-skills problems that are likely to arise in a given assignment.

In the facial description assignment, students frequently fall into a list-making style, describing the face feature-by-feature. As a result many sentences are written in the same noun-verb-modifiers pattern, which gets monotonous. Another problem that often arises in this assignment is the use of mixed metaphors.

To focus the class on these two problems, enter a few excerpts on a word processor that exemplify the problems, print them out, and bring them to class. (If there is a large screen or enough video screens available for everyone to read the text, you won't need to print out the examples.)

The Activity: Pass out the duplicated excerpts, or get them up on the video screen, and ask students if they can detect what's wrong with them. Here's an example of repetitious sentence structure:

> . . . The mouth is partly open. The corners droop lifelessly. The lips are parched and pale only partially revealing the slightly yellowed teeth. The lower portion of the face bears a darkened look starting in front of the ears just below the hairline and continuing down the sides to eventually meet at the chin. . . .

Here's an example of mixed metaphors:

> . . . Immediately, one is drawn to her eyes, which glow like those of a Siamese cat in pitch blackness. They are almost hypnotic, as if you are standing along the beach on a bright day, and the sea's perpetual greenish blue waves are rolling in.
> Next are her teeth, white as caps on the waves of the sea and perfectly aligned like rows of chairs in an auditorium. . . .

After discussing what's wrong with these examples, help students rewrite the first one so that the sentence patterns have more variety. When it comes time to discuss the mixed metaphor example, suggest that there are a few ways to avoid mixing metaphors. One is to use metaphors only occasionally, for emphasis. Use concrete, descriptive detail for the most part, adding metaphors only where they can be most effective. Another solution is to use metaphors that blend together into an extended metaphor, such as the following:

> When he smiles, his thick nose points down like a perfect equilateral triangle, while the lines around his mouth bend as large parentheses.

> The most distinguishing feature of his face that immediately intrigues most people is his magnificent, aquamarine eyes. The indigo outer circles melt into a rich and mesmerizing deep sea of glass. As his skin is so brown, these placid pools resemble small inlets of a turquoise Caribbean Sea surrounded by a dark tan beach.

Ask students to revise and print out another draft of their facial expression descriptions, keeping the day's lesson in mind. Since the teacher has already read and written comments and suggestions on these papers, it's not necessary to repeat the process in the peer editing groups as well.

Character Sketch

PURPOSE: This activity helps writers further develop their ability to observe detail by directing them to examine not only the physical features of the subjects, but also the way they act. In a character sketch the writer presents the person to readers by showing that person in action.

PREPARATION: Find a few character sketches to read to the class as examples for the writing assignment. If you wish, duplicate them for students to keep; however, it's not necessary for this activity. The following are two student-written examples of character sketches:

GRANDPA

As we walked down the magnolia-lined dirt road, it was as if the sun was lighting a candle on every treetop. In one hand, Grandpa would carry the fishing poles, the tackle box, and the plastic bucket to keep the fish in. I'd carry the small wicker basket filled with peanut butter sandwiches, potato chips, oranges, and the brownies that Grandma would bake fresh that morning and sneak into our basket.

The sun would rise higher as we slowly walked down the road. When I looked up, it seemed to form a halo on Grandpa's cloud-white head. I remember how tiny my hand would feel in his. Those hands, warm and calloused, would gently cup over mine.

The road would take us to our secret place—a pond, hidden by Eucalyptus trees and hip-high jungle grass. Actually, it was more like a large mud puddle than a pond. I was never quite sure if there were any fish living there, but it never mattered. We'd hook the squiggly worms, cast our lines out into the muddy water, and wait.

When the sun had climbed to the top of the sky, we'd rest our fishing poles by the log at the edge of the pond and eat our lunch, if there was any left by then.

Then Grandpa would lean back against his favorite tree, close his eyes, and tell me stories about his boyhood. I'd lie on my belly with my chin resting in my palms, listening to the music of his voice and watching his hands act out the lyrics. I'd try to picture him as a little boy and would giggle because Grandpa's head and Grandpa's hands looked so funny on the body of a six-year-old.

He taught me how to whistle "Yankee Doodle" and I remember how he clapped his hands when for the first time, I tied my own shoes. What a feat it was to whistle and to tie my own shoes.

I'd tell him how we could build a boat out of magnolia trees and sail around the world. How I'd have a farm just like Grandpa's when I grew up. How there would be at least ten ponies on that farm. There was no dream too trite to share with Grandpa. He'd hold them all in his hands, nourish them, caress them with his fingertips.

Always too soon, the sun would turn into a pink-orange haze and we'd know then that the day was over. We'd gather our things—the wicker basket, the fishing poles, the tackle box, and the empty plastic bucket. As we stalked back through the jungle grass, I'd feel for Grandpa's hand. We'd walk and whistle down the road to home.

MOTHER

She lives in a four-bedroom, two-and-a-half bath townhouse on the west side of a big city. Not many people enter her domain except for the maid who comes in once a week. Two college degrees hang framed on the wall above her bed, yet she doesn't work. Whenever they hang the least bit crooked, she immediately straightens them.

During the day, she busies herself with errands. She drives through the city in a sparkling clean, copper-colored Mark V that has a mere two thousand miles on the speedometer. Usually, her errands take her to the bank, or to the stockbroker's office, or to the grocery store. Her days are functional and for the most part cheerful; but when the sun departs, it takes with it the brightness of her day.

As darkness fills the house, she goes to the liquor cabinet, opens it, and takes out a fifth of Scotch. Within an hour, the contents of the bottle are nearly gone. She sits on a couch, with an ashtray very near, overflowing with cigarette butts. There isn't any light present in the room, yet a shadow is cast on the space by light from other rooms. The stereo plays low classical music. She hasn't had dinner yet. The bottle sitting on the table next to the cigarette butts is dinner.

As she puffs on a cigarette, she carefully caresses the gold medallion hanging around her neck and fondly thinks of Greece, the place where she purchased the treasure. Her long, slim fingers house many gold objects as do her arms. She rarely takes these prized possessions off, not even when she sleeps. She says she wants to be buried with them.

She sits almost stonelike on the orange couch. Long, slim legs are crossed, and her feet are bare, with toenails painted orange like her fingernails and lips. An untucked shirt reveals rolling flesh. All parts of the woman's body are long and thin except for her protruding middle which has nurtured four children and much alcohol. Her face is streaked with the make-up that she has forgotten to remove. Purplish bags lie beneath brown, fawnlike eyes, and framing them, her auburn hair is cropped short and caked with the remains of that morning's hair spray.

With midnight approaching, she gets up from the sanctuary to refill her glass once more and to empty the ashtray. As she makes her way to the kitchen, she stumbles and the five-foot seven-inch body tumbles to the ground. Cigarette butts scatter and the glass explodes into many tiny pieces. As she lies there, cheek pressed to the cold floor, tears fall out of the dark, glossy pools. She thinks of her children and her possessions and her life. Many minutes pass, and her thoughts turn to the future. As she drifts off into oblivion, she dreams of the new day and how bright it will be.

THE FIRST ACTIVITY: Begin this activity with a little exercise in observation. Ask students to watch carefully as you walk across the room. Then, walk as if you were a soldier marching, and while you're marching, ask students to write down descriptive words that describe the manner of your walk (strut, stride, tread, march, pace, step, tramp, stamp, etc.). Next, walk like a 90-year-old person, and ask students to jot down descriptive words. Then walk like a person who has just stolen something . . . then, like an adolescent who is going home (or to school), but doesn't really want to get there. Perhaps students can suggest other types of walks that you, or they, can demonstrate.

Next, repeat the exercise using different sitting positions. For example, sit like a girl in finishing school (while students write descriptive words) . . . then, like a person at a baseball game when the score is tied and the bases are loaded . . . like a kid who's just been told her favorite toy has been smashed . . . like a person who's just about to go in for an important interview . . . like a lady wearing a very short skirt, and so on.

Next, ask students to come up with interesting and original descriptive words that describe the ways people laugh, cry, talk, eat, dress, etc. At this point it probably won't be necessary to demonstrate each of the behaviors, but do continue if the dramatic interest is still high.

When these exercises are finished, discuss with students the need to use specific words and concrete examples of behavior when presenting characters to an audience. It is not effective, for example, simply to tell readers that Joe is mean. Why should anyone believe it? A writer must *show* the reader that Joe is mean by presenting him in action:

> Joe took $2.00 from his sister's bureau drawer and spent it on candy for himself. When his sister found her money missing, Joe said he saw her friend, Sara, take it.

Write down the following opinionated statements on the chalkboard or word processor:

Sid is jealous.

Susan is a wizard.

Henry is a brute.

Mary is terribly shy.

Ellen is stuck up.

Penny is a flirt.

Frank is the weirdest person I've ever met.

Sara is dishonest.

Marge is such a good friend.

Ask students to pick one of these statements and write a paragraph during class that demonstrates the particular character trait indicated. The opinionated statement should not appear anywhere in the paragraph, nor should any other abstract judgment. The writer's job is to present the evidence, allowing readers to make their own judgments.

Read a few of the paragraphs aloud, and discuss how successfully each provides concrete examples of behavior. Here are a couple of examples:

> Last year Susan won every college math competition in the country. The kid can even remember major characters in novels she read years ago in junior high school. Once I saw her complete the Times crossword puzzle in thirty-two minutes flat!

> Hands clenched to the chain wall of the tennis court, Sid watched him play with the sharp eye of a hawk, waiting for his prey to falter. Every day Sid studied the serve, stance, footwork, and swing of his rival. When the stalked player gained a point, Sid's brows slammed together; then, his teeth glistened when the player missed a ball and lost the point.

Assign a character sketch for homework. Ask students to select a subject and study that person's behavior for a while—the way he or she walks, talks, sits, etc. Suggest that students record some of these observations in their journals.

Discuss ways they can organize the character sketch, for example:

Introduction—presents the character with a brief physical description.

Main Body—reveals the person's character by presenting specific information and examples of behavior.

Conclusion—leaves the reader with a certain familiarity with one or two aspects of the character, and a sense of completeness about the piece of writing.

Be sure they understand that there are a variety of ways to organize the paper and that, in fact, the example character sketches that you'll soon read aloud, will probably show alternative methods of organization. Ask students to enter first drafts on a word processor and bring their disks to class on the day the paper is due. Conclude by reading a few example character sketches. (If you duplicated them for students, pass them out before you begin reading.)

THE SECOND ACTIVITY:

Preparation: Prepare and duplicate a list of *Evaluation Criteria for Character Sketches* such as the following:

1. Content
   - Did the writer use effective detail to help the reader *picture* the character?
   - Did the writer present examples of the character's behavior, so the reader could get to know at least one or two aspects of his or her personality?
2. Organization and Sentence Structure
   - Do the ideas progress smoothly, or is the organization unclear? Do any sentences or paragraphs leave you confused? Help the writer improve the flow of ideas.
   - Does the piece have awkward or vague sentences? Help the writer identify them and revise them.
3. Grammar and Mechanics
   - Help the writer correct the spelling, punctuation, and grammatical errors in the paper.

This kind of handout does not cover all the problems editors will encounter in the papers they critique; however, it does help them begin thinking about how to approach the critiquing of a paper and gives them a focus.

The Activity: When the class begins, tell students that this class period will be primarily spent in groups, critiquing and revising the first drafts of their character sketches.

Ask them to meet in their editing groups and begin reviewing one another's papers. A teacher or tutor should spend time with each group helping them go through the entire process with one of the papers, and leaving them to do the rest by themselves.

Following this activity, students can revise and print second drafts to pass in to the teacher. Ask the editing groups to choose one or two of the most successful papers to share with the class.

After the teacher has critiqued second drafts, she may find it necessary to request further revisions and third drafts to be completed. Student editing groups often don't catch all the problems, especially at the beginning of the term.

The teacher may also find it necessary to spend considerably more class time training the editors to do their job effectively. Learning to critique and edit is by no means easy; it's a whole new skill for most students to learn, and it requires lots of practice to be effective.

Describing a Place

PURPOSE: Describing a place is like describing a person in that it uses precise details to create a picture of the subject in the reader's mind. The difference is that for some writers, it's a little more difficult to convey a sense of mood or "character" in a place and make it interesting. This activity will give student writers more practice in observing and communicating clear images to their readers.

PREPARATION: Locate a few examples of effective place descriptions and duplicate them for students to use as models, if you feel it would be helpful. Bring them to class on the day you plan to do the activity.

The following are two student-written examples of place descriptions:

GRANDFATHER'S PIZZA PARLOR

It is 7:30 on Friday night and Grandfather's pizza parlor has reached its normal level of hysteria. Behind the counter the staff bustle back and forth like ants after their hill has been trampled. There are seven of them pounding dough, cutting vegetables, filling pitchers of beer, and bussing tables. Each is wearing the brown short-sleeved shirt which bears the name of the establishment in yellow writing. Occupying the larger tables in the center are three or four groups of men in their late twenties. Each group is dressed the same. These are softball teams; they've come here to eat a little pizza, drink a lot of beer, and make as much noise as they possibly can. Around the sides of the room sit the couples who've come for dinner. They are watching the people in the middle. Some of them are amused, but most appear somewhat annoyed.

Over in the far corner are the video games. Surrounding the machines are all types, ages, and sizes. At this hour the bunch consists mainly of kids in their early or mid teens. Each of the machines is humming, clicking, buzzing, or beeping away under the control of one while the others look on. At the top of each machine is a neat row of shiny silver quarters belonging to those awaiting their turn. This method of waiting in line is a courtesy among avid video fans, and a violation of this system is looked on with extreme distaste. A strong smell of cigarettes pervades this portion of the room. The pay phone in the corner rings frequently; each time it is answered by the nearest free hand, and the name of the person being called is shouted above the confusion. Some of the video players turn occasionally to glare in disgust at the noisy jocks who are pounding on their tables and yelling constantly. A collective groan arises each time one of them stumbles to the juke box and replays the same song over and over again.

SMALL TRAGEDY

He peeked through the window of the motor home and noticed the shredded sun visors, and the chewed-apart dashboard. The thought of vandalism tore through his mind until he noticed the door was still locked. When he inserted the key and turned it to the right, a shiny aluminum door flew open, and the stagnant smell of a dog kennel rushed out of the gap. The one plush brown carpet was covered with chunks of foam rubber that had escaped from the cushions on the couch. Sections of hard black plastic had been gnawed until only the metal frame shown on the steering wheel.

The room looked as if someone had a raging party. But there were no empty beer cans thrown in the corner or cigarette butts smoldering in the carpet. Only foam rubber, shredded cloth, and torn screens remained.

The battle for survival was over. There were no longer the sounds of cloth tearing or screens ripping, only the mournful whimpering of a young boy could be heard.

The silver door handle on the inside of this death chamber was gouged and scarred, but it didn't give way. Curtains which had hung so elegantly over the windows were torn in uneven strips on the floor.

The boy made his way past the veneer-covered dining table and headed toward the compact bathroom. A voice rose over the cries of the boy and told him not to go any further. The boy was oblivious to the warning and he entered the tan colored bathroom. In the fiberglass tub lay his dog, cold and finally at rest.

The last student-written example is a description that introduces both setting and characters, as the introduction of a short story or novel would do.

There is a place where crisp dresses hang in rainbow assortment. Below them are red and white saddle shoes and black Mary Janes, pushed up into a patent leather mound. In the corner a little girls sits and plays with her dolls, in silence.

A bright yellow bedroom, with a four-poster canopy bed and a handmade lace bedspread, stand in constant display. The little girl can only sleep there. Along with the four-poster canopy bed is a chestnut vanity that has a matching roll-top desk. Everything in the room matches perfectly.

Behind the closet door, the little girl has built her dolls a house out of old shoe boxes. On her hands and knees, she peeks her head into the box and tucks the tissue tightly around her sleeping dolls. The little girl giggles at the sound of her mother's voice calling her name. Her mother doesn't know about her new hiding place.

While she waits for her dolls to wake up, she fixes them a meal of blueberry jam and bread. She didn't have time to steal a knife from the kitchen, so she spreads the gooey jam with her finger. Her mother's footsteps pound down the hallway. The little girl pulls the closet door shut and tells her dolls to be very still if they happen to awake. She loses her balance while shutting the door, falls against it, and stains her dress with sticky jam. In darkness and in tears she hopes her mother won't find out about the only place she can play. Footsteps thump into her bedroom.

Quickly, the little girl hides the jam and bread underneath the hill of party shoes. Silently, she leans down and kisses her sleeping dolls. Angrily, her mother looks under the four-poster canopy bed. The little girl's heart pounds against her dress that has been stained with jam and fear. She hears her mother's fingernails scratch the closet door open.

THE ACTIVITY: Begin the class by asking students to write a one-paragraph description of the classroom. Read some of these aloud and discuss what mood or "character" the writer conveyed about the classroom. After reading a description, ask the class if it contained any opinionated words or vague generalizations. If so, ask students to help revise it, using specific words that don't contain overt judgments, but do more subtly convey a mood or feeling about the classroom.

Discuss why and how authors use place descriptions in their work, such as short stories, novels, interviews, etc.

Explain that the next writing assignment will be a place description. Remind students to use descriptive detail, and try to create images that involve all the senses. Readers should be able to see, hear, smell, taste, and feel certain parts of the place being described.

Ask students to limit their subject to one small place, such as one room, the front of a building, one small spot at the beach, because if they attempt to describe a larger place they won't be able to present adequate detail.

Discuss how to organize a place description. For example, one could take the reader on a tour of the place—enter, walk around and absorb its contents, then leave the room. Or, one could lie on a couch and take the reader around the room the way the lounger's eyes would move from place to place inside the room.

Ask students to enter first drafts on a word processor and bring their disks to class when the assignment is due. Read (and pass out, if you have duplicated) the previously selected examples of place descriptions.

When students arrive in class with first drafts, spend some class time going over what editors should look for in the critiquing session (i.e., the points mentioned above) and send them off to review papers in their editing groups.

A teacher or tutor should again visit each group and help facilitate the critiquing process. When the papers have been reviewed and suggestions have been made, students may revise, print out, and pass in second drafts.

After reading these drafts and making further suggestions you'll probably ask students to revise and print a third draft. Be sure to pick a few of the best descriptions to share with the class.

First Person Narrative

PURPOSE: This activity helps students learn about the structure of a short story through reading and analyzing short stories and then writing one.

PREPARATION: Locate a few very short stories that are written in the first and third person points of view and that relate experiences with clear-cut climaxes and resolutions. Stories like "Appointment in Samarra" by

W. Somerset Maugham, "The Sniper" by Liam O'Flaherty, "After Twenty Years" by O. Henry, "The Open Window" by Saki, and "A Very Short Story" by Ernest Hemingway, are good examples to use because they demonstrate that stories can be very short in length, yet still have all the necessary ingredients to make them structurally complete narratives.

Duplicate one or two stories that are first person narratives for students to use as models while writing the assignment.

The following two examples are student-written first person narratives:

TRUCKERS' DELIGHT

It was gettin' on about three a.m. in Rosalee's Good Eats Cafe off I-80 somewheres in Nevada with Tammy Wynette cranked up fierce on the jukebox and a couple o' lonesome Jakes filterin' Sanka black through their guts when I walked in all stiff-like from a long haul up from Virginie way. Now, these dudes were truckers clear through—I could tell by the way they sat on the swivel counter stools with cigarette melt-holes in the red vinyl cushions of 'em, with their legs all spread out—they was just drownin' their lonesome highway blues. They all had them trucker's wallets too; you know the kind with a chain attached? Yeah, those chains ain't no good iffen somebody gets it in mind to take your dough, but they sure lets you know in time to get out your Barlow an' let some blood. Sure gets 'em thinkin' when that blade flashes. Yeah, oh . . . sorry. Any-how, I come in all sore from haulin' straight through from Kansas an' kinda pissed-off on account of my log-book being way behind, so I ordered up some brews and kicked back at the bar, hopin' to get some re-laxs.

Then up outa nowhere comes this broad with a set of hallelujah headlights like Dolly Parton or Miss goddam America. Truth is, though, she was ugly. Mug face, you know? You woulda had to tie meat around her neck just to get the dogs to look at her, but I had some Bud in my brain.

"Hi there, Mister," she says. Yecch.

"Ma'am," I says, trying to keep my eyes offa them jugs she was totin'.

"What brings you to the Eats so early in this lonesome part of the country?"

Now I've seen all this before, and once you hear the ol' "lonesome parts," you better take off, or look out. So all I said was, "My Kenworth . . . Ma'am."

"Would y'all be planning on resting here a spell?"

"Not likely, Ma'am, see I gotta make my run, and I gotta get caught up on my schedule."

"Why surely you aren't in any hurry, oh, and my name is Bessie Mae. Bessie Mae Moocho."

"Billy Bob." I tipped my Stetson.

Now right about then I wanted to get about a hundred-thousand miles between me and ol' Bessie Mae Moocho, so I scused myself and made off for the pisser. It was a nasty ol' truck-stop john with them long wall fixtures with soggy cigarette butts in 'em and Skoal and Red Man spat on the wall and those urinal mints tossed in but as don't do any good. Cracked yellow tiles on the floor and a cracked mirror over the rusty sink looked like somebody sneezed on it. Real high-class head, though. Had music piped in from the juke and it was playing "Bony Fingers."

Then in comes this dude all sore-like, bloodshot eyes looking for me—gonna break my face for messin' with his dame. Just figures.

Don't ever try to reason with a drunk kicker—they just get meaner. He comes up to me with, "You been messin' with my sweet patootie!"

"Your *what?*"

"My gal." Now he's lookin' at me all squinty.

"Look fella, I'm just here to be off the road, I'm not lookin' for trouble and my own girl somewhere else. Better lookin' too."

"I saw you makin' eyes at her!"

"Now hold on one single minute, there guy. That broad rolled up to *me* and gave *me* the time of day."

That's when he swung. Connected too, right in the jaw. I guess I got mad and we went at it. At the end, I got in a couple of good ones and he fell into the stall and onto the turlet, out for the count, real natural-like. I came outa there quick, laid a five on the counter and made ready to split when a chair hits me right on the back. Sonovabitch!

I grabbed that sucker and rang his chimes and tapped his head real friendly-like up against the bar there. Then I ran him out the door into a post, and I was kinda upset, so I was fixin' to stomp on his miserable face with my Tony Lamas when, well, that's when you came up to me, officer.

A CASE OF MISTAKEN IDENTITY?

"Moonlight, wine, and roses" I croon along with the love song playing on the transistor radio. Going about my pre-date ablutions, milky bath, powder, make-up, and perfume, I like to talk to the cat and daydream. "This is the night that will change our lives, Kittycat. No more tuna for you, it will be trout on a silver platter from now on. No more thrift shop clothes for me. Goodbye one-room apartments, ratty furniture, and complaining neighbors. Goodbye bounced checks and GOODBYE to you, single life!"

Everything must go right tonight. I've been eyeing this beauty for months. Linen suits, gold watches, and Jerry Brown haircuts. Funny . . . somehow I just can't picture his face. . . .

I'll open the door. His long, lingering gaze will travel slowly up and down my svelte body, his will tense with longing; he'll bring me roses. A bundle of 'em. Probably twenty-four. He'll bring champagne which we'll drink in his Rolls out of long-stemmed crystal glasses. We'll go to a secluded French restaurant, the kind with candles and white linen tablecloths. We will hold hands and gaze with longing at each other over the tabletop. It will be so sweetly sad and romantic—just like a Harlequin romance!

I slide into silk stockings and my brand new, bought-for-this-occasion blue silk shantung dress. A touch more lipstick . . . and there's the doorbell!

I open the door slowly, majestically.

There he stands . . . frozen pizza in one hand, a six-pack of beer dangling from the other. "Didn't I tell you? The fights are on tonight. Ali against Norton. Where's the tube?"

THE ACTIVITY: Explain to students that since they have already written pieces that develop characters and setting, the only other major element they need in order to write a story is a plot. Discuss with them the definition of *plot*, helping them understand it as a series of events that occur in time, leading up to and including a climax and a resolution. Explain that a plot also needs some sort of conflict that either gets resolved, or doesn't.

Draw on the chalkboard an illustration of a plot and label its parts (Fig. 5.1).

Explain that many ordinary events in life fit into the story form. All the form requires is one or more characters who face a particular conflict; the conflict ultimately reaches a climax, which is followed by some result or resolution of the conflict. Situations like this occur frequently in our daily lives, and could be material for a short story. Here's an example of an ordinary situation that could be transformed into an interesting story. . .

> Two dogs, who happen to be out for a walk in the park with their respective owners, get into a fray. The owners, who don't know each other, begin fiercely arguing over whose dog started the fight. Eventually, the argument evolves into a conversation and the two discover a common love for Mozart. They decide to go to a concert together that evening, without the dogs.

Spend some time talking about point of view, explaining that if a story is written in the first person point of view it means that the story teller is a major or minor character in the story (thus the pronoun "I" is usually evident in the story). If the story is written in the third person point of view, the storyteller is outside the story as an ordinary human observer, or as an all-knowing, omniscient observer. Ask them which point of view they feel would be most appropriate for a story about the park experience described above, and why?

Refer the class to familiar examples of stories in the first and third person points of view, and then read aloud previously selected short stories that illustrate different points of view. Identify the point of view used in each story and discuss how it would change if told using a different point of view. Also discuss the plot, identifying the conflict, climax, and resolution in each story.

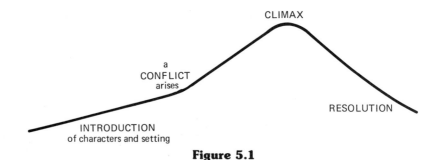

Figure 5.1

Explain that the next assignment will be to write a first person story using themselves as the major character. Ask students to pick a significant event in their lives, such as the most embarrassing thing that ever happened to them, the funniest, the saddest, the nicest, the worst, etc., and retell the experience as a story with an introduction, a conflict, a dramatic build-up, a climax, and a resolution.

One effective way to demonstrate the process they'll go through in completing this assignment, is to pick a salient experience from your own life and retell it in story form. The following is one teacher's personal experience that was retold orally to a class:

> "When I was a senior in high school I performed in the school play, *Finian's Rainbow,* as one of the singing and dancing chorus girls. . ."
>
> (The teacher continued the tale by describing particular tension-building details and events that preceded opening night. She described the costumes—hers was a floor-length evening gown that draped casually over one shoulder. Then she described the dance routines and a few other details that came to mind at the time.)
>
> ". . . .Eight o'clock arrived on opening night; all the seats in the theatre were filled, and pretty soon the show began. . . . . The first act was just fine. The actors were pleased with their performance and so was the audience."
>
> "The curtain went up for the second act and it continued with the same intensity as the first. Toward the end of the second act the chorus did a dance that required the girls to leap-frog over the guys, and then the guys pulled the girls through their legs and up to a standing position for the second act finale. . . . I leap-frogged over my partner and he pulled me through and up, right on cue."
>
> (The storyteller demonstrated this leap frog routine with a student in the class.)
>
> "However, my partner was standing on my dress, and as he pulled me up, the dress stayed down. I stood in the center of the stage facing 200 people in my underwear.
>
> "When the show was over, the director asked if I'd be willing to do it again, tomorrow."

Ask students to pick an experience, identify its climax and resolution, and make a list of the plot details they plan to include. Then they can revise the list and use it as an outline for the narrative. Ask them to compose a draft, enter it on a word processor, and bring the disk to class on the day it's due. After the assignment has been carefully explained, pass out and read the duplicated examples of first person narratives.

When the class meets next, ask a few students to read their stories aloud and ask the class to identify the different parts of the story (i.e., conflict, climax. . .).

Have students meet in editing groups to critique their papers. Hand out a previously prepared printed list, or write on the chalkboard some specific things they should focus on in the critiquing sessions, such as tense switching, awkward sentences, and weak transitions between sentences.

Ask students to revise their papers after these sessions and print out a second draft to pass in. After you read these papers and make further suggestions for improvements, students can revise and print a final draft.

Fantasy Story

PURPOSE: Inventing a fantasy story provides students with the opportunity to develop characters and a plot just the way they wish, without having to worry about distorting the truth. Writing fiction also forces them to intentionally create all the essentials of a story because nothing already exists in a fantasy until the writer invents it.

PREPARATION: Locate a few short fantasy stories—fairy tales, science fiction, fables—to read aloud to the class on the day you do this activity. Stories such as "Thus I Refute Beelzy" by John Collier, "The Princess and the Tin Box," "The Rabbits Who Caused All the Trouble" and "The Bear Who Let it Alone" by James Thurber, and any of Grimm's Fairy Tales, serve as useful examples of fantasy stories.

In addition, duplicate one or two very short fantasy stories to serve as models for the writing assignment. The following are two examples of student-written fantasy stories.

FAIRY FABLE

Once upon a time in Fairy Land there was a beautiful princess named Alexandra. Her flowing brown hair and soft shy smile, combined with soothing blue eyes and a 37C bust, made her the sight of the land. Here she stood in her five-foot seven-inch curved frame waiting, just waiting to be whisked away by some gallant prince. But alas, there were no gallant princes. Every gallant prince that she knew of was already reserved for a later story, or he was married, living in California and playing a lot of tennis. So Fairy Land was definitely short of gallant princes. There were a few princes, but nothing gallant.

The beautiful princess was heartbroken, all this virgin talent unused. Finally she got an idea! Fairy Princess Alexandra sent a telegram to other countries asking for gallant princes to come to Fairy Land and make an appointment for a personal interview. Well, they came by the thousands, by the hundreds of thousands! There were dragon slayers, war heroes, knights of bold, knights of gallant, princes of poet, even the King of Wall Street was there! Nowhere else could she find such a better selection of gallant men. After two years of interviewing she finally narrowed her selection down to two; Sir Henry Ganse of Tulipesville and Sire Walter Yuddle of the well-known Yuddle Lillies (a very renowned family).

Princess Alexandra was in a jam. First, no gallant princes and now too many gallants. "What's a beautiful and rich princess to do?"she uttered. Once again an idea came to her. She would have these two meet for the first time at a clearing in the forest. Dressed in full combat gear, a battle would be fought to the death. Left in the clearing would be the princess' vast fortune and a single horse enabling the winner to ride out a rich gallant hero, and whisk the beautiful princess off her feet.

Battle day was set and the gallant princes trained very hard. The day came. The two tramped into the thick forest and met. They eyed the priceless treasure and then each other behind walls of steel. With swords drawn the battle began; grunting and yelling and blows of steel could be heard throughout the land. Sir Ganse was struck in the head by a swift blow; he then crashed to the ground. All the metal encaging his body acted as a weighted death trap. Sir Ganse lay on the ground—helpless, knowing that death was about to conquer him. Sire Yuddle, standing over him with the heavy sword raised above his head said, "You know this must be." The reply was a courageous, "Yes, but before I die remove thy mask to let me see better the victor." This Sire Yuddle could not refuse. Taking off his mask, he then reached down and removed Sir Ganse's helmet. The two had never seen another perfect man before. Handsome, muscular, tall, and most important of all gallant, they were without a doubt, the cream of all the countries. Silent, the two stared—and stared. They were in love! How could Yuddle possibly kill someone he loved as much as himself! The two, hand in hand, picked up the vast riches and mounted the horse, leaving the beautiful Fairy Princess Alexandra waiting to be whisked away.

About a year later the Princess received a candy-gram from her two gallant men thanking her for the riches (most of her vast riches anyway) and for her part in getting them together.

As of this date, the beautiful Fairy Princess has sagged a little, but is still a sight to see. As for Sire Henry and Sire Walter, they are now a gallant company, "Ganse and Yuddle," abbreviated G-A-Y and are living in California, working hard for gay rights and playing a lot of tennis.

Moral of the Story: It is sometimes hard to distinguish gallant men from fairy princes.

GRATITUDE AND SPAGHETTI

The room is dark except for the dim light of the table lamp beside me. I sit in the deep, cushioned armchair, waiting for him to come home. I have always waited. Again I look around the small, neat house. The coffee table has been polished well. The long white couch has not a speck of dust on it. The old wooden floor has lost its shine but it is clean. Every corner, every crack has been carefully swept. All the windows have been washed twice today. I can see my reflection through the glass. No, the windows could not be cleaner. He likes our house to be neat and clean. It has always been neat and clean.

I hear the old grandfather clock chime in the next room. It is six o'clock. I wait and listen. Soon, I hear the sound of his shoes clicking against the cement pathway to our door. I count the footsteps, six of them altogether, then I push myself up from the chair and try to smooth the fine wrinkles of my dress. It is his favorite dress. There are two shuffles against the bristly welcome mat, silence, then the screen door opens and shuts with a metal clang. A shadow fills the doorway and moves into the darkened light. He is home.

I go to him and take his hat and coat. He bends down to kiss my cheek. He is a tall man, almost six foot six, with a lean but muscular build. His hair is thick and black and just slightly touched with grey. He is very handsome. He has always been handsome.

I hang the hat and coat in the closet and go to the kitchen. When I return he is seated at the far end of the supper table, reading the evening paper. On the table there are two porcelain coffee cups and a large bottle of Chianti. In the center there is a tiny glass vase with one red rose which I picked from our garden this morning.

I place a plate of steaming spaghetti in front of him and spoon out a mound of thick, lumpy red sauce. He puts down the paper and tastes the spaghetti. He looks up at me as he chews and smiles. I pour some of the dark Chianti into his cup and place it before him. Again he tastes, again he smiles. Everything is just right. He is pleased.

I sit down at the other end of the table and quickly eat my spaghetti. When I finish, I drink my Chianti and watch him over the rim of my cup. He puts a large forkful of spaghetti in his mouth and slowly chews. Then he places the fork down, wipes his lips with a napkin and takes a sip of Chianti. I love to watch him eat for he savors each bite, first with his eyes and then with his mouth. I pour Chianti in my cup and wait.

He pushes the empty plate aside, wipes his lips again and places the soiled napkin on the table. I quickly get up and shuffle back to the kitchen and bring out the cake I have baked for him. It is chocolate, his favorite. Three layers of rich, creamy chocolate cake. He smiles but shakes his head and rises from the table. He comes to me and again I point to the cake. He pats my arm and brushes a kiss to thank me. Yes, he has always thanked me.

I get up from the table and carry the dirty dishes to the kitchen. Then I hear the screen door cry open and shut again. I listen to the six hollow footsteps on the pavement and then, once more there is silence. I wash each dish carefully by hand and put them neatly away in the cupboard. I go back to the dining room to get the cake and carry it back to the kitchen. Such a beautiful cake. It will spoil if no one eats it. I take a clean knife from the drawer and slice a large piece for myself. As I eat my cake, I lean on the counter and stare at my reflection in the newly cleaned windows. I am old and fat.

THE ACTIVITY: Read one of the example fantasy stories out loud and discuss what makes a fantasy different from other narratives. Ask students to identify specific parts of the example story's structure, including the introduction of characters and setting, the conflict, climax, etc., and also ask them to identify the point of view.

Read one or two other short fantasy tales and discuss them in the same way. Pick short ones (such as the ones suggested in the Preparation section) that can be read in five or ten minutes. If you can find Thurber's "The Princess and the Tin Box" (from *The Beast in Me and Other Animals*, by James Thurber), read that one aloud too, but stop before the last few paragraphs. At that point ask students to write a short ending of their own, before reading Thurber's. Give them a few minutes to do this and then read a few of their endings out loud. After that read the author's published ending. This exercise is fun and helps writers get into a fanciful spirit for the next assignment.

Explain that they will write a fantasy story—any type they wish, as long as it involves imaginary characters, setting, and plot. Suggest that they first brainstorm ideas for a situation and characters, and then develop an outline for the plot. Ask them to compose the first draft on a word processor and bring the disk to class on the day the assignment is due.

Hand out and read a least one short, student-written fantasy story for students to use as a model, before sending them off to write one on their own. When students bring their drafts to class, invite them to share the stories with classmates, if they wish. Then have them meet in editing groups to begin critiquing their stories. One or two more drafts will probably be necessary to develop them into effective and interesting fantasies.

Dialogue

PURPOSE: Spoken language is typically different from written language, and although students need to concentrate on learning the more formal written language for success in their academic and professional lives, examining and attempting to reproduce authentic conversational speech is a very useful exercise. It helps writers understand the differences between written and spoken languages and it helps sharpen their skill in listening to, as well as in accurately reproducing, spoken language. Writing dialogue is also a useful exercise because it forces writers to present everything they wish to communicate through conversation.

PREPARATION: Locate a few example short stories that use a lot of dialogue, such as "The Chaser" by John Collier, "The Other Wife" by Colette, and "Snake Dance" by Corey Ford. Duplicate at least one very short dialogue so students will have a model of the format while they write their own. The following is a student-written example of a short dialogue:

THE FIRST TIME

I was walking down the hall to my history class when I saw it. That crooked metallic smile. I pretended not to notice, turned quickly around, and headed in the other direction.

"Hey, Julie!"

"Oh Alex, hi."

"You haven't forgotten about this afternoon, have you?"

"This afternoon? Oh yeah, this afternoon. Listen Alex, I . . ."

"You're chickening out huh?"

"No. No, I'll be there."

"Good."

"Alex?"

"Yeah?"

"Do you think we should?"

"Sure, you'll really like it."

"But what if someone sees us?"

"Stop worrying. Just remember—behind the Texaco station in the grove at 3:15."

It was impossible to concentrate through my last two classes. "Sure, you'll really like it," he had said. Most of the girls in my class had tried it and liked it. I hated being the odd-ball, the weirdo.

When the 3:00 bell rang, I walked slowly down the hall to the bathroom. I carefully combed out an imaginary tangle in my hair and stared in the mirror. It was now or never.

I waited in the grove, watching the red and black Texaco sign spin around and around. Maybe he wasn't coming. Maybe he forgot.

"Are you ready?" I saw the crooked smile again as he stepped out around the station.

"Sure. . . . Alex?"

"Yeah?"

"I—uh—I've never done this before."

"You're joking."

"No. Will it hurt?"

"Nah. I'll be careful."

"I don't know, I. . ." He reached out to hug me. I felt his clammy hands grip my bare arms. And then his spongy lips were on mine. He had lied— it did hurt. His braces scratched my lips. Thank God he couldn't get his tongue through the rubber bands on his braces. Thank God I didn't have braces or we might have been stuck there forever.

"Let's go sit down over there."

"Let's just go, Alex."

"What's the matter, didn't you like it?"

"Loved it, but let's not overdo it."

"O.K., I'll see you tomorrow, same place, same time."

"Alex, I. . ."

"See ya." He started walking off toward the station, then turned around so I could see his crooked metallic smile one more time.

THE ACTIVITY: Begin this activity with a few short improvisations to help students focus on dramatic dialogue. Ask for student volunteers to act out roles that you assign. Then explain the hypothetical situation they are in, and let them begin speaking and acting as characters in that situation. Here are a few example situations students might improvise:

- *Characters:* a parent, a neighbor, a teenager
- *Situation:* The parent and teenager are sitting in the living room when a neighbor arrives. The neighbor is furious because a window in his house has been broken, and he's sure it was the teenager who broke it. The teenager claims he (she) didn't break the window.
- *Characters:* Two friends of the same sex
- *Situation:* The friends are having a conversation over lunch which eventually shifts to the topic of a very special party coming up on Friday. Both of them have been invited to the party and are supposed to

invite a friend (of the opposite sex) to accompany them. Suddenly they discover they both want to invite the same person. They are very close friends, so they don't want to injure their relationship, but on the other hand, they both really want to take this special person to the party.

- *Characters:* A teacher and two students

  Situation: The teacher has asked the two students to come to his office after school to talk privately. When they are alone the teacher explains that he's heard that some individuals at school are selling drugs to students, and that if it doesn't stop soon the principal has threatened to call the police in to handle the problem. The teacher believes that one or both of the students know which students are involved in selling drugs, and the teacher wants to find out in order to talk with those students.

Before doing the improvisations ask students in the audience to pay attention to the language being used by the characters. How does it differ from written language? How does the spoken language differ in each situation and with each type of character? Ask them to think about how the audience learns about the background of each character and about his or her personality. Discuss these and other issues after each dialogue, so that by the last one the students should be fairly sharp at listening and observing.

Then discuss how the writer faces an even tougher problem in communicating a situation when characters can only be presented through conversation, without the aid of facial expressions and actions—as in a written dialogue.

Explain that their next assignment will be to write a dialogue between two (no more than three) people. Ask them to think of a situation for a conversation that includes some kind of conflict between the two people in the dialogue. The dialogue will report their conversation using spoken language appropriate to the characters involved. The spoken conversation should be a means for communicating certain aspects of the characters' personalities to the reader. The dialogue should also include some of the other elements of a story, such as climax and resolution. Suggest that the students spend the rest of the day carefully listening to other people speak, and recording their exact words whenever possible, to provide practice in writing conversations the way they are actually spoken.

During this class, or in a follow-up activity before the paper is due, go over the written form used for writing a dialogue. It would be helpful to distribute a handout and/or refer to specific pages in a grammar book that carefully explain the correct use of quotation marks. Explain also, that when recording a direct conversation the writer should start a new paragraph every time a different person begins speaking. At this point, pass out the duplicated example of a short dialogue for students to use as a model when they begin writing. Read this and other examples of dialogues and discuss how the writer managed to express significant ideas in the dialogue as well as give readers a glimpse of the characters' personalities.

Suggest that students first pick a dramatic situation to write about; then the characters and the words will fall into place more easily (as in the improvisations). Ask them to compose first drafts and enter them on a word processor. Ask them to bring their dialogues to class on the day they're due, along with as many printed copies as there are characters in the dialogue.

On the day the assignment is due, have students meet in editing groups to critique their dialogues. In these editing sessions it would be appropriate for members to read the dialogues aloud to the group, to see how successfully each resembles an authentic conversation.

When editing groups have critiqued all members' dialogues, ask them to select one or two of the best to perform for the whole class. Or, the teacher might choose to wait until after the next drafts have been completed before suggesting that they be performed.

One-Act Play

PURPOSE: This activity helps students further develop their skill in writing dramatic dialogue. To write a one-act play they will have to combine story-writing skills and dialogue-writing skills to put together a successful play.

PREPARATION: Locate one or two short plays to use as examples for this activity. A play such as Strindberg's "The Stronger" is particularly suitable because it has only two major characters and it is very short. Student-written plays are also useful examples, as they demonstrate for young people what's possible for student writers to accomplish, as well as what problems they might face. Duplicate as many scripts of each play as there are characters in it. Make sure that every student has a copy of one play to use as a model for the writing assignment.

The following is an example of a student-written play:

NO SMOKING, PLEASE

CHARACTERS: **Older Woman**—a middle-aged non-smoker
Woman—a smoker in her mid-twenties
Friend—a woman who is eating with the Woman in the restaurant
Young Woman—a non-smoker in her early twenties
Two Men—Neither has any lines of script. One accompanies the Older Woman and the other accompanies the Young Woman.

SETTING: The play is set in a small restaurant at lunchtime. The Woman and her
friend are seated at a table. They have finished their meal and are talking
over coffee. One of the women reaches into her purse and pulls out a pack
of cigarettes. She takes one out and lights it with a gold lighter. The Older
Woman, sitting at a nearby table with her husband, turns to the two women.

Older Woman: Excuse me, but do you think you could extinguish your cigarette? It really irritates me while I'm eating.

Woman: *(turning to the older woman)* Oh, I'm sorry. *(She puts her cigarette
out in the ashtray, then looks at her friend curiously, then back to the older
woman.)* Wait a minute. Isn't this the smoking section?

Older Woman: Yes, it is, but it's the only seat we could get. The non-smoking section is full.

Woman: Well, the smoking section is for people who want to smoke. You
should have waited for an available table in the other section. *(She takes
out another cigarette and lights it.)*

Older Woman: Please put your cigarette out. It really bothers me.

Woman: I enjoy having a cigarette after a meal. I have the right to smoke
in this section of the restaurant. If it bothers you, move.

Friend: Joan, maybe we should go if it bothers these people.

Woman: *(voice raises)* No. I'm sick and tired of all this nonsense about
smoking. They should have known people would smoke in this section.
Time after time, I'm asked to put out my cigarette. I have the right here—
they don't. *(She blows smoke in their direction.)*

Older Woman: *(fanning the smoke with irritation)* We would have waited for
another table, but we have to be somewhere in a half an hour, and we
didn't have time to wait. *(to husband)* It's just the principle of the whole
thing. She can't even wait to smoke until she gets outside. Some people
just have no will power. Oh, Harold, I feel sick. I can't even finish my meal.

Woman: Okay, then leave. You aren't making me feel guilty. *(She looks directly at the older woman.)* That is what you are trying to do, isn't it?

Older Woman: I just thought you could be considerate enough to wait until
we had left or until you were outside. I guess you like being obstinate and
rude.

Woman: *(She puts out her cigarette, takes out another and lights it.)* I feel
you are the one being rude. It's the principle of the matter. I have the right
to smoke here and you are violating my right by asking me not to smoke.

Older Woman: Oh, this is ridiculous.

Woman: Isn't it.

Older Woman: Let's go, Harold. *(They get up.)*

Woman: Toodles. *(As they pass, she blows smoke in the older woman's direction. The older woman glares and storms past.)*

Friend: Joan, don't you think you were overdoing it a little?

Woman: Hell no. I do have the right to smoke here. I swear it's a never-
ending battle with all this smoking business, and I'm sick of being so polite
all the time. I have just as much right to smoke as they have to tell me not
to. *(A waitress seats a young couple next to them. Joan takes a puff of her
cigarette and blows out the smoke.)*

Young Woman: Excuse me, but do you think you could put out your cigarette? I'm allergic to smoke. . . .

Lights fade . . . Curtain closes. . .

THE ACTIVITY Begin this activity by performing one or two very short plays in class. Give a copy of the script to each student who will play a part and spend a few minutes with the participants explaining the plot of the play and the roles they will be taking. Then have the "actors" read the play before the class.

Discuss the differences between a story and a play and ask them what they think are the particular advantages of each. You might do this by dividing the chalkboard in half and labeling one side *Plays* and the other side *Stories*. Then list the elements that are comparable. For example:

Plays

- Characters must be developed completely through their speech and actions on the stage—the playwright cannot provide narrative descriptions to characterize them.
- Body language and tone of voice are vitally important in characterizing on the stage.
- Characters are visible—very little about their physical appearance is left up to the audience's imagination.
- Settings cannot change often and they are limited to what's possible to build on stage.
- Plays must be clear and comprehensible at the first presentation because the audience can't re-read it, or slow it down.
- The audience must be kept interested for the duration of the performance. People watching the play can't skim it, or skip over the boring parts, so they'll leave if it doesn't sustain their interest.

Stories

- Story writers often use lengthy text descriptions to help develop characters and describe setting.
- Story writers can't make use of body language or tone of voice, except through text descriptions.
- Characters are not visible; the reader is free (forced) to imagine what characters look like from the text descriptions.
- The setting can change often and there is no limit to the kinds of settings an author can use.
- The text doesn't have to be crystal clear at the first reading because readers can slow down or re-read the text.
- The story writer also needs to keep the audience interested, but not to the same degree as a playwright, because while reading a story, indi-

viduals can skim or skip over parts that don't interest them.

- Reading a story is more often a personal, solitary experience, whereas going to a play is a large group, social experience.

Tell students that their next assignment will be to write a short, one-act play that includes no more than two major characters.

Pass out a copy of a short play (if all students don't have one yet) and examine the format:

Title

Author

Cast of Characters (in order of appearance) names the characters and gives brief information such as age, title, and relationship with one or more of the other characters.

Setting briefly describes the place (stage setting) and who is on stage when the play begins.

The Script (dialogue) identifies the character followed by his or her lines.

Acts and Scenes are the playwright's devices for changing time or place in the play.

Ask students to pick a situation for a play and suggest they draft it first as a dialogue. Then they can develop it further into a short play. Have them enter a draft on a word processor and bring it to class on the day it's due, with as many additional copies as there are characters in the play.

When students arrive in class with their plays, allow enough time to act out a few of them. Some students may choose to postpone the performance of their plays until after editing groups have critiqued them, and they've had a chance to perfect them.

Go through the critiquing and revising process and then act out more of the plays.

Poetry

PURPOSE: Writing simple poetry helps students sharpen their senses and gives them the opportunity to practice creating sensory images and poetic comparisons. Playing with the kinds of literary devices used in poetry entices students to "loosen up" and begin experimenting with interesting and unique ways to express their ideas. A new, poetic approach to seeing and communicating often tends to freshen up their prose writing, too.

PREPARATION: Read through this activity and select the poems you wish to duplicate for students. Duplicate a number of your own favorite published and unpublished poetry, too, enabling students to have an ample supply of models for the writing assignment. Try to locate one or two informal poems that describe the essence of poetry, such as "How to Eat a Poem" by Eve Merriam.

THE ACTIVITY: Begin this activity by reading a poem or two that help define poetry and the experience of reading poetry. Then as a class tackle the question: What is poetry? Be sure the following points are included in the discussion:

- Poetry may or may not rhyme.
- Poems include words or comparisons that suggest emotions, attitudes, values, or experiences.
- Poets often use words with multiple meanings, so the poem says more in fewer words.
- Poets are concerned with the sounds of words; thus they carefully choose words with sounds that suit the mood and meaning of the poem.
- Poetry does not always convey specific values or a moral, and it is not always beautiful. It communicates experience.
- Poetry is a multidimensional language. It has:
  —an intellectual dimension
  —a sensory dimension
  —an emotional dimension
  —an imaginative dimension
- The difference between poetry and other forms of literature is degree. Poetry is the most condensed communication of experience.

Pass out a few poems by published and unpublished poets that use metaphor or simile as a major poetic device. (If the class hasn't done the activity entitled *Simple Metaphors and Similes,* do it in conjunction with this activity.) The following are a few student-written examples:

Sometimes
   When it's raining
   The sun still shines
   In your eyes
     And wishes
      Slide down rainbows
Releasing thoughts
Of time,
When happiness
Was walking through
Mud puddles.

I spit out anger
Like watermelon seeds
A juicy mouthful stored—
Then blasted rapid fire.
When the battle is finished
I wait a long while
For the next childish feast.

Cool calm breezes rustle
Through hanging trees, burdened
With polluted sorrows
Carelessly created.

RISING IN THE MORNING

Suddenly alerted—mind blinks, eyes flutter, jump up. . .
Like toast pops and abruptly cools, as it
    leaves the warm place into a fast-food world

Anger broods inside
Caged,
Like a trained wild beast
That sits within
When the door is
Open.

Read the poems out loud and discuss the content and meaning of each one. Ask students to explain the metaphoric comparison in each, and point out what imagery the poet uses to stimulate which senses.

In addition, you might pick a poem that's a bit more complex than these and ask students to write a paragraph that paraphrases the poem. This is a useful exercise for discovering how significantly individual interpretations actually do differ.

Next, ask students to look around the room, choose an object and compare it to something else, making a simple metaphor or simile. To help get them started, write a couple of examples on the board, such as these:

THE KEYBOARD

Over its rectangular back
lie rows of shiny scales
with letters.

Bright yellow words on the chalkboard
whisper
to foul phrases that
shriek
from the wall outside.

Computer mirror at my desk
Who writes better than the rest?

The smell of a burning 100 watt bulb
Is mildly chemical
As the smell of a cellophane-wrapped pie
Is mildly apple.

Holds together thoughts of brilliant men
A simple paper clip.

Then have the class invent other metaphors and similes that may have nothing to do with the classroom, such as the following student-written comparisons:

That first kiss;
A thousand avenues open.

California Fall
Like a birthday child waiting
For presents of rain drops.

My daughter is like a door that says
"Private Do Not Enter"
My soul is closed
To you.

Too much to do
Urgent deadlines to meet.
I feel
Like a blender whirling
Still ridiculously twirling
Though the substance has
Clogged.

A love affair is like a piece of chocolate
So sweet, yet quite
Unnecessary.

Show them some examples of poems that rely primarily on sensory images, rather than metaphorical comparisons, to convey meaning, such as the student-written poems that follow. Then ask them to try inventing some, too.

As I ate the strawberries I felt a
Shimmering tingle go down to my toes.
They were rich   red   fat   and juicy
Squishing through my teeth
Making my glands water
And slowly
    sliding
       down
          to my
              stomach.

Bored
Sipping coffee
Sucking candies
'Till I'm bloating
Mad.

LAST MINUTE OF CLASS

Tense bodies edge forward
Waiting for teacher's nod.

WHEAT HEADS

Clusters of fluffy wheat heads—
Coquettes—
toss yellow locks
in the morning breeze.
But
soon they sit still and
bake brown by a desert sun.

A sudden dust storm
ages blonde curls with gray dust.
And
terrified, they cling
to cracked soil while
wind blasts threaten to uproot them.

For homework, ask students to write a few more poems that use images and comparisons to convey particular ideas. Ask them to enter their poems on a word processor and bring them to class on the day the assignment is due.

After the homework assignment has been given and explained, you might share with them some other poems written by students. The following two examples combine a variety of poetic devices, including imagery, metaphor, and simile. They both make strong statements that express the writer's attitude concerning certain kinds of people.

HOUSEWIVES

Every morning
I wheel up the long avenue of
palms and sprinklers and housewives
in bandanas and gardening gloves.
They never once look
up from their weeds.

They live in the walls
of small houses, sealed in
dust-free carpets.

Their hearts vacuumed,
dreams thrown out with the garbage,
their eyes are as empty
as sucked eggs.

I watch them,
line by line, like clothes
strung out in winter.
Then I go home
and chase rainbows.

SOUVENIR

Bent iron and twisted steel
grow like a vine
around the telephone pole
as thousands of sparkling glass diamonds
peer wickedly
from the calloused pavement.

People, crowding close
to see the blood,
make their awkward, foolish comments,
push nearer to see
the most interesting thing in life—
Death.

The burnt rubber tires askew on their axles
like dilated eyes, spin
unfocused.
Plush leather seats are streaked with red—
lips kiss the dashboard.

A small boy pushes out from the crowd
and looks at the blond hair
tangled in the jagged window.
He stops to pick up a splinter of glass—
as a souvenir.

When students come to class with their poems, invite them to share one or two with the class. Perhaps this can be one writing assignment that does not go through the peer group reviewing process. Critiquing poems and advising peers about how to improve their poetry is a skill that's a bit more advanced than helping one another edit and revise prose assignments. This assignment may be better handled as a large group experience in which students share their poems with classmates and then hand them in to the teacher.

You could leave poetry writing after this brief, informal activity, or you could pursue it a good deal further with an in-depth study of other poetic devices, such as rhyme and meter, personification, assonance, consonance, alliteration, and irony. If you choose to continue with further poetry writing activities, spend some time helping students learn to read and critique one another's poems, keeping in mind that it's more difficult to provide supportive criticism and suggestions for improving poetry than any other writing genre.

Process Analysis

PURPOSE: This activity helps students learn to be accurate and complete when writing instructions or any other procedures that require detailed analysis and/or explanation.

PREPARATION: Duplicate enough copies of the graphic image illustrated in Figure 5.2 so that everyone in the class can have one. Have them on hand when you do the activity, but keep them concealed until the moment they are needed.

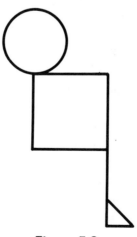

Figure 5.2

THE ACTIVITY: Begin this activity with a classroom game. Ask for three student volunteers, and then send them out of the room. Tell them that it will be ten or fifteen minutes before they'll be needed, but they should stay close enough to be called back at any time.

Back in the classroom, take out the duplicated graphic illustrations and hand one out to every student. Explain that their task is to examine the drawing and write instructions so that a person who has never seen it could reproduce the exact same drawing just by reading the instructions. Hence their written instructions must be perfectly clear, accurate, and complete. Ask them to write the instructions on a separate piece of paper (not the sheet with the drawing).

When they have finished, ask them to put away the drawings. Move a student desk that's not being used to the front of the classroom and turn it around so it's facing the wall. Call back one of the exiled volunteers and ask her to sit down at the desk facing the wall. Give the student a pencil and blank sheet of paper. Now explain to her that another student from the class (pick one) will read a set of directions out loud to the newly arrived student. All she has to do is follow those directions. If the listener doesn't hear something clearly, or is confused, she may ask the reader to repeat the instruction, but that's all. No additional words or explanations may be spoken besides what was originally written in the directions. No one is allowed to talk or prompt in any way. (The listening student is not facing the class.)

When the drawing is finished, hold it up for the class to see. Then call in the next student and go through the exercise again, asking a different student to read his or her directions. Repeat the same process with the third student.

How closely do the students' drawings resemble the original one? How closely do they resemble each other? In light of this exercise, discuss once again the need for clarity, accuracy, and completeness when writing an explanation of a process.

Tell students that their next writing assignment will involve another process analysis. Ask them to pick a process that they know how to do very well. Some examples follow.

- How to write an essay
- How to survive at [Greendale High School]
- How to lose weight
- How to stop smoking
- How to manage a restaurant
- How to raise a child
- How to sell a boat (car, stereo, bicycle)
- How to train a dog

- How to grow a garden
- How to get along with a brother (sister, roommate, employer)
- How to read a book
- How to study for an exam
- How to avoid theft

Advise students to pick a process that is relatively uncomplicated, so that they can explain how to do it in no more than two or three double-spaced, printed pages. (Topics such as how to play bridge or how to build a computer, for example, are too complex.)

Advise students to write a list of the steps involved in the process, in the order in which they are executed—before they begin composing. They can then use this list to help organize and compose a first draft. Ask students to enter their drafts on a word processor and bring the disk to class on the day it's due.

On the day the assignment is due, ask editing groups to meet to critique the first drafts. This writing assignment is fairly easy for students to critique because the organization of a process analysis paper is straightforward, and its success is related to how well a reader can understand the process after it is explained. Therefore, it might be a good opportunity to direct editing groups to focus on a few basic-skills problems that often occur in this type of paper, such as repetitious sentence patterns and pronoun switching.

Compare And Contrast

PURPOSE: Comparing two objects or ideas is a method of analysis that we often use when making decisions, introducing unfamiliar objects or ideas, presenting opinions, and so on. This activity helps students learn more about how to use the compare-and-contrast method of analysis effectively in their own writing.

PREPARATION: Locate a comparison essay to read to the class as an example. This one was written by a student.

PAST AND FUTURE LAWS FOR MINORS

Crimes such as vandalism, shoplifting, reckless or drunken driving, and drug use, are committed every day by people of all ages. The punishments given for these offenses depend on the age of the lawbreaker and the severity of the crime. Punishments for offenders under 18 years of age is now typically so lenient that the convicted teenager does not hesitate to repeat the crime.

In California, a proposal has recently been drawn up to deal with young law-lawbreakers. The underlying assumption of the proposal is that if minors feel they can get away with committing petty crimes, they will advance to more severe and serious offenses as they get older. The following paragraphs present the current laws for minors and the new, recommended laws for minors, concerning acts of vandalism, shoplifting, drug use, and reckless or drunken driving.

Ripped-up lawns, spray paint on the sidewalks, broken windows, and egged fences are just a few ways that people vandalize public or private property. In the current laws, vandals are given a choice of punishment: they must repair the damage, pay to have it repaired, or be assigned to community service. Doing community service work involves working up to thirty hours in activities such as caring for the elderly, cleaning the streets, and working in the police station.

The new proposal forces vandals under 18 to either pay or fix the damage. If the minor is not capable of personally making repairs, he must supply the money that is necessary to have the repairs done professionally. If the offender cannot supply the money, his/her parents will be held responsible. The vandal will also be assigned up to forty hours of community service work. This proposal not only provides definite punishment, it also involves the vandal's family, who should be fully aware of the crime their child has committed.

The current law states that shoplifters over 18 are automatically fined and/or taken to jail. However, the punishment for a minor who is caught shoplifting depends on the police, the parents, and the store involved. Shoplifters' parents are called right away, but many times the punishment ends there. The police who are called into the store to handle the situation can decide whether the minor needs to be taken to court. The parents also help decide on the punishment. If they insist that their child has never had any problems in the past, and that they will be able to straighten everything out themselves, the police will typically let the child go, possibly with community work assigned. If the parents refuse to take responsibility and if the child has already been involved in other crimes, the police can take the child to Hillcrest, a temporary juvenile jail that keeps and counsels lawbreakers under 18. The latter of these punishments is very rare. Most often, the store drops the charges and the shoplifter walks out of the store feeling a bit nervous, but frequently not nervous enough to refrain from trying again.

The new proposal for shoplifters under 18 warrants that every criminal be sentenced to a specific type of punishment. The first offense will result in thirty to forty hours of community work. The second offense results in double the amount of community work and the shoplifter is put on probation for three months. The third offense will automatically put the minor in Hillcrest for as many as thirty days, regardless of the value of the stolen object.

The use of illegal drugs is fairly common among teenagers. According to today's law, it is impossible to lock up a person of any age for the possession of marijuana. If caught with this drug, the minor is usually put on probation and/or assigned up to thirty hours of community service. If the minor does not fulfill this obligation, he/she still cannot be put in jail. However, the possession of any other narcotics causes immediate arrest. Possession of cocaine, for example, means three to four years of imprisonment at Camp Glenwood, a ranch that has a special school for problem children. The ratio of students to teacher is 15:1, thus giving the lawbreakers the extra attention they normally don't receive in public school.

The new proposal for lawbreakers under 18, who are caught with any type of narcotics is as follows: the offender must attend a weekly drug abuse class, is put on probation, and must attend special counseling sessions at Glenwood every weekend for one year. A second arrest means the offender will be sentenced to four years at Glenwood.

Reckless driving is a major cause of automobile accidents, but the punishment does not give the driver any reason to stop speeding or driving through flashing red lights at 2:00 in the morning, for example. Depending on the mood of the police officer present, a ticket may be given, the driver may be taken to jail, or just a simple warning may be issued. If the reckless driver injures a pedestrian, the driver is taken to jail, the parents are called in, and a date is set for a court appearance.

The new proposal for dealing with reckless drivers suggests that these lawbreakers be automatically sentenced to a three-month probation with one full weekend of traffic school. They will also be fined $50 and receive a ticket that will go on his/her driving record. If a reckless driver injures another person, the driver will lose his/her license for six months and will spend two weeks at Hillcrest.

Reckless driving is often caused by alcoholic beverages. When a minor is pulled over and accused of driving "under the influence," the police officer can make an arrest, or just extend a warning. If arrested, the minor is taken to juvenile court and assigned community service and alcohol abuse counseling. The driver's license is often suspended, although if a drunken driver is caught with an already suspended license, he/she can be sentenced up to six months at Glenwood.

The major change in the new proposal for drunken driving insures that every minor who is pulled over is brought to court. The police will not have the choice of deciding whether or not to arrest the suspect. If proven guilty, the driver will have to attend driving and alcohol abuse classes. When a drunk driver injures another person, he/she must pay for the damage, plus pay a fine of up to $1,000. The driver's license will be suspended for up to a year and he/she must attend alcohol abuse classes.

These new proposed laws are designed to make potential offenders think at least twice before going ahead with an unlawful act. Many of the current laws do not put enough pressure on soon-to-be criminals. A warning, or telephone call to parents is not enough. The specific punishments outlined in the proposed laws will hopefully stop many minors from committing any sort of crime now, or ever.

THE ACTIVITY: Read aloud for the class the example essay that compares two objects or ideas. Then discuss how effectively the writer makes his or her points by using comparison. Does the writer argue that one of the things being compared is preferable to the other (as in the example essay above), and how? How clearly and completely does the writer present the two subjects being compared?

Examine the structure of the essay; for instance, are the two subjects compared point-by-point through the essay, or is one subject fully explained, followed by an explanation of the second? In the example essay above, the current and proposed laws are compared point-by-point; first the laws for punishing vandals, then shoplifters, then drug abusers, then reckless and drunken drivers.

Brainstorm topics that would make good material for a comparison essay and write them on the chalkboard or word processor. Some examples include the following:

- Cross-country skiing and downhill skiing
- Watching news on television and reading news in the newspaper
- Two magazines on the same topic (e.g., *Glamor* and *Mademoiselle*, *Popular Computing* and *Personal Computing*, *Time* and *Newsweek*, *Sport Magazine* and *Sports Illustrated*)

- Reading a novel and watching it on television
- Small colleges and large universities
- City living and country living
- U.S. educational system and another country's educational system
- Huck, in *Huckleberry Finn* and Holden, in *Catcher in the Rye*
- Checkers and chess
- Sailing and motorboating

Ask students to choose one of these topics for the classroom activity that will follow. Let's take the topic, "Cross-Country Skiing and Downhill Skiing," for example. Divide the chalkboard in half and make two columns, labeled: *Cross-Country Skiing* and *Downhill Skiing*. (A center column that overlaps both, labeled *Characteristics of Both Sports*, would also be useful.) Then ask students to name all the characteristics of these two sports that they can think of that are comparable.

Characteristics of both sports

- They both are winter sports that get you outdoors in the snow (if and when there is snow).
- The purpose of both sports is to glide on a pair of skis.
- The equipment used in both sports is fairly similar.

Cross Country Skiing

- There are no ski tows; you have to climb up the hills. Much of the sport involves traveling on fairly flat trails.
- It consumes more energy.
- It's less expensive because you don't have to pay for a ski lift.
- There are fewer people involved in this sport, so you generally can enjoy more peace and quiet while skiing.
- You don't have to travel long distances to get to a special ski area with ski tows; you can ski anywhere there is snow.
- There are some equipment differences; for example, the skier's heel is not clamped down to the ski, the skis are longer and thinner, etc.
- The equipment is somewhat less expensive.

Downhill Skiing

- The sport generally involves traveling downhill, rather than on flat trails.
- There are ski tows or lifts; you don't have to climb up the hills.
- It doesn't require quite as much energy.
- It is more expensive because you have to buy a ski lift/tow ticket, but it's worth it not to have to climb up the slopes.

- There are generally more people at a downhill ski area, so you're more likely to meet new and interesting people.
- Downhill skiers enjoy the unique feeling of flying when skiing down a hill.
- There are some equipment differences; for example, the skier's heel is clamped down to the ski, the skis are shorter and wider, etc.

Next, ask students to help group the entries into categories. Examples include similarities, the kind of movement involved, equipment, pleasure.

Discuss the method of organization that would be most effective for this essay. Would writers compare the two sports category by category, or would they describe one sport first and then the other? After they've decided, have them arrange the notes in an appropriate order of presentation. Finally, ask them to compose a thesis statement that states the two subjects being compared and leads the reader into the comparison. Here's one suggestion:

> Cross-country skiing and downhill skiing are two winter sports that are extremely popular with Americans. However, just because they both involve skis and poles worn by people who travel across snow-covered terrain doesn't mean they are the same. [*thesis statement:*] In fact, they are strikingly different.

Here's another suggestion:

> [*Thesis statement:*] There's a social war going on at Greendale High School between the downhill skiers and the cross-country enthusiasts. Every day at lunch, from November 'til March, the two armies sit at opposite ends of the cafeteria, firing comments about the virtues of their preferred sport, or the deficiencies of the other.

After they have the essay planned, explain that their homework assignment is to pick their own topic for comparison and go through the same steps they've just completed in class. Writers may choose one of the topics from the list, or invent a new one. Ask them to compose a first draft, enter it on a word processor, and bring in the disk on the day the assignment is due.

After students have critiqued their first drafts in editing groups, they can revise them and hand the second drafts in to the teacher. Some of the most successful ones may be shared with the whole class, before or after the final drafts are completed.

Cause And Effect

PURPOSE: This activity helps students learn to recognize when to use a cause-effect method of analysis and presentation in their writing, and it provides practice in using that writing technique.

PREPARATION: Locate a cause-effect essay to read to the class as an example of this writing method. Periodicals are good sources for this kind of essay.

THE ACTIVITY: Read your example essay to the class and discuss how effectively it uses the cause-effect method of analysis. Would another method of analysis and presentation be more effective? How else could a writer approach the topic being addressed? Ask students to identify the thesis statement. Discuss the specific causes and effects pointed out in the essay and ask students to pinpoint the writer's arguments, and evaluate how successfully they are expressed. Can students think of other causes or effects that support or refute the writer's opinion?

When you've finished discussing the example essay, list other topics that could be effectively presented using the cause-effect method. For example:

Causes-Effect:

- Reasons for joining a 4-H Club (swim team, fraternity or sorority, the Peace Corps, etc.)
- Causes for failing an English exam (math exam, history exam, etc.)
- Reasons for selecting a particular college (spouse, career, place to live, etc.)

Cause-Effects:

- Effects of moving to Riverdale
- Effects of being execssively good-looking (smart, athletic, etc.)
- Effects of being excessively good-looking (smart, athletic, etc.)
- Effects of spending my junior year in France

Pick one of the topics for class discussion, and ask students to name the causes leading up to a result, or a cause that created many effects. List these on the chalkboard or word processor. For example, if the class picks the topic "reasons for joining the Peace Corps," the list of causes might look like this:

Reasons For Joining The Peace Corps

- I like to travel.
- But, I prefer to stay in one place for a long time, rather than move from place to place like a tourist.
- I'd like to become familiar with another culture, and learn its language, social habits, educational system, and so on.
- I enjoy projects that allow me to use my hands and force me to invent

ways to successfully complete them without spending money on materials.

- I enjoy the challenge of living on little money.
- I enjoy helping other people improve their own lives.

Also list the arguments on the other side:
Reasons For Not Joining The Peace Corps

- Two years is a long time to be away from friends and family.
- I'm not very good at learning foreign languages.
- I'm not particularly good at fixing and building things with my hands.
- I like American food.

Plan how to organize this information into a cause-effect essay, assuming that the effect is that the writer has decided to apply to the Peace Corps. Some of the negative arguments would wisely be included in the essay too, so the piece would be more realistic and less like an advertisement for the Peace Corps.

Ask students to suggest a thesis statement for the hypothetical essay. Here's one possibility:

> After six months of surviving in the scorching flatlands of southern Malawi, I tried to recall my original reasons for joining the Peace Corps.

Ask students to choose their own topic for a cause-effect essay that they will write as a homework assignment. Advise them to go through the same planning process the class just completed before they begin composing a draft of the essay. Have them enter first drafts on a word processor and bring the disk to class on the day the paper is due.

When students come to class with the assignment, ask them to meet in editing groups to critique the essays, and then have each group pick one or two of the most successful papers to share with the whole class. After critiquing the second drafts, teachers may ask students to revise them further in a third draft.

Emotive Language

PURPOSE: This activity helps students learn to recognize biased, emotional words and phrases that are commonly used in written and spoken language, and to understand how they distort the truth.

PREPARATION: Locate a couple of periodical articles that contain numerous slanted words which attempt to appeal to the readers' emotions and prejudices. Advertisements, reviews, and letters-to-the-Editor are good sources for this kind of language. Duplicate one for class discussion and save another on a disk for a classroom writing activity.

THE ACTIVITY: Draw a picture of a fat woman on the chalkboard—a rough sketch will do just fine (Fig. 5.3). Now ask the class for words to describe the shape of this lady, who happens to be their most beloved aunt. Examples include plump, full-figured, robust, round, hefty, heavy-set, big boned, solid, large-framed, portly.

Next, tell them that the woman is that neighbor who always complains about the loud music coming from your upstairs window or the bike you sometimes leave on the sidewalk near her house. What words would students use to describe her appearance now. Examples might include obese, fat, gross, immense, flabby, dense, two-ton, gluttonous, a pig, a tub, a hippo.

Draw three columns on the board and label them Positive, Neutral, and Negative. Then discuss *denotation* (the literal, explicit meaning of a word, the dictionary definition) and *connotation* (the feelings and attitudes associated with the word). Scatter a few words or phrases under the appropriate headings on the board, and ask the class to fill in the rest of the columns for each word. Here's an example of what could result:

Figure 5.3

Positive	Neutral	Negative
firm, solid, stable, secure, rooted, loyal, settled, established	difficult to move	rigid, stubborn, stiff, unpliant, inflexible, stern, unyielding
thrifty, economical, careful, frugal, sparing	one who is reluctant to spend money	tightwad, stingy, skinflint, cheap, close-fisted, miserly
home, cottage, nest, chalet, castle, hideaway	house, cabin, abode, mansion, residence, dwelling	shack, dump, hut, hole, hovel, pigpen, white elephant

Read aloud to the class the following example of emotive language. The speaker is a politician delivering a speech.

> If when you say whiskey you mean the devil's brew, the poison scourge, the bloody monster, that defiles innocence, dethrones reason, destroys the home, creates misery and poverty, yea, literally takes the bread from the mouths of little children; if you mean the evil drink that topples the Christian man and woman from the pinnacle of righteous, gracious living into the bottomless pit of degradation and despair, and shame, and helplessness, and hopelessness, then certainly I am against it.
>
> But if when you say whiskey you mean the oil of conversation, the philosophic wine, the ale that puts a song in their hearts and laughter on their lips, and the warm glow of contentment in their eyes; if you mean Christmas cheer; if you mean the stimulating drink that puts the spring into the old gentleman's step on a frosty crispy morning; if you mean the drink which enables a man to magnify his joy, and his happiness, and to forget, if only for a little while, life's great tragedies, and heartaches, and sorrows; if you mean that drink, the sale of which pours into our treasuries untold millions of dollars, which are used to provide tender care for our little crippled children, our blind, our deaf, our dumb, our pitiful aged and infirm; to build highways and hospitals and schools, then certainly I am for it.
>
> This is my stand, I will not retreat from it. I will not compromise.*

Pass out and read aloud one of the duplicated articles that contains emotive language. Then ask students to underline all the loaded words they can find.

What effect does using this biased, emotional language have on the reader? Discuss this, and the need to be clear, honest, and logical when trying to persuade an audience to accept your way of thinking. Some persuasive writing deviates from the truth in order to appeal to the prejudices of an audience, but writers who use too much slanted language eventually lose credibility with their readers. Many respected writers do use an emotional appeal successfully to persuade others, but they use is moderately. Logical arguments and factual evidence are the most effective techniques of argument.

As a classroom writing activity, have students meet in their editing groups to work on a biased article that has already been entered on a

---

(*from "The Prohibition's Last Stand" by Kenneth Vinson, published in *The New Republic*, October 16, 1965. Reprinted by permission.)

word processor and saved on a disk. Ask groups to read the article on the display screen and revise it, conveying the opposite bias (or, you could ask them to write it with neutral words that contain no bias). Have them save the rewrites using a different file name, so they will have both versions on the disk.

An alternate classroom writing activity would be to divide the class into groups of four students. Have one pair of students in each group collaboratively compose a letter or speech on the word processor that advocates something they feel strongly about. Ask the second pair in each group to compose a letter or speech that severely criticizes the same thing. Have them save these entries on a disk. The following day, have the group members trade disks and rewrite the pieces with the opposite bias. Each pair should then save their rewrite using a separate file name so that all four versions are still available.

Pick a few of these to read to the class and then discuss how the arguments would be stronger if the writers used logical and factual information to support their position, instead of an emotional appeal. If students did slip in some good logical arguments, point them out, and use them as leads into the next writing activity. . . .

Ask each group of four to work together in composing a speech or letter on the same general topic as before, but this time they will all take the same position and support it with logical arguments and examples rather than emotional language. Ask them to save their final version on the original disk, using a separate file name. Collect the disks and read them over to check whether students have, in fact, learned to make the distinction between emotional appeal and logical persuasion.

The homework assignment is similar to the first classroom activity. Pass out another of the duplicated articles (or ask students to find an article themselves) that uses a considerable amount of slanted language to persuade. Ask them first to underline the biased words and phrases. Then they should rewrite the article on a word processor, changing the words to convey the opposite bias (as in the whiskey speech). Then attach the original article to the rewrite before handing in both articles.

Persuasive Writing

PURPOSE: Persuasive writing may well be the kind of writing that readers are exposed to more than any other; it's used in advertising, campaigning, marketing, and public relations, as well as for presenting proposals, defending positions, and advocating causes. Being able to persuade an audience to adopt a particular opinion, idea, or proposal is powerful but a difficult skill to learn. This activiy will help student writers learn to compose effective persuasive essays.

PREPARATION: Find one or two persuasive essays that use logical arguments, supported by factual information and examples, in order to persuade an audience to adopt the writer's point of view on the subject. Have these on hand to read to the class on the day you plan to begin the activity.

"A Modest Proposal" by Jonathan Swift, is a dramatic example of a persuasive piece of writing. The student-written essay concerning punishment for lawbreaking minors (see the *Compare and Contrast* activity) is another example of persuasive writing. The following is a student-written speech designed to persuade the audience to adopt a new proposl for high school education:

A PROPOSED HIGH SCHOOL EDUCATIONAL SYSTEM

When you think about the most memorable times of your life, chances are you'll remember your high school years. After all, during that time you may have met some lifelong friends, enemies, sweethearts, and possibly your spouse. You may have enjoyed brief fame as a basketball player, President of the Student Council, or Junior Prom Queen. The recollections of the school dances, football games, and other events further enhance these memories. But when you come right down to it, did you learn anything during your four-year stay at Metropolis High? Well, if you're not too sure whether you did or not, you might be in favor of a more academically oriented high school experience for your children. The paragraphs that follow propose a new high school eductional system that will both teach kids academics and enable them to enjoy their time at school.

As we have all heard, many of the high school systems are now beginning to revert back to emphasizing the 3 R's—reading, 'riting, and 'rithmetic. This is due to major studies done a few years ago that showed many college freshmen are deficient in basic skills.

The proposed required classes for a new high school system would put a great deal of emphasis on these needed skills. It would include a minimum of four years of English, which includes essay writing, world literature, spelling and grammar, business writing, and speech. The proposed system emphasizes the importance of being able to express oneself verbally as well as on paper; these required English skills are designed to help sutdents learn to communicate better with peers in the working world. Math is also emphasized in the new system. Students will be required to take two and a half years of mathematics. A half year of basic math, a half year of business math, and the other year and a half of upper division math (e.g. Algebra, Geometry, Trigonometry). This will help the student later in life when he/she will be required to fill out tax forms, balance checkbooks, etc. History is also of prime concern in the new system. Students will have to take three years of history. This includes one year of U.S. History, one year of state and local history, half a year of U.S. Government, and half a year of Psychology. Computer Science is also of prime concern. Since computers are now being widely used by businesses and individuals, we feel that there should be a class to teach the basics of computing. Upper division courses would also be offered. Students should take a minimum of two years of Science, including one year of Introductory Biology and the other year in an upper division class like Biology II, Chemistry, Physics, or Computer Science.

The last required course is Physical Education. Students would take two years of P.E., or one year, if he/she participates in a competitive sport such as football, baseball, tennis, or swimming. Students need to be educated physically, of course, but not to the extent that they have been recently. The proposed system does not discourage physical fitness by any means, but it does put a greater emphasis on academics.

The grading system in the proposed high school system will set "C" as the passing grade for all courses. However, there will be various levels of most courses offered, so that students will be able to enroll in the courses that suit them best. There will be Math, English, and Science "lab times" so that students can obtain extra help whenever they need it. The labs will be run by college students who are majoring in the subject they will be tutoring. Tutoring by the subject teachers will also be available when the students request it.

The requirements for graduation are basically that all the mandatory courses must be passed with a grade of "C" or better. Also, students must pass competency tests in reading, writing, and mathematics before graduation. The tests will by no means be easy; therefore, classes to help students pass these tests will also be available.

Class size is another issue addressed in this proposal. No class may exceed twenty-five students. When necessary, another section of the class will be added to accommodate the overflow. Every required class will also have lab sessions for students to attend in order to get extra help. The labs will be open one hour before school and two hours after school. The school will make every effort to insure that students get the help they need.

Other regulations include a strict set of rules designed to maintain order in the school at all times. The purpose is to keep kids out of trouble, while giving them all fair treatment. The length of the school day will be seven hours, from 8:00 to 3:00. The classes will be 55 minutes long, with a ten-minute passing time between classes. A fifteen-minute break will be held between second and third period and lunch will be one hour long. Freshmen, sophomores, and juniors will be required to take six periods, while the seniors, who are holding jobs or taking classes at a community college, will be required to take two classes. Seniors who hold jobs will also be required to take a Work Experience class. The campus will be open during lunch and closed at other times of the day.

Attendance is also an important element of this proposal. Students are allowed two tardies per class during a semester. Every two tardies after that will result in the reduction of the student's grade by half a grade. However, the tardies may be worked off by doing chores around the school (e.g., painting, clean-up work, etc.). Cutting a class will be considered equal to two tardies. If a student is caught loitering off campus, two hours of work will be issued to the student and a cut will also be recorded in the teacher's records. When students are sick or otherwise absent with a parent's permission, the student must bring a note from a parent within two days, or the absence will be recorded as a cut. The school will enforce these rules without exception.

Two final regulations that pertain directly to students are a dress code and rules about the possession of illegal drugs. No shorts (mid-thigh) will be allowed at school and no other revealing attire will be tolerated. Hair length will be left up to the students' discretion. No illegal drugs are allowed on campus; if any student is caught possessing illegal drugs, he/she will be immediately suspended from school. The same rules apply for weapons. The school will enforce these rules without exception.

All teachers that are hired after this new system is adopted, will be certified by the state and will have majored in the subject they are assigned to teach. Teachers will have to be on campus from 7:30 to 3:30 every school day, except on the days when they are scheduled to be in the lab—on those days they will be at school longer. Teachers will have to submit weekly attendance records, as well as reports of the curriculum material covered and the assignments given during the week. These will be filed in the administration office. One of the anticipated benefits of this procedure is that students who have been absent and need to catch up on past lessons and assignments, can get this information for all their classes at the office.

This proposed high school educational system is one that we could adopt without huge expense to the taxpayers—no new buildings or expensive equipment are being proposed, only a new way of operating the already existing facility. The proposed system is tougher and stricter than the present one because it stresses academics more and maintains a higher degree of discipline. But after all, high school is supposed to be primarily a place to learn academics—having a good time is something that will happen quite naturally in the process.

The next example is an editorial written by a college sophomore for a junior college newspaper.

STUDIO UNION 54

Last night I was sitting in my room thinking about the Student Union. This is not something I do all the time, but I began falling asleep while I thought about it. Admit it, "Let's go and hang out at the Student Union for a while," is seldom heard at Marlow. There must be a reason for this, and I think I know why.

Basically, the Student Union needs *pizazz*. It really has no excitement or appeal; my apologies to the architect and the decorator (if there was one). Right now there are very few uses for the Student Union, and I, for one, go over there only when necessary.

Now, when I say pizazz, I don't mean turning it into Studio Union 54. God, can you imagine that? Pulsating lights, Donna Summer moaning, and big lines at the door with a bouncer turning away people because "They just wouldn't fit in with the crowd?" For some reason, I wouldn't want to see that.

The Student Union needs good, good, good, music, and a nice atmosphere. Now I actually feel guilty when I buy something at the Snack Bar because it's exacly the same as the cafeteria food I'm already paying for. Wouldn't it be great for once to be able to order a really good avocado sandwich? I wouldn't feel a bit guilty about that. There should be a snack bar with a varied menu of "homemade" food. Let's hear it for hot pastrami and a beer.

Music, if nothing else, draws people together and the Student Union has lots of room for it. I can see the headlines of the Marlow Press now. . . "The Rolling Stones Appear at the Student Union—One Night Only." Hey, come on, don't be a skeptic—you never know what can happen.

I am constantly overhearing people say, "I wish there were a place where I could go to meet people and just sit and talk." The Student Union could be the answer, if it were designed correctly. Pinball machines, interesting guest speakers, a juke box, backgammon tournaments, performances by Marlow musicians, and countless other ideas could be put into use for the betterment of the Student Union. Another thing that should be changed is that dull name: Student Union. It conjures up boring thoughts right away. But for now, let's just think of ways to fix it up.

Some day, I hope one will be able to hear a group of people driving down Main Street saying, "Oh, wow, I wish I went to Marlow College. They've got the most terrific student union—every other weekend they host a band concert and informal

dance."
Oh hell, I guess I'll go and get an Eskimo Pie before I go to sleep.

THE ACTIVITY: Read an example persuasive essay aloud and ask the class to identify the writer's thesis statement or paraphrase the position being advocated. Then ask students to relate the specific arguments presented in the essay. How effective are the arguments? In the first example essay above, for instance, the writer proposes a plan for a high school, but falls slightly short of defending it with logical arguments that explain *why* the proposed plan is desirable. What arguments could be made against the writer's proposal? Does the writer anticipate those arguments and present counter-arguments?

The second example essay is written to an audience of peers, and it therefore doesn't attempt to present the school administrators' arguments, such as cost, fire laws, etc. The intended audience is almost certian to be sympathetic and so the writer feels free to be informal and humorous.

Introduce and discuss the steps one would follow when planning and writing a persuasive essay:

1. Choose a controversial topic that you feel strongly about and know something about.
2. Brainstorm ideas and gather facts, examples, and other information pertaining to the topic.
3. Plan the method of argument (i.e., an inductive or deductive approach).
4. Organize notes into a rough outline by grouping them in categories and arranging them in the order of presentation.
5. Compose a first draft.

Now, lead the class through these steps as a demonstration activity. Brainstorm together some possible topics for a persuasive paper. Examples might include:

• Working while attending school
• The credit card system of buying
• The value of a liberal arts education
• Treatment of the elderly
• What to do about alcoholism
• Police protection
• The role of women (men) in our society
• Cheating in the classroom

- Ethics in American business
- Trial marriage

Have the class pick a topic for this exercise and then discuss how a writer would go about gathering information pertaining to the subject.

Explain that to be convincing a writer should present a logical argument which includes a coherent collection of facts and examples that are arranged to lead to a particular conclusion. There are two methods of argumentation that are commonly used in persuasive writing—inductive arguments and deductive arguments. *Inductive* arguments begin with a series of statements that include factual information and/or examples that lead up to and conclude with the writer's stand on the topic. *Deductive* arguments begin with a general statement and conclude with a particular statement that expresses the writer's position on the topic, followed by supportive, factual information and examples. This deductive form of argumentation is the one most student writers tend to use in persuasive essays. The writers of both the example essays above used the deductive approach. Discuss which approach would be most appropriate for the topic the class chose for this exercise, and how they would go about organizing notes taken on the topic.

Explain that although a persuasive paper should be soundly based upon logical arguments and factual supportive information, a writer must also consider the emotional impact of the presentation on the audience. Even though writers are advised not to rely on emotive, slanted writing that appeals to the prejudices of an audience, an occasional emotional plea can be effective (such as the suggestion of an avocado sandwich or a hot pastrami and beer, in the second example essay).

When the planning exercise is finished, ask students to chose their own topic for a persuasive paper and begin doing the research for it right away. You may decide to expand this activity into a larger project that includes groups of students working collaboratively to do research and prepare major proposals involving controversial topics. Groups could then present their proposals to the class in formal panel presentations. Alternatively, you might organize debates on various topics that would involve teams of students preparing arguments which would defend opposite sides of the issues.

After the first drafts are entered on a word processor they should be critiqued by members of an editing group, panel, or debating team. The topics chosen for this assignment are typically interesting and provocative, and therefore students usually do an effective job of identifying the strong and weak arguments in classmates' papers. The assignment is particularly good for encouraging students to work together, and getting them to spend time and energy critiquing one another's work. You might have the most success with this activity if you present it to students in the middle of a semester, as the sudden change of task tends to stimulate fresh energy and enthusiasm in peer groups that have been developing a fairly uniform pattern of operation for a couple of months.

Negative Criticism

PURPOSE: This activity helps students learn to examine what elements are included in effective criticism, and the assignment provides practice in writing a critical piece.

PREPARATION: Locate a couple of examples of negative criticism and duplicate one for students to use as a model when writing the assignment. The following two examples are editorials written by college sophomores for the school newspaper:

SPORTS ARE NOT EVERYTHING

Once again the Olympic Games are about to take place, and once again political controversy is prevalent. The Olympics only represent one example of how sports affect everything and everyone. We have all been led to believe that sports, either through participating or spectating, are not only healthy, but also a positive force in our society.

Sports have provided recognition for Blacks, whose exposure through media has speeded up integration in this country (or so we are told). But for every Black sports hero, like O.J. Simpson, Kareem Abdul-Jabbar, or Reggie Jackson, there are thousands, and maybe millions, of Black youngsters who devoted their energies to sports when they should have been directed toward careers in other areas. Because the success of several athletes was publicized, many more kids spent their time on the playground until it was too late for them to qualify for anything above marginal work.

Our society has distorted sports to the point where the winner is more important than the game. Athletics are structured around certain values, such as hard work, honesty, and extreme dedication—these are the steps to success. Obviously, these values are not limited to the sports realm exclusively, for they are also prevalent in our everyday dosage of America's way of life. Unfortunately, these values are but a definition of manhood, and not necessarily a proven solution to the task of being successful.

A New York sportswriter summed it aptly when he stated: "Here in America, sports' insidious power is imposed upon athletics by the banks that decide which arenas and recreational facilities shall be built, by the television networks that decide which sports shall be sponsored and viewed, by the press that decides which individuals and teams shall be celebrated, by the municipal governments, which have, through favorable tax rulings and exemptions from law, allowed sports entertainment to grow until it has become the most influential form of mass culture in America."

JOHNNY WILL LEARN

First, Johnny's mother told him enthusiastically, "You're going to go to school today!"

"Why?" Johnny asked quite curiously.

"So you can meet lots of people and make lots of friends and have lots of fun," she answered, straightening her dress that looked rather like the kind the First Lady liked to wear.

"Why?"

"So you can get an education. And I wish you wouldn't say 'why' all the time, Johnny." Johnny was always asking why, and it annoyed everyone. Johnny's mother had to admit that although she loved Johnny very much, he was becoming a bit of a nuisance, and she would be glad to have him out of the house while school was in session. "Besides, it's only for a few hours a day," she thought.

"What's education?" Johnny asked. She didn't know the answer, so she said, "You'll get to learn about arithmetic and—"

"What's arith . . . arith—"

"—and the alphabet, and—"

"But I already know the alphabet. A, B, C, D, E, F . . ."

"Johnny, please!" She rolled her eyes and sighed. Johnny looked down at his red and white canvas tennis shoes. "It's very good that you already know the alphabet, because now school won't be as hard for you. Don't worry, you're going to like school. I promise."

Later, when Johnny saw the ugly buildings and all the crying children and the frowning parents, he said, "Mommy, I don't like school."

"Nonsense!" she said abruptly. "You're *going* to like it. You'll see."

Holding Johnny by the hand, his mother marched him up to the little beige bungalow that said KINDERGARTEN on a piece of construction paper taped to the door. A name tag on a woman's dress said, "Virginia Brooks, Kindergarten." The woman's hair looked like the First Lady's.

"Hello, Mrs. Brooks," Johnny's mother said. "I'm Loretta Jenkins."

"How do you do, Mrs. Jenkins. And, oh, this must be John."

"Johnny!" the little boy blurted out. A bit embarrassed by her son's correction, the boy's mother smiled at the teacher and said, "Johnny, say 'how do you do,' to Mrs. Brooks."

"How do you do, Mrs. Books."

"My name is Mrs. Brooks, John, and it's very nice to meet you. I'm going to be your teacher."

"My name's Johnny," the boy said. "are you my new mommy?"

Johnny did not want his mommy to leave him there, and he told her so, but she left him anyway. Still, he wasn't as upset as some of the children. He had come to trust his mommy, even if he did not know exactly what a mommy was.

Besides, when he looked around the classroom, he liked what he saw. He saw colorful building blocks and lots of paints and "millions and millions" of crayons. He liked to draw with crayons and he had never seen so many before. On the wall of the classroom were several crayon drawings that he knew had been drawn by children. He wondered if he would get to draw with crayons. He looked around for some paper to draw on, but something caught his eye. There in front of him was a slate with his name on it: "John Jenkins." Best of all, the slate was resting on a chair, a chair that Johnny thought was the most beautiful chair he had ever seen, for this was the first chair Johnny had ever seen that was just his size!

He began to sit down in the chair when something else commanded his attention. On one wall, above the chalkboard, was written the alphabet on a long piece of paper. Johnny recognized all the upper-case letters; he even knew how to write them. But he did not recognize the lower-case ones. Just as he thought he would use the slate with his name on it to try to copy the letters he didn't know, the teacher called out to him, "John, pick up the slate in front of you and sit down in the chair."

He wondered if he had done something wrong. The woman's voice, to Johnny, seemed a bit mean, but he did what she told him. He felt embarrassed. It hadn't occurred to him that, because all the other boys and girls were sitting down, he should sit down too. He would remember to follow them from now on.

The teacher had each of the children tell his name to the class, and, covering their slates with a sheet of paper, asked if they could write their names. Almost all of them could, including Johnny.

For the next fifteen minutes, the teacher had them play with the building blocks. Then she made them stop. Then she had them paint for half an hour. Then she made them stop. Then she told them it was recess. "Time for milk and cookies!" she announced with fake enthusiasm.

She gave everyone two cookies and a tiny carton of milk. Johnny was not hungry, and he told her so, but she made him eat the cookies and drink the milk anyway. "They're good for you!" she said.

After recess, the teacher told the class that it was "nap time." She had the boys in the class stack the little chairs and cover most of the floor with the padded, brown mats they were to sleep on. Johnny wasn't tired, and he wanted to tell her so, but he did not want to be embarrassed again, so, following the rest of the class, he lay down and closed his eyes, pretending to be asleep.

After the fifteen minutes, the teacher made them put the mats away and get their chairs, and for twenty minutes she had them draw with crayons. Then she made them stop. Then she had them copy the alphabet on their slates. Then began fifteen or twenty years of repeat-after-me's.

The next year Johnny would learn about grades. The year after that he would learn how to take an exam. Then he would learn about cheating. Then he would learn about truancy. Then he would learn about drugs. Then he would learn about sex. Then he would learn about college. Then he would learn about Skinner.

THE ACTIVITY: Some persuasive writing presents negative criticism without offering suggestions for improvement. When writers criticize, they are essentially trying to persuade others to share their negative position. Written criticism sometimes offers recommendations about how to improve the subject of criticism; very often it does not. Letters-to-the-Editor, editorials, and negative reviews are common examples of this kind of persuasive writing.

Read to the class a couple of examples of persuasive writing that primarily criticize. After reading each one, discuss the method the writer used to criticize, and discuss the effectiveness of the presentation. Do the writers use emotional words, or do they use information and examples to persuade readers to agree with them? If you read "Johnny Will Learn," discuss the writer's use of satire.

Ask students to pick a subject they have very strong negative feelings about and write a letter-to-the Editor or editorial that attempts to persuade others to share that position. Go through the regular editing group critiquing process with these papers, too, and read some of the most effective ones to the class.

News Reporting

PURPOSE: This activity helps students become familiar with the inverted-pyramid style of writing commonly used for news articles. Writers will also get further practice in distinguishing fact from opinion, as their job in writing a news article is to report the facts, not their opinions.

PREPARATION: Locate a few news articles in a current newspaper that clearly demonstrate the inverted-pyramid style of writing, in which the essential *who, what, when, where* information is located in the first paragraph. Bring in the articles to read aloud and/or duplicate copies for everyone in the class. Try to find articles in the local city newspaper as well as a school newspaper.

The following is a student-written example of a news article:

CO-ED HOUSING AT LAST!

The Board of Trustees approved a proposal March 12 for co-ed housing options to be offered in the fall. The plan will put men in suites of Howell and Mitchell halls and women in a wing of Collins Hall, a floor of Krause Hall, and eventually one side of Peterson Hall.

Although the Trustees and Administration have long disapproved of the idea, the proposal went through because, said President Robert Riley, "Marlow is finally ready for it."

A year ago, a group of students, headed by now-alumna Sandra Atkins, drew up an extensive plan for the establishment of co-ed housing at Marlow College. The proposal included a campus poll which showed that an overwhelming majority of students were in favor of co-ed options. According to the sponsor of the final proposal, Dean of Students, Richard Thompson, "A great deal of the information in the proposal that went to the Trustees was taken from Sandra's study, and the most persuasive part of the proposal was the fact that students had made such a good case." The Dean added that the idea did not become a reality years ago probably because the Trustees "were not convinced that students were serious about that change."

In the fall, students may still elect to live in a single-sex dorm, and participation in the co-ed program will be based on selectivity in the screening of student co-ed housing applicants.

President Riley stated: "I think the co-ed housing option will provide a more serious academic environment."

Locate an example of a poorly written news article that contains opinions, vague language, and poor organization. Duplicate this for students also, or bring it to class to read aloud.

The following is an excerpt from a poorly written news article:

WOMEN'S VOLLEYBALL BEGINS

"We have a lot of young and inexperienced players, some of which have never played on a varsity team before. But they really do have a desire to play and they've improved 100 percent since the beginning," said the Assistant Coach for the women's volleyball team, Susan Hill. There are thirteen women on the team, all trying to do their best.

Sue is a physical education major and her position as Assistant Coach gives her the practical experience she needs for certification. She remarked, "I really like working with Judy (the head coach) and the girls on the team." Sue was also Assistant Coach for the men's volleyball team last year while she played on the women's team.

Sue and Judy have positive expectations for the team. "They've improved so much since the beginning, I'm impressed with each and every one of them. I'm very excited and anxiously await . . .

For comparison, the following is an excerpt from an article that is similar in nature, but the writer is more successful in organizing the piece and presenting meaningful quotes.

VANCE'S UPHILL CLIMB

"It helps my studying, it puts me in a disciplined mood, it gives me lots of exercise, and most importantly, I enjoy it," said Marlow freshman Vance Moorley. Vance is a bike racer; he has ridden in approximately twenty races and leads a regular training schedule, riding an average of 275 miles per week.

Vance started riding only two years ago; three months later he was riding his first race. "Someday I'd like to take it as far as I can. In three years I want to ride the Red Zinger, where the top Olympic racers are invited. It'll take me six years before I should reach my peak. I'd like to try to make it to the 1988 Olympics, if possible."

As an Interim project . . . well, you guessed it . . . he rode. He kept a regular schedule for training; during the weekdays he rode about thirty to forty miles a day, and on Sundays he rode eighty miles, usually over to Half Moon Bay. Towards the end of the month he broke his arm, but that didn't stop him. He had his cast fitted to the handle bars. Also added to his schedule is a diet of well-balanced meals and relaxing nights; no late parties. Due to his schedule and his seriousness about racing, he does have to sacrifice most activities on campus such as joining any clubs. "It will pay off," he said.

When asked how he got started in racing, he replied, "In 1976 I saw the Red Zinger Bicycle Classic. These racers were held next door to me in Denver, Colorado. A year later I was able to ride with these same racers."

Vance's decision to come to Marlow . . .

THE ACTIVITY: Pass out the well-written news articles to students (if you duplicated them) and read one of them aloud. Explain that in a news article the most vital information (what happened, when it happened, where it happened, who it happened to, and who was involved) is located in the beginning, and that this is called the *lead*. Then ask them to point out the lead in the article you just read.

Read the first and second paragraphs of other example news articles, and discuss how the information is arranged from most important, to less important, to least important. Discuss why it's done that way. For example, readers often don't have time to read more than the first few paragraphs of each story; editors frequently cut the ends of articles to make space for late-breaking news, and so forth.)

Explain that newspaper reporters are trained to report just the objective facts, not their own opinions. However, they may interview people involved in the event being reported, and quote their stated opinions.

Pass out an example of a poorly written news article (or get it on a screen display) and read it aloud. Ask the class to help you identify some of the problems. In the example excerpt above, the reporter seems to be confused about which is the focus of the article—the volleyball coach or the volleyball team. She begins the article with a long and cumbersome quote (that suspiciously doesn't even read like a person's natural speech) and then jumps from point to point with little continuity. Readers are left confused and bored. The reporter needs a focus for the article and some more newsworthy quotes. Ask students to try to create a stronger lead, and suggest how the article should be organized to support the lead.

Write on the chalkboard or word processor the following rules to keep in mind when writing news stories:

- Know what you want to say.
- Write an effective lead—one that's clear, includes the vital information, and catches the reader's attention.
- Put good quotes near the beginning.
- *Show* the news, don't talk *about* it.
- Use concrete nouns and active verbs.
- Limit adjectives and adverbs to a minimum.
- Write the facts and omit judgments.
- Write clearly, coherently, and briefly.

Discuss each of these "Rules for Reporters" and suggest that students also make note of them, to use later when doing the writing assignment.

Next, as a class activity, ask students to describe an event that recently happened at school. Ask them to list the *"what, when, where, who"* information concerning the event on the chalkboard. Then have them continue listing other information they think should be included in the article. Ask them to number the items from most important to least important.

Then go to a word processor or another section of the chalkboard and ask students to suggest a lead for the article. When they've dictated a lead they are happy with, continue writing the article collaboratively, following the numerical order of your notes.

So far, the article has no quoted remarks from a participant or observer. Do they want to include such information? Why? Where? How would they get it, or how should they have gotten it at the time of the event? If they feel interview information would be advantageous to the article, then invent some appropriate people and their comments to add to this sample article. (You'd better explain how dishonest and dangerous the act of inventing quotes, or even misquoting, would be in a real news article.)

When the imaginary news article is finished, print out copies for everyone. Suggest that in addition to this rough draft article, they should also use articles from the front page of any reputable newspaper as models for the next assignment—to write a news article.

Ask students to pick an upcoming local event to report on—one that's of interest to them. Explain that they should go to the event with notebook in hand, in order to take detailed notes about what happens, and to write down important or interesting statements made by others involved. Stress the importance of reporting what people say accurately.

Have them compose first drafts, enter them on a word processor, and bring a copy of their paper for everyone in the class. (It's a wise idea to go through the critiquing process occasionally as a whole class, because it provides a fresh model for editing groups to follow in their critiquing sessions.)

On the day the assignment is due, select one to review and pass the duplicates to students. Read the paper out loud; ask for positive comments about the general structure and content. Then ask for suggestions. Next, go back to the beginning and examine the lead. Does it contain the essential information? Is it clear and strong, and would it entice a reader to continue reading? Ask for suggestions.

Continue through the article, examining and making supportive suggestions for improving the order of information, clarity and accuracy of language, use of quotes, etc. Conclude the critique of the first paper by summarizing some of the major strengths and weaknesses and pointing out a few of the major areas that need revision in the next draft. (Student writers should also be taking notes on their individual copies of the article during the critique.)

Go through the same process with one or two other papers, and then pass the remaining ones around so that students have copies of their classmates' papers. For homework, ask them to critique and write comments on four or five of the papers. You might assign specific ones to each student, thus ensuring that everyone's paper gets a complete critique by several people. Students may go on to revise and print second drafts as soon as they receive their critiqued first drafts.

Interview

PURPOSE: This activity helps students learn how to interview someone and report the information accurately and effectively.

PREPARATION: Arrange for a guest to come into the classroom for a short interview. In addition, find a few examples of newspaper articles that rely heavily on interview material. Try to find a feature article that focuses on a single individual being interviewed and a news article that focuses on the newsworthy information obtained from an interview. Duplicate copies of one or two of these for students to use as models when writing the assignment.

The following student-written article is a news article, yet it also focuses on the two individuals being interviewed.

DEPARTING DEANS DISCUSS GOALS FOR MARLOW

Though many students aren't aware of it, Marlow will lose two deans effective at the end of this semester. Both Dean of Students Richard Thompson and Business School Dean John Dennis have decided to pursue other directions. Richard Thompson is retiring, while John Dennis will move on to Metro University as Associate Dean of the School of Education. Both men expressed their reservations in leaving Marlow, and discussed their hopes for the future of the college.

Richard Thompson told the Press, "I would like to see the students raise their standard of priorities more towards studying and also show some intellectual curiosity." S.B.A. Dean Dennis would like to see "increased use of cases, instead of lectures or textbook approaches, and more courses stressing quantitative and qualitative approaches simultaneously." He also felt that "Business students are spending a lot more time studying and there is increased seriousness, but the level of business writing could be improved." Dennis added that there should be a full-time business writing staff.

When asked about his replacement, the Dean of Students replied, "He or she should be interested in students, forthright, and consistent in his or her judgments." Thompson's responsibilities included those of the Director of Athletics, but, he felt, "It is not necessary for [my replacement] to take on both responsibilities as long as separate Deans cooperate with each other."

Both Deans agreed they will miss the contact with students that they enjoyed at Marlow.

Richard Thompson, in his ninth year here, spent 29 years in the U.S. Marine Corps as an aviator, and was a commanding officer in the Naval R.O.T.C. He also spent three "controversial" years during the Vietnam Era as the Professor of Naval Science at Stanford University.

John Dennis, who became the Dean of the Business School four years ago, received his Master's Degree in Business at the Harvard Business School and his Doctorate of Education at Stanford University.

Selections for the two Dean positions are to be made prior to the end of the Spring semester.

THE ACTIVITY: Ask the class to imagine that they are reporters who have just been given the assignment to write a feature story on Mr. Scott for example, because he has an interesting hobby—he likes to climb sky scrapers. Tell them that you have arranged for Mr. Scott to come to the classroom in a few minutes for an interview about his hobby.

Discuss with the class what a feature article is and how it differs from a news article. Explain that a news story *informs;* a feature story *entertains.* A feature story typically is not written in the terse, inverted-pyramid style; instead it invites the reader to relax and enjoy the story.

However, a feature is like a news story in that it has to be accurate, clear, and keep the reader interested.

Discuss with students what questions they should ask Mr. Scott and ask them to write down these questions. (Ask them to take notes during the interview as well.) Help them see the value in asking direct questions, such as "Why do you scale tall buildings?" instead of more vague ones such as "How do you like climbing tall buildings?" And, "What do you think about when you're three-quarters of the way up?" instead of "How does it feel to be way up there?"

Encourage them to follow up vague answers with more specific questions. For example, if they ask: "What training did you get to learn to climb buildings?" Mr. Scott might respond, "Oh, a friend showed me how." Then ask follow-up questions such as, "What skills do you need to climb?" and "How long did it take you to learn?" and "What equipment do you need?"

When Mr. Scott arrives, have students raise their hands to ask questions, press-conference style. After the interview is over and the guest has left, ask students what they thought were the most important and most interesting things Mr. Scott said. Do they agree, for the most part? Ask them to read one or two of the quotes they wrote down. How accurately did they note the quotes?

Ask students to help devise a list of the points they would include in a feature article about Mr. Scott. Write these on the chalkboard or word processor and then arrange them in order of presentation. Compose a lead that would entice others to continue reading.

Then explain that their next assignment will be to interview someone whom they think would be an interesting subject for a feature article. Tell them to write down some questions beforehand, and then bring the questions and a notebook to the interview. Suggest that they follow the same planning and organizing steps the class just did, before beginning to write.

Ask students to compose a draft, enter it on a word processor, and bring the disk to class on the day the assignment is due.

Hand out and read the example interview articles and examine with the class how successfully the writers use direct quotes and interview material in the articles.

When the students come to class with their assignment done, have them critique their articles in editing groups. Then ask the editing groups to choose one or two of the best to share with the class. Students can then revise, print, and hand in the second drafts.

Review

PURPOSE: Students do the preliminary work for writing a review every time they critique one another's papers. However, when they critique classmates' papers they put the emphasis on making suggestions for improvement; in a review the work is finished, so the emphasis is on judging its relative success. Another difference is that students' critiques in editing groups are communicated orally, with two-way communication and ample opportunity to clarify and refine their remarks. When writing a review, students are forced to organize their comments and criticisms, and communicate them clearly and effectively in writing.

PREPARATION: Collect a couple of well-written, short reviews of movies, books, plays, computer software, restaruants, etc., that would be interesting to students. Duplicate them to use as models for this activity.

The following is a student-written, negative review of a movie. (See the *Writing a Review* activity in Chapter 4 for an example of a positive review.)

"HARDBODIES" FLASHES 90 MINUTES OF TASTELESS TRASH

The ads promise that *Hardbodies* is "more hilarious than *Gandhi.*" Well it is, at least a little bit. But then, *Gandhi* is not comedy. And to put it simply, neither is *Hardbodies.*

Hardbodies is likely to be the most tasteless movie of the year. The plot is almost nonexistent, the characters are ridiculously exaggerated stereotypes, and the acting is revoltingly inept.

The movie deals with three wealthy, sex-starved businessmen, played by Garth Wood, Michael Rapport, and Sorrels Puckard, who lease the best house on the beach and try to meet girls.

Of course, they are hopeless—until they meet Scotty Palmer (Grant Cramer), the "hunk" of the town. Scotty generously agrees to teach the men to get "hardbodies" ("the foxy little things on the beach," Scotty explains) for a mere $600 a month plus full use of the house.

Scotty teaches them "dialogue" and explains how to offer girls a "B.B.D." or "Bigger and Better Deal." Predictably, all three are hopeless at first. But they improve with practice, as well as haircuts and completely new wardrobes, all chosen by Scotty.

The three then decide to have a party, with all the hardbodies invited. The party is a smashing success, as are the three now-capable men, who each gets a girl. They continue having more of these parties, and therefore, more of the girls.

The movie continues in this moronic fashion until one man, Hunter, becomes a bit over-zealous in his pursuit of the opposite sex. Scotty sides with the object of Hunter's lust, so Hunter promptly fires him. In addition, Hunter gets Scotty's girlfriend, Kristy, to break up with Scotty.

Eventually, but not soon enough for anyone watching the movie, Kristy realizes that Scotty is the only man that she (along with just about every other girl in the town) truly loves. So she returns to him and decides to go back to college and to live with Scotty.

The ostensible stars of the movie are the four men. But the real star is *skin,* because that's almost all that anyone wears throughout the movie. It seems that the girls of this town enjoy nothing more than tearing off their clothes at any given time or place and jumping into bed with the nearest male. And when they do have clothes on, they generally limit themselves to bathing suits that leave almost nothing to the imagination.

I think I laughed about three times throughout this hour and a half of mindless drivel. *Hardbodies* is about four cuts below the last major teen sex flick, *Porky's*, if that level of trash can be imagined.

In short, *Hardbodies* is probably the worst way to spend five dollars available. For a "B.B.D.,' watch the break-dancers in the parking lot. They're free.

THE ACTIVITY: Begin by distributing and reading one of the example reviews. Ask students to state the reviewer's opinion of the movie (or whatever the subject of the review might be) and the reasons for liking or disliking it. See if they can locate a thesis statement that summarizes the reviewer's opinion. Ask students to evaluate the review on the basis of how successful it was in convincing them, for example, to see (or not see) the movie.

Examine the organization and the writing style. How do they compare with other forms of writing the class has studied? Does the writer avoid using biased words and slang? Explain that reviews often include a fair number of biased words and slang. Examine how much of the movie was re-told or summarized in the review. Was it too much, too little?

Hand out and examine a second review together, using the same process of analysis. Are the two reviews similar in writing style, organization, and amount of summarization? Which one do students feel is more convincing, and why?

Explain that for their next writing assignment they will choose a book, movie, restaurant, or other appropriate subject, and write a review of it. Explain that later, when they critique their reviews in editing groups, classmates will go through the same process of analysis and evaluation with their papers that they did in class today. Therefore, they should keep these evaluation criteria in mind while planning and drafting their reviews.

Suggest that students keep the example reviews handed out to use as models. Ask them to compose first drafts, enter them onto a word processor, and bring the disk to class on the date the review is due.

On the day the assignment is due, have students meet in editing groups. Write on the chalkboard or word processor the evaluation criteria they will use (the same procedures they went through in class) to help focus their comments and suggestions while critiquing the reviews. After the editing groups have finished, ask students to revise, print, and hand in their second drafts. The teacher can then critique these drafts and help students prepare another draft.

Final Journal Entry

PURPOSE: This activity will help students gain perspective on their writing improvement and on their personal growth over a period of a semester, or a year.

PREPARATION: Duplicate copies of the following assignment for everyone in the class.

FINAL JOURNAL ENTRY

Go back and re-read your whole journal from beginning to end. List approximately four to six subjects that you wrote about most frequently—things that kept "popping up" over and over again. For example, you might have repeatedly mentioned certain people, a concern about grades, parties, values, sports, animals, jealousies, physical health, appearance, school, politics, your future, love, death, the weather. . . .

Then, take each of these "themes" and explain fully how you feel about each one now, and whether you have developed or altered your views since you began your journal.

This final journal entry is to be shared with me, so if there are certain sentences or paragraphs that you wish to keep completely private, be sure to delete them (temporarily) just before you print a copy to hand in. Your journal entry will never be read by anyone but me, unless you choose to share it.

THE ACTIVITY: Save this activity until the end of the course. It involves students in a private, personal experience that directs them to re-read and analyze the journals they have been keeping since the first day of the writing course.

As you pass out the duplicated assignment to students, explain that they should take the assignment sheet home and plan to spend two to three hours of uninterrupted time, re-reading their journals, reflecting on the contents, and then writing responses to the assignment questions.

Ask students to enter this final journal entry on the journal disk they've been using during the semester. Have them print out a copy of this final entry to pass in; they may keep the rest of the journal. It is hoped that some will continue writing in their journals long after the course is over.

Chapter 6
THE PRODUCTION OF
STUDENT PUBLICATIONS

When word processing landed in the educational arena a few years ago, many faculty advisors of student publications (e.g., literary magazines, newspapers, and yearbooks) quickly adopted the new technology. Language arts teachers who had their classes publish literary magazines were also attracted to word processing. Pretty soon, they were clamoring for computers in their classrooms, or more frequent access to the school's computer lab. And now, more and more classroom teachers dare to attempt publishing projects now that they've started using word processing with their students. Word processing is rapidly becoming an indispensable tool for producing many kinds of school publications.

The features that powerful word processors have, such as left, right, and center justification, spelling checkers, and screen displays that show what the printed page will look like, add to the enthusiasm teachers and students have for using this tool to put together school publications. For example, the capability to justify left and right margins makes designing pages with multiple columns an easy task. Young poets, and others artistically inclined, who write for literary magazines also enjoy creating interesting visual images with lines of text that can be printed on the page in unique and interesting ways.

```
         Even ragged margins that are
              placed off the left side of
                    the page can provide visual
                          variety and attract
                                the reader's attention.
```

Journalism teachers have become especially attached to the word processor's capacity to move blocks of text easily. When they want to teach the standard inverted-pyramid style of writing, it's simple to shift the most vital *who, what, when, where* information to the top of the news article. With word processing, teachers can effectively demonstrate how to reorganize articles into the inverted-pyramid style. Then students can practice it by rearranging sentences and paragraphs in their own work.

The following sections present specific examples of how particular schools have managed to use word processing to assist in the process of publishing a school literary magazine, newspaper, or yearbook (Fig. 6.1). In addition to addressing the students' particular use of word processing, the examples also focus on how individual student groups were organized and, in some cases, how students and advisor felt about the whole process of producing their publication.

Literary Magazines

Some schools publish a literary magazine as a formal, school-wide project. Often a faculty advisor and group of student editors work as a team—planning, collecting, editing, and publishing the best writing produced by students in the school that year. Some schools even put out two or three issues per year. A special student editorial board typically entices other students in the school to submit their best quality short stories, essays, plays, character sketches, poems, and even drawings. In addition, the editors often solicit classroom teachers to submit the finest of their students' work for consideration. Some schools hold writing competitions with prizes for the winning entries, as well as promise literary fame through publication in the school magazine.

Once the magazine editors have accumulated more submissions than they need, they review them all carefully and select what they consider "the best." Prior to making final choices, however, they probably consult with the advisor concerning the criteria for judgment. Issues such as whether entries accepted for publication must be grammatically impeccable, or whether creativity and reader interest are the primary requirements for acceptance, must be resolved by the group. The board also must decide how much variety of genre they wish to include. Do they want an issue of all poetry, all short stories, or a balance of several different genres, writing styles, and topics? Also, will they include the

Figure 6.1 Five student publications. *(Courtesy of Saratoga High School, Saratoga, CA; Winchendon School, Winchendon, MA; Crittendon Middle School, Mountain View, CA; Menlo College, Atherton, CA; The Intercultural Learning Network, San Diego, CA)*

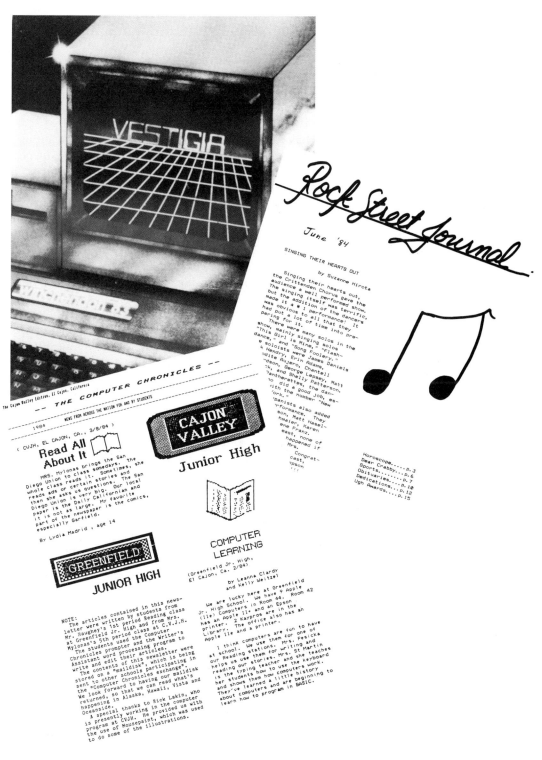

VESTIGIA

WITCHCRAFT

The Cajon Valley Edition, El Cajon, California

-- THE COMPUTER CHRONICLES --

NEWS FROM ACROSS THE NATION FOR AND BY STUDENTS

1984

(CVJH, EL CAJON, CA., 3/8/84)

Read All About It

MRS. Mylonas brings the San Diego Union to class somedays. The whole class reads it. Sometimes, she reads ads or certain stories and then she asks us questions. The San Diego Union is very big. Our local paper is the Daily Californian and it is not as large. My favorite part of the newspaper is the comics, especially Garfield.

By Lydia Madrid , age 14

CAJON VALLEY
Junior High

GREENFIELD
JUNIOR HIGH

COMPUTER LEARNING

(Greenfield Jr. High, El Cajon, Ca. 2/84)

by Leanna Clardy and Kelly Weitzel

We are lucky here at Greenfield Jr. High School. We have 9 Apple (IIe) Computers in Room 44. Room 42 has an Apple II+ and an Epson printer. 2 Kaypros are in the Library. The office also has an Apple IIe and a printer.

I think computers are fun to have at school. We use them for one of our Reading stations. Mrs. Pesicka helps us use them for writing and reading our stories. Mr. St Martin is our typing teacher and she teaches her students how to use the keyboard and shows them how computers work. They've learned a little history about computers and are beginning to learn how to program in BASIC.

NOTE:
The articles contained in this news-letter were written by students from Mr. Haughey's 1st period Reading class at Greenfield Jr. High and from Mrs. Mylonas's 5th period class at C.V.J.H.

The students used the Computer Chronicles prompter and the Writer's Assistant word processing program to write and edit their articles.

The contents of this newsletter were stored on a "maildisk", which is being sent to other schools participating in the "Computer Chronicles exchange".

We look forward to having our maildisk returned, so that we can read what's happening in Alaska, Hawaii, Vista and Oceanside.

A special thanks to Rick Lakin, who is presently working in the computer program at CVJH. He provided us with the use of Mousepaint, which was used to do some of the illustrations.

Rock Street Journal

June '84

SINGING THEIR HEARTS OUT

by Suzanne Hirota

Singing their hearts out, the Crittenden Chorus gave the audience a well performed show. The singing itself was terrific, but the addition of the dancers made it a # 1 performance! It was obvious to all that they had put a lot of time into pre-paring for it.

There were many solos in the show, mainly singing solos. "This Girl is Mine," "Flash-dance," and "Song Foolery." s soloists were James Daniels r Hendry, Erin Adams, odite Aujero, Chantell dson, George Lepsey, Matt ok, and Shelly Patterson.

Pantherettes, the dan- o did a good job, es- with the number "New ork."

panists also added rformance. They son, Matt Hasel-hmaier, Karen ene Franz, east; none of happened if Mrs.

Congrat-cast, pson

work of students from every grade level, or will it be a magazine that features the work of only a few talented upperclassmen? What about artwork? How much of the issue will be text and how much visual art? These are a few of the decisions the editorial board will have to make in the preliminary stages of publication.

Once the editors have planned the sort of magazine they want and picked the material to be included in the issue, the truly challenging editorial work begins. All the copy has to be entered on a word processor and every sentence carefully proofread. At this point, editors must determine just how much they can alter and revise another person's writing. Will they make suggestions and then send the piece back to the writer for revision; or, will they revise it and then check with the author afterwards? At some point the edited material goes back to the author for approval. Delicate negotiation between editor and writer may be necessary during this phase, and this is when it's a superb advantage to have editors who are not only competent at editing, but also tactful.

The next stage involves designing and preparing the layout for each page of the magazine. Here the word processor is a vital asset once again. Let's take an example page. The person responsible for laying out the page takes any illustrations or photographs that go on the page and arranges them attractively on an 8 1/2 × 11 inch planning sheet. When she settles on an arrangement of artwork that looks just right, she'll draw lightly around the artwork indicating its borders and leaving the rest of the page free for text.

At the word processor she can experiment with different designs for the text—narrow columns, sentences that surround the artwork, diagonal columns—whatever looks aesthetically interesting. When the final layout design is finished, she pastes the artwork and text on the planning sheet, which is then "camera-ready" and set to go to the printer.

The editorial work is done. Students can now concentrate on marketing the product, gathering student responses to the publication, planning another issue, or, perhaps, catching up on the homework from their other classes. . . .

Informal Magazines

Many language arts teachers have their students generate a much more more informal publication as a class project. In one elementary school, for example, kids composed various types of writing on the word processor regularly for a few months, and the teacher simply saved it. Then she introduced her plan for the class to produce a literary magazine. She explained that each member of the class would have at least one piece of written work included in the publication, which would be distributed to every child in the sixth grade, plus extra copies for other classrooms and the school library. The kids were pleased and a little apprehensive, as never before had they viewed themselves (and their writing) as worthy of school-wide recognition.

The teacher met privately with each student in order to decide which of the student's work would be included. They also discussed how the writing could be further revised, expanded, or improved to make it perfect for the magazine. Some of the kids decided to add computer graphics or pencil drawings to their stories. The class even held a drawing contest in order to get the best possible artwork for the magazine cover. Members of the class chose the cover design by secret ballot and then decided to include several of the other popular artistic entries inside the magazine, too.

When the students finished making all the necessary text revisions, and the computer printouts confirmed that the copy was free from grammatical and mechanical errors, they were ready to plan the layout. This class chose to print two columns on each standard 8 1/2 × 11 inch page. Column space had to be provided for the graphics and illustrations, and sometimes the artwork had to be adjusted so that everything fitted neatly on the page. When the layout was perfect, students pasted the artwork on the computer-printed master pages.

After school the teacher took the camera-ready master pages to the local quick-print shop and had one hundred copies offset-printed overnight for around $50.00. The next morning there were twenty-five brilliant faces and twenty-five young writers eager to do another. . . .

Newspapers

There are not many schools below the college level that publish newspapers so often that members of the press face oppressive pressure to meet deadlines. But whenever there are tight deadlines, word processing certainly can be a big help in producing copy fast. Professional newspaper journalists typically work under continual pressure—occasionally they're expected to complete several writing assignments within a single day. (This information may be useful to mention to student writers who complain about strict deadlines.)

Young journalists would do well to practice drafting newspaper articles on the computer keyboard, rather than taking time to write a draft by hand before entering it on a word processor. At journalism school, students typically compose on the keyboard and are pressed to complete assignments before leaving the classroom. The ability to plan, write, and revise on the spot is a valuable skill, and one that's appropriate to practice in a journalism class. The word processor, of course, helps facilitate this activity enormously.

If you're in a school that has word processing equipment, and perhaps even a typesetting machine available for journalism students, then you may well adopt a demanding and discriminating approach to creating a student newspaper. The following paragraphs provide a glimpse of how one class of very diligent journalists put together a rather sophisticated high school publication.

The *Eagle* is a biweekly newspapar published by specially selected high school sophomores, juniors, and seniors. To get into the journalism class that meets daily to produce this eight-page paper, students must be recommended by their English teacher. The recommendation process is as follows: Every spring the journalism teacher sends a form to all English teachers asking them to indicate students in their classes who are: (1) excellent writers; (2) responsible (e.g., the kind of student who gets homework in on time and doesn't give excuses for why things weren't done); (3) able to accept criticism; (4) able to work with other students well; (5) willing to put in a lot of time after school and on weekends. Using these and other references, the journalism teacher (who is also the *Eagle*'s faculty advisor) builds a class list for the following year.

When the course begins in the fall, students learn to use the word processing system right away, because they're expected to turn in all copy on a disk. (The journalism classroom has microcomputers and a typesetting machine.) In addition, students learn basic newspaper terminology as well as the typesetting commands necessary to give appropriate printing directions to the typesetter. Editors and staff writers also learn standard editing symbols and use the Associated Press stylebook as a reference.

Some reporters compose their articles on a word processor, while others draft them by hand and enter them later; they say it depends on how close they are to the deadline.

The advisor appoints an editor-in-chief just before school closes in June; she or he takes over the paper in September. The other editors are selected in the fall, after "it becomes clear who's good at what," says the advisor.

The first issue doesn't come out until October, so during the first few weeks of class the advisor teaches common writing styles used by journalists for news articles, features, reviews, and editorials. According to the advisor, however, the kids mostly teach one another; the editors work with the staff writers, and "in my eight years of teaching I've never seen such improvement. Those editors are ruthless." The advisor adds, "Editors in this class are very competent, I don't have to worry about that. In fact, the advisor before me didn't even look at the paper until after it came out. I decided to edit it, at least the first time. Well, I discovered that my corrections were almost identical to the copy editor's."

The *Eagle* is run completely by the students. Says one staff member, "If it wasn't that way it wouldn't be a good paper. There would be nobody here after school. There would be nobody here on weekends." The editors give the article assignments and establish the deadlines. Reporters enter copy on a word processor, and then the appropriate editor reviews it and returns it to the writer for corrections. Next it goes to the copy editor, who corrects the grammar and mechanics. Finally the disk is turned over to the typesetter. (One or two students learn this skill and become the official typesetters.) When the copy is unusually late, it can be edited right on the typesetting machine.

The typesetting machine converts the copy to standard columns, which are then cut, waxed, and pasted on the layout sheets. Photos and ads are half-toned, sized, waxed, and put on the layout sheets, as well. Then the hairlines and heads are added, and this practically camera-ready copy gets a final proofreading before it's delivered to the print shop.

During second period, every other Friday, the paper is distributed to everyone in the school. Then, during the class session following its publication, the staff critiques the strengths and weaknesses of the issue and makes assignments for the next. After each issue staff members also complete a self-evaluation form on which they itemize everything they did for the issue and give themselves a grade (optional). The advisor and editors meet to review the evaluations and determine staff members' grades for the issue. Individual students may be present during the discussion of their grade. According to the advisor, this evaluation process provides an excellent opportunity for students to learn to communicate more effectively with peers.

Except for the cost of hardware and software, the *Eagle* is supported entirely by student-raised funds. Staff members, led by their business manager, raise money though ads solicited from the student body and the local community. Evidently they no longer have room in the paper for all the requested ads, and this past year the records showed a $2500 surplus!

What's the difference between using word processing equipment and an ordinary typewriter to produce copy for the newspaper? Staff members who have used both respond:

- "You can write faster. Stories can come in later and still go in."
- "You can make more corrections on the screen, so now we have very few blue-pen corrections on the final copy."
- "It's much easier to compose on the computer keyboard, and also, it's more fun because we have more freedom of composition and layout."
- "Having computers doesn't change the interpersonal stuff. We still have knock-down drag-outs. Having computers just makes us want to do more. . . ."

Informal Newspapers

If your school doesn't have a large enough budget to afford the sophisti-phisticated equipment used to create a paper like the *Eagle*, you certainly can produce an informal newspaper on a shoestring budget, one similar to the elementary school literary magazine described earlier in this chapter. Use a word processor to edit copy and print columns which can then be pasted on standard 8 1/2 × 11 inch paper or longer 8 1/2 × 14 inch paper. After the camera-ready masters have been prepared, you can duplicate them in great quantity on any photocopy machine or offset print machine for a very reasonable price. Figure 6.2 pictures the sports page and an activity page from a photocopied edition of *The Rock Street Journal,* an informal, middle school publication.

Telecommunications

A computer system can be used to send letters, reports, messages, and even news articles across distances electronically. When a hardware device called a modem is connected to a computer, the modem can convert information from the computer into a form that can be transmitted by phone lines, satellite, etc., to another modem, which changes the information back to a form the receiving computer understands. This capability empowers the user to send and receive written messages electronically. The process is called telecommunications.

There are a variety of ways to use the computer's facility to telecommunicate. . . . You can receive and send electronic mail directly to another computer that's connected to a modem. You can call up a public bulletin board to leave messages for others, and read messages left by others. You can also join a particular electronic network, which would enable you to use the members' electronic mail and bulletin board services, and in some cases the shopping, banking, newswire, data bank, and other special services available to network members. Many people subscribe to commercial network services, such as CompuServe [R], The Source [SM], Dow Jones News/Retrieval [R], etc., to obtain access to some of these special services.

A few schools around the country are exploring the computer's capacity to transmit news articles electronically to produce a school newspaper. In fact, one such telecommunications endeavor involves schools from other countries such as Mexico, Israel, and Japan, in its news wire network. Patterned after adult news wire services, the Computer Chronicles Newswire Network is designed to store students' telecommunicated stories on disk and makes them available to schools that subscribe to the news wire service.

Each school site publishes issues of the *Chronicles,* which include articles written and edited by classmates, as well as articles off the news wire that are written by students from distant schools.

The young journalists write articles about many things—from their elementary school's Good Attitude Lounge and their favorite pastimes, to housing facilities in Wainwright, Alaska, and babysitting safety. Some writers use an interactive software program, The Computer Chronicles Prompter, to help them organize the articles while they write. The program asks the student to enter the category of the article (news, sports, weather, fun, life, or sharing); then, as he drafts the article, the program

WINNING AND LOSING

by Kristen Badger

As I ran across the court, sweat dripping off my face, I knew we were behind. It was the championship game for the seventh grade Crittenden girls' basketball team. We were doing well until we got to the final game. Out of ten games we played before the final game, we had only lost three. When we got to the play-offs, I was thrilled. The game was at Jordan School although we were to play the seventh grade Wilbur girls' basketball team.

Since we had won seven straight games, we knew that our luck wouldn't last. Wilbur was an easy team, but we had some bad breaks. For instance, one player had to sit on the bench for one reason or another, and none of us were working well together.

We lost. I never felt so bad in my whole life. Now I know what "the agony of defeat" means.

There were seven girls on the seventh grade team. The starting five were Phoebe Aujero, Suzanne Hirota, Jeanella Pablo, My Trang Tran, and Kris Badger. The substitutes were Maria Muyco and Diana Saucedo.

CAN A TEAM BE TOO BIG?

by Guido Hajenius

If there are too many basketball players on a team, it is very hard for the coaches and the starters. In the beginning of a game the coach is going to play the starters first, then switch off with the second best players till the second quarter.

However, when it is a close game, the coach wants to keep the best players in the game. This leaves about ten players on the bench who don't even play at all. If he puts the other players in, the team has less of a chance to win.

Which is more important, winning the game or having all the players play?

Andy Miranda said, "It all depends on the game, because when we are behind by two or three points, we want to win. Tommy Griffin said, "It all depends on our record because, if it is not impressive, I would want to win.

Figure 6.2 Two pages from the Rock Street Journal. *(Courtesy of Pat Dusterhoft, Crittendon Middle School)*

PUNK FASHIONS

by Robert Duniphin

What is in:

Tails
Spikes
High top colored
 Converse
Died hair
501 jeans
Vans
Cut-up shirts
Green lipstick
Odd Shaped earrings
Writing on your hands
Bandanas
Stripes
Varries

What is out:

Bell bottoms
Penny loafers
Cords
Long stringy hair
Slacks
Michael Jackson songs
Sweaters
Plastic shoes
Zody's clothes
Toughskins
Mickey Mouse Watches

ALFRED STEEP

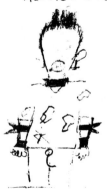

SCRAMBLED SONGS

by Sharon Hansen

1.   RTIHELRL
2.   YSA ASYSYA
3.   PTSRI
4.   MPUJ
5.   ABRK TA HTE ONOM
6.   ACMRA MAIELAC
7.   OFIND
8.   RNUIN TIWH HTE INGTH
9.   OS ADB
10. 99 ERD LOBAOLSN

JOKES

by Tommy
Griffin

1. Mother: You say you were
          fighting to pro-
          tect a little boy?
          Who was he?
   Little boy: Me!

2. Teacher: Jerry, please make
           a sentence using
           the word "lettuce."

   Jerry: Please, let us out of
          school early.

3. Angry Father: What does this
                "C" mean on your pap-
                er?

   Little boy: I think it's a
              moon. The teacher
              ran out of stars.

prompts him to include the kind of information that's appropriate for the type of article he's writing.

To produce an edition of the *Chronicles,* an editing board at each school site reads the stories submitted by students from their own and the other schools. The board votes on each story, discusses it, and then votes again to make a final decision. Every decision to accept or reject an article must be supported by specific reasons. "It's too short," for example, isn't an adequate reason. The editors must identify specifically why the content of the article isn't satisfactory. "It doesn't include enough explanation of the topic to make it understandable for readers outside California" would be a fair reason.

After articles have been accepted for publication, they are often further edited and revised. (Articles initially rejected by the board may also

After articles have been accepted for publication, they are often further edited and revised. (Articles initially rejected by the board may also be revised and reconsidered for publication later.) Articles that come across the news wire frequently need editing, too. In fact, this long distance reviewing process provides an effective learning experience for both the writer and the reviewers, especially considering that English is a second language for many participants.

What is different, and particularly advantageous about using telecommunications to produce a student publication? According to one study done on the *Chronicles* project,* the student journalists involved were:

> learning about life styles and customs that were different from their own. They were beginning to understand the role that newspapers play in a society and how such communication networks function. Students were forming their ideas about what makes a story "newsworthy," they were dealing with issues of what is appropriate and inappropriate for this medium, and they were beginning to understand what things about their own environment were special or different. (p. 17)

Figure 6.3 pictures a News Features page and a Sharing page from *The Computer Chronicles.*

Yearbooks

High schools and colleges have been making "memory books" for over a hundred years, say the yearbook publishers. And in the past couple of decades yearbooks have become so popular that junior high and even el-

*From a paper, "Muktuk Meets Jacuzzi: Computer Networks and Elementary School Writers," by James Levin, Margaret M. Riel, Robert D. Rowe, and Marcia J. Boruta. Laboratory of Comparative Human Cognition, Univ. of California, San Diego, La Jolla California, 1984.

NEWS FEATURES FROM WAINWRIGHT ELEMENTARY

HERE IN WAINWRIGHT WE HAVE TO CONSERVE WATER. THE REASON WE DON'T HAVE A LOT OF WATER IS BECAUSE WAINWRIGHT IS A COLD DESERT.

EACH HOUSE GETS ABOUT 400 GALLONS OF WATER A WEEK. WE GET THE WATER FROM A WATER TRUCKAND THE WATER TRUCK GETS THE WATER FROM A WATER STORAGE. WE HAVE TO BE VERY CAREFUL ABOUT BRUSHING OUR TEETH. WE CAN'T LET THE WATER RUN. IT'S THE SAME WAY ABOUT SHOWERS AND LAUNDRY. WHEN YOU TAKE A SHOWER YOU CAN'T LET THE WATER OUT YOU HAVE TO PUT IN THE PLUG AND USE THAT WATER FOR LAUNDRY.IN WAINWARIGHT THERE IS USUALLY ALWAYS A WATER PROBLEM. SOMETIMES WE DON'T GET ANY WATER FOR A WEEK. BUT NOW WE HAVE A BIG WATER PROBLEM, THE TANK, FROM WHICH THE VILLAGE GETS ITS WATER, HAS ABOUT THREE FEET OF ICE IN IT. WHEN ICE FREEZES IT EXPANDS SO THE ICE IS PUSHING THE SIDES OUT OF THE TANK. NOW THE VILLAGE MAY NOT GET WATER FOR A LONG TIME. WHEN WE CAN'T GET WATER, WE HAVE TO MELT ICE THAT THE MEN CUT IN THE FALL. THEY CUT THE ICE FROM A POND OUTSIDE OF TOWN.

UP HERE IN WAINWRIGHT, ALASKA, WE HAVE A ROOM WHERE THERE ARE A LOT OF FUN VIDEO GAMES. THIS ROOM IS CALLED THE KG.A.L. WHICH STANDS FOR THE GOOD ATTITUDE LOUNGE. THE ELEMTARY STUDENTS HAVE TO EARN THE RIGHT TO GO JUST LIKE THE HIGH SCHOOL KIDS BUT WE ONLY GET TO GO ONE TIME A WEEK. THE GAL HAS 4 VIDEO GAMES, A ROCKET HOCKEY GAME, AND A SHUFFLE BOARD GAME. THERE IS ALSO A POOL TABLE AND A FOOS BALL GAME. WE LIKE TO BUY POP AND HOT DOGS. THE ELEMTARY KIDS ONLY GET TO GO EVERY THURSDAY, BUT WE SURE DO HAVE FUN!

IN OUR VILLAGE WE ONLY HAVE ONE RATHER SMALL BUT GOOD CLINIC. WE HAVE TWO HEALTH AIDS. THEY TAKE TURNS WORKING AT THE CLINIC. THEIR NAMES ARE SANDRA AHMAOGAK AND LUCY SEGEVAN. THE DENTIST AND THE EYE DOCTOR BOTH COME TWICE A YEAR. WHEN THE DENTISTCOMES HE CHECKS OUR TEETH AND IF YOU NEED ONE PULLED OR FILLED HE DOES THAT WHEN HE IS HERE. IF YOU NEED GLASSED WHEN THE EYE DOCTOR COMES HE ORDERS THEM FOR YOU!

BY JENNY GRECO   GRADE 5

HERE IN WAINWRIGHT, ALASKA WE GO WHALING EVERY YEAR. WE GO OUT WHALING IN APRIL AND OFTEN GET ONE IN MAY. WE GO WHALING IN "UMIAKS" WHICH ARE SHAPED LIKE CANOES AND COVERED WITH WALRUS SKIN. WE HUNT THE WHALES WITH HARPOONS AD BOMBGUNS. AND THERE IS BETWEEN 25 AND 10 IN ONE CREW. THERE IS 14 AND 15 CREWS. AFTER WE CATCH A WHALE WE BUTCHER IT UP. WE CUT THE BLUBBER WHICH IS GOOD TO EAT AND MEAT THEN WE BOIL IT AND THEN EAT IT. THEN WE CUT THE MEAT THEN WE TAKE THEM TO THE SHORE AND GO OUT AGAIN. USUALLY WE GET A WHALE AT 12:00 MIDNIGHT AND 9:00 IN THE MORNING.

EVERY SUMMER OR SPRING THERE IS A BREAK UP AND THE ICE ON THE ARCTIC OCEAN BREAKS UP. THEY CALL IT A LEAD AFTER THE ICE BREAKS UP AND THEN THE WHALERS GO OUT. THEY GIVE CANDY OUT TO THE KIDS FOR GOOD LUCK AND SO THEY CAN CATCH A WHALE. WHEN THEY SPOT A WHALE THEY CHASE IT AND THEY ALL HAVE WHITE PARKAS ON BECAUSE THE WHALE IS AFRAID OF ALL COLORS EXCEPT FOR BLUE AND WHITE. THEN THEY THROW A HARPOON AND IF IT MISSES THEY THROW ANOTHER HARPOON AND IF THAT MISSES THEY DON'T GET A WHALE. UP HERE IN WAINWRIGHT, ALASKA, EVERY YEAR THEY CATCH A WHALE, THIS YEAR A MAN NAMED LUKE KAGAK ALMOST STRUCK A FEMALE WHALE THAT JUST HAD A BABY WHALE. BUT THEN A MAN NAMED ROSSMAN GOT A WHALE AND KNOW THEY PUT UP A FLAY WHTH A WHALE ON IT TO SHOW THAT THEY GOT A WHALE.

BY CARRIE GRECO   GRADE 3

HERE IN WAINWRIGHT, ALASKA, THE SNOW IS JUST STARTING TO MELT. SOME DAYS IT IS VERY BEAUTIFUL AND SOME DAYS AE VERY COLD! IT IS STILL VERY NICE. TODAY IT IS ABOUT 5 ABOVE 0. THE SUN IS NOT SETTING FOR A LONG TIME. IT IS LIGHT ALL NIGHT. THE KIDS PLAY OUT ALL NIGHT SOMETIMES. THEY MIGHT JUST TAKE NAPS DURING THE DAY AND THEN PLAY OUT SOME MORE. MY LITTLE BROTHER, JEREMY, DOESN'T LIKE TO GO TO BED WHILE THE SUN IS STILL SHINING. SOMETIMES IT'S HARD TO FALL ASLEEP. IT'S FUN TO PLAY OUT THOUGH.

BY MICHELLE VANCIL   GRADE 3

Figure 6.3 Two pages from The Computer Chronicles. *(Courtesy of The Intercultural Learning Network)*

168

(CVJH, EL CAJON, CA.
3/23/84))

Babysitting Safety

by

Gala Gooden

I babysit a lot almost every
day. I have to keep a good eye on
the kids. I babysit a 2 year old and
a 2 month old baby. I babysit a girl
and a boy. It is a hard job to do if
you do not know that much about kids.
You have to keep a good eye on the
youngest kid because she or he can
get into things and put them in their
mouth and choke. You also have to
keep a good eye on the oldest kid
because he or she also can get into a
lot of trouble. for instance, they
can fall off their bike or can fall
off the swing or slide. I enjoy
babysitting and I think I am really
good at it. You would to if you try
it just once.

(Greenfield Jr. High, El Cajon,
California, February 10, 1984)

JOGATHON

On Wednesday, March 7, our
school had a jogathon. The Student
Council sponsored it because they
wanted to help raise money . The
Student Council uses the money for
school activities such as athletic
awards, school dances, field trips,
and sometimes special equipment for
classes. Any student could particpate
if he had three sponsors or more. The
runners ran around a track and 5 laps
made 1 mile. Each runner had a lap
card. Prizes were given to the
runners who ran the most laps and
those who raised the most money.

By Shawn Lint, age 15

Norman.D

(GREENFIELD JR. HIGH,
EL CAJON, CA. 3/12/84)

THE MUD RACES

by

ROBERT L. TRUFFA AND
KELLY WEITZEL

The Mud Races were held in
January, at the San Diego Jack Murphy
stadium. The mud races are a bunch
of 4 x 4's trying to drive through
mud to the finish line. The Stadium
is all muddy because the Football
season is over and the Stadium
workers sprayed a bunch of water all
over a large mass of dirt. They
created some bumps in the dirt so it
would be harder to drive through.

People have to sign up if they
want to be in the races .A truck
named ,Mud lord, came in first place
and his time was 3;55. Mud Lord was
twenty five feet tall and twenty feet
long.

ementary schools are getting into the act. Although the yearbook typically is primarily a picture book, it contains enough text to keep the writers on a yearbook staff very busy.

Here's a characteristic example of how one middle school puts together a yearbook. This school has been using word processing to create the school yearbook for three years now, and according to the advisor, before word processing they practically had to beg kids to sign up for the yearbook class. Parents were called upon to type all the copy for the yearbook on typewriters, and the faculty advisor (with the help of other teachers and very few students) did everything else. This year, however, over one hundred students signed up for the twenty-three spaces available in the class. The yearbook has recently won awards for excellence, and becoming the editor-in-chief of the yearbook is now the most prestigious honor in the school.

This is how they organize. . . . The class is a full-credit elective class that meets regularly for the whole year. They work on the yearbook until February, when the last pages have to be turned over the the publisher; after that they spend the rest of the year producing a literary magazine. Typically the class is composed mostly of "seniors" (eighth graders in this middle school), until mid-year when a few underclassmen are invited to join, so they can be trained to hold responsible positions in next year's yearbook class.

The faculty advisor selects the *editor-in-chief* and *copy editor*. Then together they choose the other editors. The editor-in-chief is responsible for managing all the other editors; therefore, he or she must be academically competent, responsible, and able to supervise peers tactfully.

The next in command, the copy editor, must also be a good manager, but this person must specifically have excellent word processing skills because it's the copy editor's responsibility to see that every member of the class learns how to use a word processor. This school has a computer lab with about thirty computers and a well-established peer tutoring system for teaching computing skills, including WordStar word processing. Therefore the copy editor must arrange for all the yearbook staff members to be paired with tutors. In addition, the copy editor helps the other editors follow through with their responsibilities, such as working with the promotions editor to be sure staff members remember to put up posters and write speeches for an upcoming publicity event. The copy editor also proofreads copy handed in by writers and double-checks such details as the spelling of students' names.

Other editors include: a *managing editor* who keeps track of finances, a *photo editor* who is responsible for collecting all the pictures, an *art editor* who takes care of acquiring artwork, a *face editor* who makes sure the faces in the photographs do indeed match the names in the captions, and a *layout editor* who oversees the design of the whole book. In addition, there is an *activities editor* who makes sure all the important school activities and organizations are covered, and a *promotions editor* who handles the publicity, fund-raising events, contests, and any other activities she or he can invent to create interest in the publication, so that people will buy it and read it.

Once the editors are picked and understand their special responsibilities, a "Ladder" is planned and posted on the wall. The Ladder is the backbone of the yearbook; it's essentially a page-by-page list of what will appear on each page. Staff members then divide up the pages, each taking several page assignments to be responsible for completing before the publisher's deadline.

Working on a page entails gathering the photographs and information to be included on that page (in cooperation with the photo editor, activities editor, and any other editor pertinent to the content of the page), writing copy, and entering it on the word processor.

Next comes the cut-and-paste routine; the photos, illustrations, and copy all must fit on the page and look attractive. To do this a staff members cuts blank paper into exactly the size and shape of each photograph or illustration as it will appear on the page. She takes a planner sheet and arranges the visuals on the page. When she finds an aesthetically pleasing design that will also work well with the written material, she traces around the paper cutouts to indicate the borders of the artwork.

Next she plans where the text will go, leaving suitable margins and white space on the page. After constructing specific areas for the text, she takes the planner sheet to the word processor. There she can arrange the text in columns of any size with justified margins. Or, she can design whatever arrangement of text she wants—triangle, circle, snake, or whatever. She'll probably experiment a bit, making several different printouts, and then when she's decided on one or two, take them to the layout editor for the final choice and/or approval.

Finally she pastes the text on the planning sheet along with paper cutouts representing the artwork. The result is a dummy of the design for the printed page. When the deadline arrives for that page to be finished, the artwork is placed in an envelope, attached to the planner sheet, and sent off to the publisher.

To raise money and create student enthusiasm for the yearbook, this class sponsors several activities during the year. At one event, for example, staff members give little speeches at an all-school gathering during lunch. They present their plans for the yearbook and invite suggestions. Then they announce the results of the annual school polls, including the "Most Popular," "Most Likely to Succeed," and so forth. The final activity at this event is to draw a half-dozen donated photographs out of a hat. These "winners" are the senior-class baby pictures that will be published in the yearbook. Other scheduled events include a cartoon drawing contest and poetry writing contest, as well as the customary money raisers, such as bake sales and paper drives.

One of the perks enjoyed by the members of this yearbook staff is the much envied "Press Pass" that gives them license to enter and leave other classes freely whenever they're on an important and timely assignment. If abused, of course, the pass is repossessed by the advisor, but evidently it works out rather well.

Some high schools produce very slick, thick, and expensive yearbooks in cooperation with yearbook companies that have their own standards and do much of the photography and sometimes final touches on the text and layout themselves. Even so, the job for the student staff is tough; they have to plan and prepare every one of those 200+ pages and meet the publisher's rigid deadlines.

One high school staff that created an elaborate 216-page volume had to work out a number of problems before the final deadlines were met and a superior yearbook actually rolled off the press. This particular yearbook class faced intense differences of opinion about what to include in the book. One faction wanted to focus on the artistic and academic aspects of school life, with thought-provoking text written in sterling prose. The other faction wanted to focus on sports and social activities, with plenty of pictures of themselves and their personal friends. Besides this problem, they also had to deal with the large discrepancy in the writing competency of staff members, many of whom were simply inadequate as writers.

Attempting to deal with these internal problems has lead the faculty advisor to initiate a recommendation system for choosing future yearbook staff members, in order to ensure an appropriate level of competency. The advisor has also decided to urge sophomores and juniors to join the staff (instead of almost all seniors) so the staff won't have quite such an intense, personal interest in which activities and pictures are included.

Another problem this yearbook staff faced was that the coeditors were extremely opinionated. The advisor had to exert considerable effort in teaching them to be more flexible and tactful. "I had to help the editors learn not to tell somebody that their work stinks," explains the advisor. They did learn, however, and by the end of the year the whole group was able to work together cooperatively.

Most of the staff members had not learned word processing skills adequately by the time the first deadline arrived, so the submitted copy was in rather poor shape. Writers forgot to delete the old parts of their files, or they duplicated parts, so there were several copies of the same paragraph on a file. A few other writers, who hadn't learned word processing at all, got their friends to enter the assignments. The advisor let it go, "mainly because I was up to my eyeballs trying to get the others' files untangled." After that first deadline things got much better and by the third deadline (out of a total of five) everybody was using word processing with some degree of proficiency.

The staff members say it wasn't difficult to learn word processing and even though most of them use two-finger typing techniques, they claim they're now pretty quick on the keyboard. Students also say that they learned the hard way about deadlines. They claim that when under pressure if there's any possibility of having a problem, it will happen. By the end of the course, however, they say they learned to plan ahead.

Other Potentially Useful Software

At least one yearbook staff has recently experimented with using a data base program to develop a master list of the senior class. The list includes every senior's name, address, phone number, parents' names, club and activity memberships, and honors awarded, as well as such information as the date their portrait is scheduled to be taken, whether they've ordered a yearbook, and whether a deposit for it has been made.

They also use the data base program to help organize the copy for every page. For each page, they record the page topic, the staff member responsible for the page, and the printer's deadline. Since the page deadlines are due on different dates, this feature is useful in helping the editor-in-chief keep track of all the pages and make sure they get to the publisher on time.

Another text processing capability of the computer that these students use is its ability to count the number of characters typed. Someone had to write a short program to measure the length of a string of characters in order to get this information, because it wasn't available on their word processing program (or on most word processing programs). A character-counting program is useful when the text is limited to a specific number of characters, and often there is a character limit for photo captions or for the personal write-ups that are typically placed near each senior's picture.

Needless to say, a spelling checker is a vital asset in preparing any printed publication. Most of the powerful word processing packages have compatible spelling checker programs.

Some yearbook companies have come out with software programs that are specifically designed to help students put together a yearbook. The Micrographix Series™ from Josten's yearbook publishing company, for example, includes a software program that assists students with designing page layouts and another that provides a data base format for collecting the appropriate information on students (see Fig. 6.4). The word processing program has ordinary text editing features as well as the addi-

Figure 6.4 The photo on the top shows the layout program. The photo on the bottom shows the word processor program. *(Courtesy of Josten's Printing and Publishing Division)*

tional capacity to count characters, calculate the size of copy blocks, display copy in specific blocks, and check spelling.

Reflective Comments

Some educators do not believe that providing an optional student publication class is important. They don't believe that students learn core curriculum skills in such a class, and they don't believe that the management and communication skills students do learn are important enough to use up class time. Other educators, of course, differ. Teachers who actively participate as publications advisors would argue that students do learn specific language arts skills, as well as certain management and communications skills that are vital to a person's education.

In a typical secondary level publications course, editors get considerable experience in managing business affairs and governing other student staff members. They often have to orchestrate large events, handle budgets, plan promotions, give public speeches, collect and organize libraries of photographs and illustrations, and much more.

Most student staff members involved in a school publication obtain experience in planning a major project that requires team effort and cooperation, which means completing assignments, volunteering when the pressure is on, and asking for help when needed. Class members get substantial practice with word processing, writing, editing, and proofreading skills. They learn principles of design and how to lay out pages. They also learn what it means to struggle hard to reach professional publication standards and deadlines.

The following comments by student staff members offer personal evidence of the kind of emotional growth that's commonly experienced by members of a publication class:

- "In the beginning of the year I thought the editors were really kind of snotty. But now, afterwards, I think they really helped us a lot."
- "At the beginning of the year I came to this class and looked at certain people and said, 'Oh God, I never want to talk to that person.' Then later, I ended up depending on that person. That's what's so neat about working on both of the publications [yearbook and newspaper], you end up making friends with these people."
- "The best part of it probably was the late nights. People sit in here and work with each other and talk, and it gets really late and everybody's tired and trying to get their work done, so everybody gets a little punchy and out of hand. And we become a close group, I guess like a family."

- "I learned a lot about writing in general, and being creative. And because we're so pressured to write for the newspaper it also helps me write under pressure in other classes. It helps me deal with other kinds of pressure situations too, I know that."
- "It gives me a good feeling knowing that I put out something that kids are really excited about."

The following Introduction to a creative writing magazine was written by student staff members. It also helps convey the feelings that students experience when working on a school publication.

> This is an introduction. It will be brief. . .what can be said about a creative writing class like ours? That it was great? That it was fun? It was. That it had a charisma of its own? It did.
>
> I'll give you two words that sum it up: inconsistent and self-centered. Inconsistent in that no two class periods were ever exactly the same, and self-centered because the writing exercises were designed to help the individual master a particular aspect of the creative writing process.
>
> So, this magazine is a panache, a goulash of pieces selected by each writer reflecting what is in each case, an effort-and-a-half. You, the reader, may find dialogues, poetry, fantasy, stories, plays, descriptions, etc., etc., etc.
>
> Oh, I just remembered to tell you this: our class was divided into editing groups. Each group gave the writers a chance to try out ideas on a small circle of friends who took the time to read and critique each other's work. We tried to be wizards of words, and these papers are our craft works—spells, illusions, and perceptions. The works reveal as much of the writer as desired by the writer. This is the way of words.

Certain student publications advisors were essential in the creation of this chapter: Art Adams, Pat Dusterhoft, Jim Levin, Diann Richards, Margaret Riel.

Chapter 7

ADAPTATIONS FOR

CHILDREN WITH SPECIAL NEEDS

Children simply do not learn at the same rate, nor do they reach certain stages of intellectual (or physical) development at the same age. Yet the nation's public school system is designed with the assumption that youngsters of a specified age should be ready to learn a designated set of skills and that they should learn them at about the same speed. Consequently, classroom teaching is typically geared for the average pupil who fits into this prescribed pattern. There are many children who don't fit neatly into these patterns, however, and sooner or later the difficulties they have in meeting classroom standards become so significant that something needs to be done.

The federal government periodically passes laws and issues guidelines concerning how states should identify and establish special programs for students who learn at a rate that far exceeds the norm, or for those who learn more slowly than the average, or who have physical handicaps that require individual assistance or special equipment in order for them to learn. Using the federal laws and guidelines, individual states design their own regulations concerning how school districts must handle learning disabled, physically handicapped, and gifted and talented children. School districts then set up specific programs and hire specially trained educators to identify and teach those children who fall far above or below the established norm. As a result, programs for these children differ considerably across the country, depending on current state and federal laws, funding available for particular programs, and local attitudes toward the need to provide special programs.

Some districts develop sophisticated programs with a staff of special education teachers, separate classroom facilities, and special curriculum materials. Some districts deal with the problems of special needs students by pulling them out of the regular, herterogeneous classrooms for extra help in specific areas. Some districts try to provide flexibility within the normal classroom environment so that students who are far slower or faster than the norm can still be challenged at their own comfortable rate of learning. The federal government now requests that handicapped children be placed in the "least restrictive environment" whenever possible. According to Public Law 94–142, in order to receive federal funding, states must establish:

> procedures to assure that, to the maximum extent appropriate, handicapped children, including children in public or private institutions or other care facilities, are educated with children who are not handicapped, and that special classes, separate schooling, or other removal of handicapped children from the regular educational environment occurs only when the nature or severity of the handicap is such that education in regular classes with the use of supplementary aids and services cannot be achieved satisfactorily.*

No matter what strategy a school system uses to provide special programs for students who need them, the addition of computers and word processing will enhance students' learning. The sections that follow discuss the use of word processing for students with each type of handicapping condition, and mention some of the hardware modifications available for students who need them.

The needs of *mentally retarded and multihandicapped* children are not addressed specifically in this chapter because their disabilities are typically so severe that they aren't likely to use word processing systems independently, at least to any great extent. *Other health impaired* children with health problems such as a heart condition, tuberculosis, or rheumatic fever, and *seriously emotionally disturbed* children with emotional handicaps that interfere with learning, are also not specifically addressed because their disabilities do not require specialized computer equipment. Many students with these handicaps are also learning disabled; therefore, the section immediately following may provide some helpful information and suggestions for educators working with these young people.

Learning Disabled Students

> "Specific learning disability" means a disorder in one or more of the basic psychological processes involved in understanding or in using language, spoken or written, which may manifest itself in an imperfect ability to listen, think, speak, read, write, spell, or to do mathematical calculations. The term includes such conditions as perceptual handicaps, brain injury, minimal brain dysfunction, dyslexia, and developmental aphasia. The term does not include children who have learning problems which are primarily the result of visual, hearing, or motor handicaps, of mental retardation, or of environmental, cultural, or economic disadvantage.*

*Section 612(5)(B), P.L. 94–142, Rules and Regulations, Education for all Handicapped Children Act of 1975.

Learning disabled (LD) students typically have average or above-average intelligence, but they have a large discrepancy between their achievement (as measured by standardized achievement tests) and their IQ (as measured by standardized intelligence tests). By the time they are identified and tested according to state regulations, they are often two or more years below grade level. The learning disability may be short-term, so that with help the child can catch up and function normally within the regular classroom environment. Or, the disability may be long-term, requiring some adjustment of learning expectations for the student.

The current theory of what causes low achievement of LD students is related to recent discoveries of how the left and right hemispheres of the brain function in the learning process. This research indicates that a person's visual, auditory, tactile, and kinesthetic processing requires the cooperative functioning of both hemispheres of the brain. Learning disabled children may demonstrate developmental and organic factors that inhibit this process. As LD children mature, their right and left brain may begin to function cooperatively; then, these children can learn normally (except that they face the problem of catching up to peers in the regular classroom). Other LD children have left and right brain hemispheres that never function cooperatively, or only begin to do so when the student is hopelessly behind.

Learning disabled children typically have problems with both reading and writing; consequently, it takes them longer to complete a class activity geared for the average pupil. They are often unable to finish an activity during the allotted class time and lack the organizational skills to follow it through to completion. As a result, many of these students develop attitude and motivation problems, and some of them simply give up.

Typically kids who fall further and further behind their classmates also develop very low self-esteem. When people suffer from low self-esteem, behavior problems sometimes begin to emerge, and such is often the case with LD students. They are frustrated and angry at themselves and ultimately at others because they feel a need to blame someone. The classroom teacher is an easy target for this anger and frustration, and often students rebel or display some other form of misbehavior in a class where they are conspicuously outside the norm.

ENTER, THE WORD PROCESSOR: Special education teachers who regularly use word processing with learning disabled students claim that the posi-

---

*Section 121(a)(5), P.L. 94–142, Rules and Regulations, Education for all Handicapped Children Act of 1975.

tive effects are remarkable. Children with handwriting problems can write much more easily on the computer keyboard, and they reportedly write much more than before. The work they do with a word processor is legible, which is also a significant and noticeable improvement. In fact, the kids get such an ego boost seeing their writing look so elegant that it often inspires them to write more. With the help of word processing, their work looks like their peers' and so they tend to feel more on a par with them.

Some learning disabled students learn computer skills—very different from writing skills—rapidly, and can help teach word processing skills to their classmates. This helps elevate their status among peers and further bolsters their self-esteem. With these positive changes in attitude, the kids who were giving up easily or refusing to do the work at all, begin to perform. As many special education teachers will avow, this alone is a major breakthrough. When these children regain their confidence, they are often ready and able to begin making progress.

Another special advantage the computer offers for LD students is that the machine is infinitely patient and can even provide positive feedback, which helps motivate children even more. Kids stick with computer assignments longer and with more enthusiasm than they ever did with pencil and paperwork.

Here's an example of a middle-school LD student's work on a one-paragraph composition. The first draft (Figure 7.1) is a handwritten paragraph about a dragon. The student crossed out each line after he entered it on a word processor. The second draft (Figure 7.2) is a printout with corrections marked in pencil. In this particular example, the teacher did not include suggestions for major content revisions. The third draft (Figure 7.3) is a printout of the the final, revised paragraph. The difference in appearance between the child's handwritten draft and the final printout is dramatic. According to his teacher, the young writer was sufficiently motivated by this experience to go through the three-draft process again right away. In later assignments, the teacher included other suggestions for revisions, which prompted further development of ideas and the expansion of a single-paragraph composition to two or more paragraphs.

Still another value that learning to use a word processing program offers LD students is the acquisition of the skill itself. Many of these students are particularly job conscious, because they plan to work right after high school or even before. Almost everyone these days views word processing as a marketable skill, and learning disabled students feel proud to be learning this professional skill, especially when they discover they can become quite proficient at it.

One LD teacher commented: "Discovering what they can produce with a word processor helps these kids see themselves as productive,

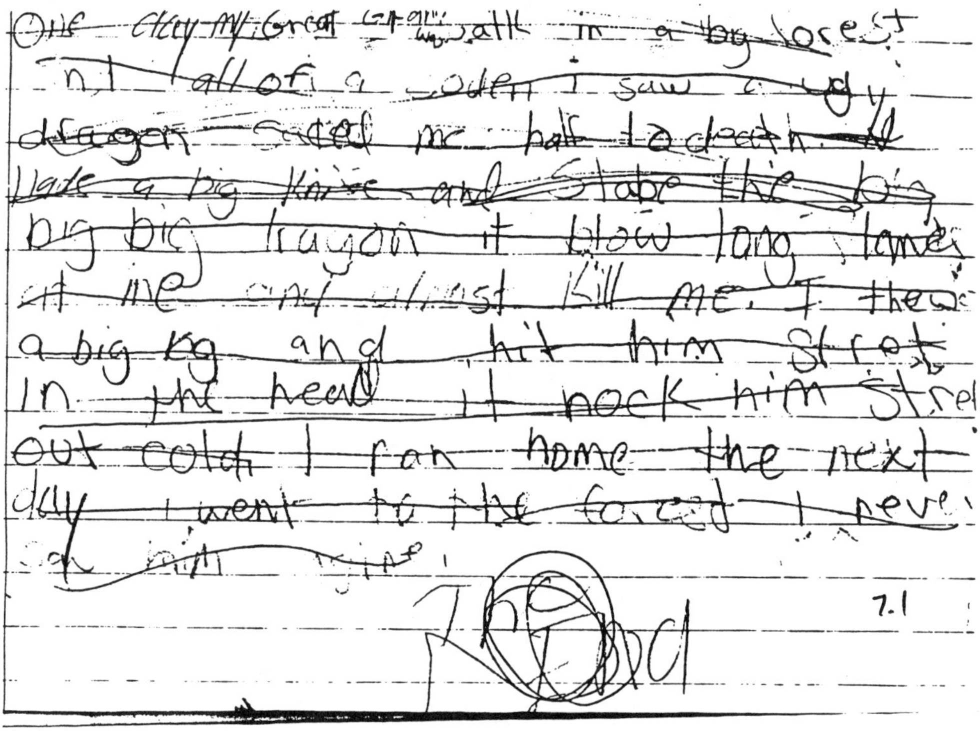

Figure 7.1 A learning disabled sixth grader's handwritten paragraph about a dragon. *(Figures 7.1–7.3, courtesy of JoAnn Hylton, Borel Middle School, San Mateo, CA)*

employable citizens. It's wonderful to watch them repair damaged self-esteem and begin to see themselves as students with academic potential worthy of respect among their peers.''

TEACHING WORD PROCESSING SKILLS TO LD STUDENTS: If the school's computers are located in a computer center, try to borrow one to use in the classroom for a couple of weeks. If you already have one or more computers in the classroom, you're all set. Demonstrate how to operate the computer and then the word processing system. Follow this up with lots of practice at the machine, individually or in small groups. At this point, if you've borrowed a computer that now has to be returned to the center, students who were once too timid to venture into computer territory will be able to enter the computer lab confidently, and begin working alongside kids from all classes in the school. In some cases they may have the opportunity to help teach word processing skills to others. (For more detailed information on methods of teaching word processing skills, see Chapter 2.)

One day my great grandfather was walking in a big

forest and all of a ~~eaden~~ ^{sudden} I saw a ugly Dragon ^{who} scared me half

to death. I had a big knife and stabed the big big big Dragon.

It blew long flames at me and almost killed me. I ~~threw~~ ^{threw} a

big log and hit him ~~stret~~ ^{straight} in the head. It ~~noct~~ ^{knocked} him out

cold. ~~Ran~~ ^{I ran} home the next day. I went to the big forest. I

never saw him ~~agine.~~ ^{again.}

THE END

Figure 7.2 The same paragraph after the student entered it
on a word processor and made handwritten corrections on the
printout.

Many LD teachers have taught their students the same "adult"
word processing systems that others in the school use, and follow the
same step-by-step written tutorials designed for everyone. It's not uncommon for students who have insurmountable problems reading *Jane
Eyre*, for instance, to march fearlessly through the tutorial instructions
presented in a word processing manual. Since LD students generally
have average intelligence but may lack motivation, word processing can
help provide that missing incentive to write.... It's certainly worth a
try.

**AFTER WORD PROCESSING SKILLS COMES IMPROVING THE WRITING
SKILLS:** When students are comfortable with the machinery and using
the text editor, it's time to begin working on writing skills. See Chapter
3 for suggested methods of organizing the classroom and Chapters 4 and
5 for specific activities. The suggested activities in those chapters are
geared for regular classroom environments; however, teachers can easily
adjust the level of expectation and the speed of delivering the material
to suit the particular students involved.

```
The Green Dragon
```

```
One  day  my great grandfather was walking  in  a  big

forest  and all of a sudden I saw an ugly Dragon scared   me

half to death.I had a big knife and stabbed the big big big

Dragon.  It blew long flames at me and almost killed me.  I

threw  a  big  log and hit him straight in the   head.   It

knocked  me out cold.  I ran home the next day.  I went  to

the big forest and I never saw him again.
```

```
THE
```

```
END
```

Figure 7.3 The third draft printed out.

Physically Handicapped Students

Young people who are blind, deaf, or have any other physical handicap
that creates an obstacle to normal academic learning are typically a few

years behind their peers. Physically handicapped children need a special educational program designed for their particular needs, and frequently they also need special equipment in order to function effectively in a classroom environment.

Recent advances in technology have produced computer attachments and modifications that help physically handicapped people use computers for writing. The sections that follow distinguish the different kinds of physical handicaps and briefly explain what specialized equipment has been developed to enable these special students to use word processing. Since physically disabled individuals often tend to have learning disabilities too, this information should be combined with the information and suggestions offered in the previous section that focuses on learning disabled students.

The Visually Impaired

"Visually handicapped" means a visual impairment which, even with correction, adversely affects a child's educational performance. The term includes both partially seeing and blind children.*

Traditional methods of providing print material for blind people are expensive and cumbersome. A third party needs to transcribe the text into braille, large print, or make an audio recording of the material.

Braille has been especially laborious to prepare because it entails producing raised dots in the paper that cannot be erased or corrected if the transcriber makes a mistake. Currently, however, it's possible to convert text into braille with microcomputer systems, and the process is completed almost as fast as the material is entered on the keyboard. A text editing and translating program such as Braille Edit (Raised Dot Computing) can be used to correct and revise text. Then the program can be used with a speech board to produce voice output, or with a paperless brailler such as VersaBraille™ to produce braille output (Fig. 7.4). A paperless braille system presents one or more lines of braille in a row of braille cell rods that come up through holes in a metal strip. Disk files can also be printed out on special printers that print hard copy braille. Using a braille system and a modem, braille text can also be sent over telephone lines or satellite relay (Fig. 7.5).

For those who have partial vision, there are computer add-ons that can be used to magnify letters on the computer screen up to 16 times their original size. The Visualtek® large print display processor, for example, enlarges letters up to 5½ inches high on a video screen (Fig. 7.6). Because few letters can be seen at a time, a joystick-type control must be used to provide control over the display.

*Section 121(a)(6), P.L. 94–142, Rules and Regulations, Education for all Handicapped Children Act of 1975.

Figure 7.4 A blind person using a VersaBraille system to produce braille. *(Courtesy of Telesensory Systems, Inc.)*

Some ordinary word processing programs, like Magic Slate, for example, have large print options that display characters that are about half an inch high on a display screen. Enlarged text written with the Magic Slate program can also be printed out on a dot matrix printer. Figure 7.7 is an example of enlarged text that's been printed out.

Speech synthesizers with appropriate software enable a person to type in text that is then converted to spoken words. At least one software program, SmoothTalker™ can convert text entered on a keyboard into speech, using the computer's internal speaker. No extra hardware is needed.

The Hearing Impaired

"Deaf" means a hearing impairment which is so severe that the child is impaired in processing linguistic information through hearing, with or without amplification, which adversely affects educational performance.

"Deaf-blind" means concomitant hearing and visual impairments, the combination of which causes such severe communication and other developmental and ed-

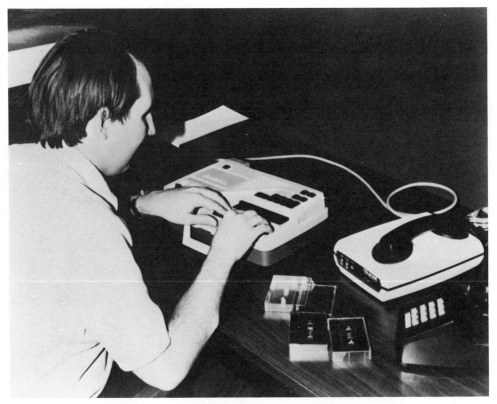

Figure 7.5 A blind person using a VersaBraille system and
a modem to transfer information over telephone lines. *(Courtesy of Telesensory Systems, Inc.)*

ucational problems that they cannot be accommodated in special education programs solely for deaf or blind children.

"Hard of hearing" means a hearing impairment, whether permanent or fluctu-
ating, which adversely affects a child's educational performance but which is not
included under the definition of "deaf" in this section.*

Unlike people who have other kinds of physical handicaps, hearing
impaired individuals are often able to use most of the available computer
hardware and word processing software without special modifications.

In order for deaf people to send and receive written messages via
telephone lines, special teletypewriter systems (TTYs), formerly used by
Western Union for text transfer, were converted years ago for use by deaf
people in conjunction with telephones. A TTY enables a deaf person to
call another TTY user and (using a keyboard) carry on a conversation by

*Section 121(a)(5), P.L. 94–142, Rules and Regulations, Education for all Handicapped
Children Act of 1975.

Figure 7.6 A large print display processor. *(Courtesy of Visualtek)*

reading the words as they are printed out or displayed on a small screen. Unfortunately, however, TTYs are not compatible with computers, so for the past twenty years they have been good only for one-on-one conversations between two TTY users. More recently, technology has been developed that enables TTY users and computer users to communicate with one another when they are both connected by modem.

A major advantage of using the newer microcomputers for telecommunications is that deaf people can now communicate with a much greater number of people, and can also gain access to national information services, electronic bulletin boards, and a variety of other telecommunications services.

Dear Mom,

This large
print sure is
easier to read than
the teensy letters
you make with your
word processing
program. The
letters on this
page are big, but
so are the spaces
between the
letters, which
makes it even
easier to read!
I love you,
Judy

Figure 7.7 A sample printout using the twenty-column, enlarged print option of the Magic Slate word processing program.

The Motor and Speech Impaired

"Orthopedically impaired" means a severe orthopedic impairment which adversely affects a child's educational performance. The term includes impairments caused by congenital anomaly (e.g., clubfoot, absence of some member, etc.), impairments caused by disease (e.g., poliomyelitis, bone tuberculosis, etc.), and impairments from other causes (e.g., cerebral palsy, amputations, and fractures or burns which cause contractures).

"Speech impaired" means a communication disorder, such as stuttering, impaired articulation, a language impairment, or a voice impairment, which adversely affects a child's educational performance.*

---

*Section 121(a)(5), P.L. 94–142, Rules and Regulations, Education for all Handicapped children Act of 1975.

People who have physical limitations that make it difficult to speak or type may use some of the available modification equipment to make typing possible. Typing sticks that are strapped to the hands make it easier to press keys for those who don't have control of the finger muscles. Alternatively, special keyguards that sit on top of the keyboard enable a user to rest the heel of a hand while poking fingers through the holes of the device to reach the keys.

For those with no hand or arm control, a pointer rod can be attached to the head for pressing keys through a keyguard to the computer keyboard (Fig. 7.8). There are also "puff-n-sip" controls which respond to sucking or blowing into a plastic tube. Other such devices respond to biting, tongue pressure, or some other bodily movement.

Accompanying the most specialized equipment is software that will let the user select from a collection of words and phrases with minimum movement. The program then assembles these words and phrases into sentences that can be stored or printed.

Remote keyboards are available that can enlarge or separate the keys and tilt the keyboard at an angle appropriate for the user. The EKEG

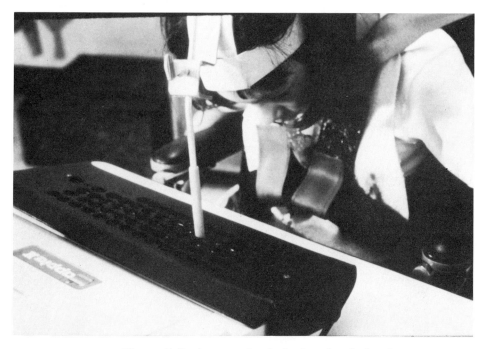

Figure 7.8 An example of a keyboard and a head pointer. *(Courtesy of Prentke Romich Company)*

Figure 7.9 An example of a remote keyboard. *(Courtesy of EKEG Electronics Co. LTD.*

Remote Keyboard also has a built-in joystick, enlarged switches, and push-button controls (Fig. 7.9).

Expanded keyboards are available for handicapped individuals who can operate a keyboard that is similar to the standard computer keyboard, only larger. The EKEG Expanded Keyboard, for example, has keys that are placed two inches apart on a flat, plastic surface (Fig. 7.10).

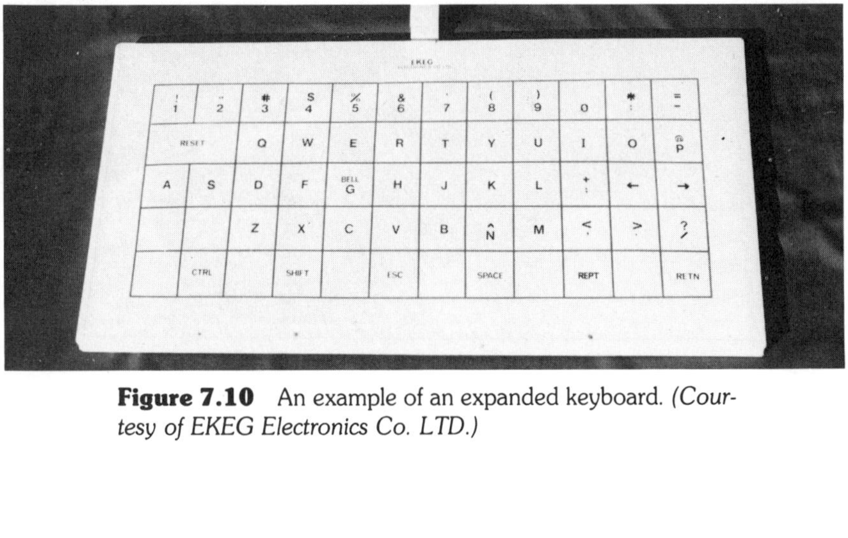

Figure 7.10 An example of an expanded keyboard. *(Courtesy of EKEG Electronics Co. LTD.)*

In addition, there are enlarged keyboards that are completely different from the standard keyboard, such as touch-sensitive boards which display pictures, words, or symbols. Some boards can also connect to a printer or speech synthesizer. The EKEG Expanded Keyboard for the BlissApple program consists of 50, 220, or 512 squares, depending on the model. Each square can be programmed to display any one of the Bliss symbols on the computer screen. Figure 7.11 and 7.12 picture the 220-square version.

Note: BlissApple, developed by the Trace Research and Development Center, is a program which allows handicapped users to write using a vocabulary of over 1,400 Blissymbols. These written messages may be displayed on the computer's video screen, spoken with the aid of a speech synthesizer, or printed out on a printer.

Alternative devices for entering information, such as joysticks, mice, light pens, and graphics tablets, are often suited to the needs of orthopedically handicapped students, and sometimes they can be used effectively without special adaptive equipment or software.

Voice recognition systems can also be used to input commands and limited information. In addition, software programs with speech synthesizers can cause the computer to speak text that's been entered on the system. (See Chapter 8 for more information on speech synthesis and voice recognition technology.)

Gifted and Talented Students

"Gifted and talented children" have outstanding intellectual ability or creative talent, the development of which requires special activities or services not ordinarily provided by local educational agencies.*

It may seem strange that gifted and talented children have "special needs," just as handicapped children do, that require government legislation to provide suitable programs. In a certain sense, however, those who learn at unusually fast rates are also handicapped in a mainstream classroom because they, too, are essentially academic "misfits." Students who operate two or more years below grade level are often frustrated and rebellious in the mainstream class, and so are the very bright children who operate years above grade level. Both groups of students often feel alienated, bored, and angry in a classroom that's geared for the average learner.

Until recently, few schools at the elementary school level singled out gifted students to advance in special education programs. Teachers

---

*From the General Provisions section of the federal education statutes, Title IV, P.L. 93–380.

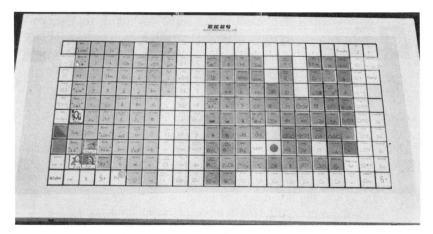

Figure 7.11 An example of an expanded keyboard for the BlissApple program. *(Courtesy of EKEG Electronics Co. LTD.)*

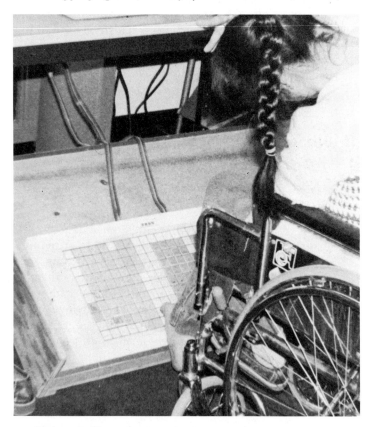

Figure 7.12 An orthopedically impaired youngster using an expanded keyboard for the BlissApple program. *(Courtesy of EKEG Electronics Co. LTD.)*

have attempted to deal with them by assigning extra work, extra privileges, or more complicated assignments on the subject being covered in class, and by using them as classroom leaders and tutors. In traditional classrooms where the teacher directs the entire class to progress at the same rate, these methods don't usually work. But in flexible classroom environments where individuals and small groups of students may work at their own speeds, gifted and talented students can often proceed with more advanced learning in the classroom, without feeling isolated.

The addition of computers in the curriculum can help even more. Having the capability to keep slower students working at rates that are comfortable for them, computer software can also move at a faster pace and challenge the accelerated learners. Both types of students can be actively learning within the same classroom.

Word processing is a special asset for advanced students. It enables them to edit and revise longer and more complex papers without significantly increasing their time commitment, because they don't have to recopy their papers.

The small-groups method of organizing a classroom, which is used so often in writing classes that have word processing, provides an ideal environment for fast learners. Teachers can arrange student groups heterogeneously and encourage individual students to progress as rapidly as they wish. The more capable students can provide a model as well as offer assistance to the group. Or, teachers may choose to arrange groups homogeneously, so that particularly bright students can be in an accelerated group with classmates who will continually challenge and encourage one another.

Resources

Following is a list of some of the many organizations and periodicals that can provide further information about computers and students with special needs.

Closing the Gap is an organization that provides hands-on workshops focusing on how to use commercial software and adaptive devices for handicapped students. It also publishes a newspaper every two months, called *Closing the Gap*.

[Closing the Gap, Route 2, Box 39, Henderson, MN 56044. *Phone:* (612)655-6573]

Communication Outlook is a quarterly journal that focuses on communication aids and techniques for individuals with communication handicaps.

[Communications Outlook, Artificial Language Laboratory, Computer Science Department, Michigan State University, East Lansing, MI 48824. *Phone:* (517)353-0870]

The Council for Exceptional Children (CEC) is a professional association for people interested in special education. The organization maintains the ERIC

Clearinghouse on Handicapped and Gifted Children, an information center which monitors, acquires, abstracts, and indexes current literature in the field of special education. The organization also publishes a print and nonprint publications for two professional journals and a variety of professionals who work with exceptional children.

[The Council for Exceptional Children, 1920 Association Drive, Reston, VA 22091-1589. *Phone:* (703)620-3660]

Deafnet is a telecommunications network established for the deaf. Users with either a microcomputer or a special teletypewriter(TTY)can link into this electronic network system.

[Deafnet, SRI International, 338 Ravenswood Avenue, Menlo Park, CA 94025. *Phone:* (415)859-3382]

The ***Education Special Interest Group (SIG)*** of the International Apple Core user's group maintains a list of special education software for Apple computers.

[International Apple Core, 908 George Street, Santa Clara, CA 95050. *Phone:* (408)727-7652]

The ***Handicapped Educational Exchange (HEX)*** is a computerized bulletin board, available to anyone 24 hours a day, seven days a week at (301)593-7033. HEX is a free service that provides information on modern technology to aid the handicapped; it lists computer hardware, software, conferences, seminars, periodicals, organizations, and related resource information.

[Handicapped Educational Exchange, Richard Barth, 11523 Charlton Drive, Silver Spring, MD 20902]

The ***Journal of Learning Disabilities*** includes articles on the use of microcomputers for learning disabled students and reviews of software appropriate for these students.

[Journal of Learning Disabilities, 1331 E. Thunderhead Drive, Tucson, AZ 85719]

LINC Resources, Inc. provides a clearinghouse to help special education teachers locate appropriate software for learning disabled students. (This service is a part of the special Education Software Center, listed below.) LINC also publishes a newsletter, *Update*, which reports on new hardware and software products for special education.

[LINC Resources, Inc., Suite 225, 1875 Morse Road, Columbus, OH 43229. *Phone:* (614)263-5464]

The ***Microcomputer Education Applications Network (MEAN)*** is a division of Education TURNKEY systems. It provides information on new developments in special education hardware and software and funding sources. It also develops some custom software for special education administrators.

[MEAN, 256 N. Washington St., Falls Church, VA 22046. *Phone:* (703)536-2310]

The ***National Rehabilitation Information Center (NARIC)*** is an organization that provides information on specialized computer devices for handicapped individuals who have little or no hand or arm control.

[The National Rehabilitation and Information Center, Catholic University of America, 4407 8th Street NE, Washington DC 20017]

Personal Computers and the Disabled: A Resource Guide is a booklet put out by Apple Computer, Inc., which presents descriptions of handicapped people at work and lists commercial products available as well as other resource information.
[Apple Computer, Inc., 20525 Mariani Avenue, Cupertino, CA 95014. *Phone:* (408)996-1010]

Special Education Community Network (SpecialNet) is a telecommunications network system for special education teachers and administrators. Among its electronic bulletin boards is information on new computer devices useful for handicapped students, as well as changes in federal legislation. SpecialNet also provides electronic mailboxes for users.
[National Association of State Directors of Special Education, 1201 16th Street, N.W., Suite 404E, Washington DC 20036. *Phone:* (202)833-4218]

The ***Special Education Computer Technology Online Resource (SECTOR) Project*** is an organization that reviews and evaluates recently published courseware and keeps an on-line data bank of information on technological advances that benefit all types of exceptional children.
[SECTOR Project, University Affiliated Exceptional Child Center, Utah State University, Logan, UT 84322. *Phone:* (801)750-1981]

The ***Special Education Software Center*** provides a software clearinghouse to help educators locate approriate special education software. It also offers technical assistance for creators of special education software, as well as an annual conference for educators, software developers, and publishers, to encourage the development of special education software.
[Special Education Software Center, SRI International, 333 Ravenswood Avenue, Menlo Park, CA 94025. *Phone:* 800-223-2711]

The ***Trace Research and Development Center*** at the University of Wisconsin has compiled an *International Registry of Systems and Programs* which lists and describes software and hardware modifications for use by handicapped people. The organization also has available *The Non-Vocal Communication Resource Book* which provides a listing of commercially available aids and systems for the communication impaired. In addition to resource material prepared by the Trace Center, the organization will also reprint material from outside sources. A bibliography and reprint order form are available upon request.
[Trace Research and Development Center for Severely Communicatively Handicapped, University of Wisconsin-Madison, 314 Waisman Center, 1500 Highland Avenue, Madison, WI 53706.*Phone:* (608)262-6966]

Special help for this chapter came from special education experts Marco Dondero, JoAnn Hylton, Jerry Krause, Terry Middleton, Pat Neu, Helen Nesbet, Diane Herrera Shepard, and Nancy Stephens.

Chapter 8
OTHER SOFTWARE TOOLS
FOR WRITERS

A respectable word processing program provides the essential knife, fork, and spoon for writers. Supplementary tools for diners, such as the soup spoon, salad fork, and butter knife, may be useful when consuming a multi-course meal, but even so, the food can be maneuvered quite skillfully without them. Some people enjoy using a rich assortment of utensils, while others think they are a bother. "Extra utensils" for writers include supplementary programs such as pre- and post-writing disks that assist students in the planning and revising stages of writing, and even more specialized writing programs that provide a format for students to compose a particular type of writing such as a branching story or a triolet.

Pre-writing programs commonly offer a series of exercises designed to help writers generate and organize topic ideas before writing. Post-writing disks help students revise and proofread a draft once it's been written; some direct the writer to reexamine organizational aspects of the written draft; and others analyze the text and point out possible problems in spelling, style, mechanics, or usage. There are even some programs that provide a format for a reviewer's comments. Some software packages for writers include a data base program for filing and storing research information for an essay or report. A few packages include an electronic mail program so that students and teacher can send messages to one another.

An increasing number of software publishers are marketing multi-program packages that include a complete word processing program and some combination of pre- and post-writing programs. The Writing Workshop™, QUILL™, and HBJ WRITER are three popular examples. QUILL and The Writing Workshop are designed for elementary and junior high level writers, while HBJ WRITER is directed toward high school and college level students.

QUILL is firmly based in the educational philosophy that maintains that creating an environment which fosters continual communication among students, as well as between students and teachers, is an effective way to teach writing. Its data base and electronic mail programs are designed to encourage sharing among classmates and provide writers with a larger audience than just the teacher. The supplementary programs in the QUILL package are shell programs, which means that the software sets up a format for the activity, but a teacher or student has to create the actual content—the questions and exercises to be completed by the writer. The Writing Workshop and HBJ WRITER, on the other hand, place their emphasis on helping an individual writer proceed through the various stages of writing, and both packages include already created pre- and post-writing aids.

The advantage of such multi-program packages is that the supplementary programs are compatible with the basic word processing program, which means that the commands in each program are similar and, when appropriate, the text is transferable between programs. Although this compatibility feature is handy, and having supplementary pre- and post-writing helpers may appear to be a real asset to students, don't go out and buy a multi-program package just because it seems to have everything a writer could need. It may not have the best word processing program for you and your students, and the extra programs in the package may be less effective than the advertisements promise. A powerful word processor is the most essential tool of all for writers, so choose one that's suitable for your class, even if it doesn't come packaged with supplementary programs.

Pre-Writing Programs

Pre-writing programs often begin by providing the writer with a format for brainstorming ideas related to a chosen composition topic. The program then helps the student organize these ideas by posing questions or offering another format for identifying major ideas and sorting them into a logical pattern for presentation. This constitutes an informal outline from which the student can begin writing.

We'll look at one example pre-writing package in detail in order to develop a picture of how this kind of writing tool works. Subsequent examples will be more terse.

Let's take the pre-writing software from The Writing Workshop as a characteristic example of what pre-writing aids have to offer the young writer. The first program, called *Brainstorming*, prompts the writer to enter a topic for the paper. As an example, we'll say a sixth-grade girl chooses to write about Wonder Woman. The program then provides a format for her to brainstorm this topic by entering any words or short phrases she can think of that relate to Wonder Woman. The format limits entries to only sixteen characters per line; so if she wants to include longer phrases, she'll have to mark the beginning of each entry with a dash or other notation. Her entries are listed below as they would be displayed on the screen.

```
                       Wonder Woman
-super human                -real identity
strength                    is obvious when
-tall                       she changes
-can jump high              clothes
-smart                      -never grows
-good                       older
-helps other                -must get cold
people                      in her skimpy
-fights bad                 suit
people                      -attracts danger
-pretty, but                -works with
not dainty                  fancy technical
-brave                      equipment
-sexy
```

The writer's next step is to arrange the entries into groups. The program makes this easy by providing a mechanism for the writer to bullet the entries she wants to include in group one, two, three, and so on. Following this, the program prompts her to give each group a label of up to eight characters. Our example writer's groups would look like this when printed out:

```
                     Wonder Woman
Physical [Features-there's no room for this word]
-super human
strength
-tall
-attractive, but
not feminine
-sexy
-never grows
older
-must get cold
in her skimpy
suit
Character [r-no room for the last letter]
-clever
-righteous
-bold
-attracts danger
Action
-can jump high
-helps good
people
-fights evil
```

```
people
-real identity
is obvious when
she changes
clothes
```

["–works with fancy technical equipment" was excluded from the screen display; evidently there wan't room for it]

The writer would then print out these notes and use them as an informal outline for drafting a paper about Wonder Woman. However, this particular writer should be further advised to include some specific examples in her paper; otherwise it's likely to contain mainly superficial generalities. (All software has some limitations, and that's only one reason why we'll always need teachers.)

Another pre-writing program in The Writing Workshop package, called *Branching*, provides an alternative approach to planning topic ideas and developing an informal outline. After the writer enters a topic heading, the program prompts her to name no more than four main ideas. The next step is to enter up to six lines of details for every main idea. The details are limited to sixteen characters per line.

Let's suppose our example writer chose to use Branching for help in planning her Wonder Woman paper, instead of Brainstorming. If we take her topic ideas and transfer them over to this program, the resulting printout looks similar to the Brainstorming printout, except that Branching doesn't provide space for all the details that our writer generated with Brainstorming. Both programs provide almost the same results; however, the approaches are different—Brainstorming helps writers with general ideas add specifics, while Branching guides those with specific ideas to develop generalities. Writers would choose one depending on whether they had a specific or a general idea for writing.

A third pre-writing program included in the package is called *Nutshelling*. This program helps students think about the essential things to include in the particular type of paper they're writing. A student selects a writing genre from the program menu: Explanatory Essay, Descriptive Essay, Letter, or Story.

Let's say our writer chooses to write an Explanatory Essay about Wonder Woman. She is then guided through four interactive writing exercises that help her think about what to include in an explanatory essay. The program prompts:

1. I will be explaining. . .
2. My reader is a person who. . .
3. To give my explanation, I'll need to. . .
4. I will end by saying. . .

Nutshelling does not limit the number of characters in these responses, so the writer is free to enter complete thoughts after every prompt. Each writing genre has its own set of prompts, and teachers can add one more writing type with up to nine idea prompts.

Our writer's Nutshelling responses for an explanatory essay would look like this when printed out:

Explanatory Essay

1. I will be explaining who Wonder Woman is and give examples that show the kinds of things she can do.
2. My reader is a person who doesn't know very much about Wonder Woman. (My readers are adults.)
[The program assumes the writer has only one reader.]
3. To give my explanation, I'll need to describe what Wonder Woman looks like, explain her powers, and show how she uses them to help people.
4. I will end by saying that Wonder Woman appears on television every week, so any readers who are interested can see her for themselves.

If the class assignment happened to be to write a persuasive essay, instead, our example student could still write about her favorite topic. She could select the Persuasive Essay writing type from the Nutshelling program menu and receive guidance in refocusing her ideas from explaining to persuading. The following shows the program prompts, with our writer's responses:

Persuasive Essay

1. My essay will be about Wonder Woman.
2. I want to persuade my reader that she is a powerful lady and does things that help other people—she's an excellent model for girls to follow.
3. This may be difficult because my reader thinks that watching Wonder Woman on tv is a waste of time.
4. Therefore I will try to convince my reader that spending an hour each week to watch Wonder Woman is not a waste of time. I can learn to be a better person, and stronger, by watching Wonder Woman.
5. I will end by saying "May I please watch Wonder Woman on tv tonight?"

The advantage of using pre-writing programs like The Writing Workshop is that they guide student writers through a structured approach to formulating and organizing ideas before beginning to compose a first draft. If the format used on a particular pre-writing disk is too specialized or limited, at least it provides a concrete set of exercises from which an individual could begin developing alternative computer assisted activities. For instance, teachers or students could enter their own pre-writing questions or brainstorming format on a disk, using a word processing program. They could then make this pre-writing helper available for other writers to use, too. Keep in mind, however, that a word processing program can only provide a format or a list for students to follow—it cannot interact with the writer, as do some of the programs that are designed for that purpose.

The Planner program in QUILL, for example, provides an open shell for teachers and students to create their own pre-writing exercises; it also handles the interaction between writer and program more efficiently than a word processing program.

Some pre-writing packages, such as HBJ WRITER, include a *freewriting* exercise that prompts the user to write continually, without pausing—even for a minute—to re-think or revise. It's sort of like brainstorming in paragraph form, and it's intended to ease the "writer's block" or "fear-of-the-blank-page" problem that some students experience. HBJ WRITER also includes an *invisible writing* exercise that involves the writer in drafting a piece without seeing it until after it's written. Invisible writing is intended to help students who become so overly concerned with editing while they compose that they lose their train of thought. By turning down the brightness control on the computer monitor, students won't be able to see their writing, and therefore can stay more focused on ideas and content.

Software that helps writers further analyze and organize ideas by prompting them to develop highly structured outlines is also available. Programs such as ThinkTank™ and MaxThink™ are sophisticated idea processors that are appropriate for secondary and college-level writers.

ThinkTank provides a flexible format for structuring a highly detailed outline and then revising it by expanding, collapsing, and rearranging headings and text. It also includes an alphabetizing feature that would enable writers to use the program to brainstorm ideas and then arrange them in order of presentation (or sort them in groups) by placing the appropriate letter before each entry.

MaxThink offers a format specifically for brainstorming ideas and sorting them, a versatile format for outlining, and an authoring capability which enables users to modify the existing formats.

Post-Writing Programs

When a first draft has been completed, writers then enter the next stage of writing—editing and revising. There are a number of post-writing software programs that can assist writers with this stage.

Let's take the Planner program from the QUILL package, as an example. *Planner* is a shell program that's intended to be used primarily as a pre-writing aid, but a class can also use the program's format to create post-writing activities, such as a checklist or series of questions and reminders for writers to go through during the process of editing and revising. For instance, a teacher might create the following Planner for middle school students who have drafted science reports on their favorite animals.

```
                    Science Report Planner
Mr. Hyatt
Science Report
After completing the first draft of your
science report, print it out and have it close by
as you answer the following questions:

1. What animal did you write about?
2. What are the two or three most important
   points you made about this animal in the paper?
3. What is the topic sentence of your
   introductory paragraph?
4. Does your topic sentence introduce one or two
   of your major ideas? If not, try writing one here
   that does:
5. What is the main idea presented in each of
   your paragraphs? (Label them parag. 1, parag. 2, etc.)
   Keywords: /Science Report/Animal Report/
```

A teacher or student could also create this kind of unstructured post-writing helper, using any word processing program. Just enter the review questions or checklist on a word processing file and give it an appropriate file name, such as Science Report Checker. You could allot one or two classroom disks to be specifically used for post-writing help, and then accumulate a number of checklists for writers to use when needed. A program like Planner, however, that is designed specifically for creating interactive writing exercises, is easier to use for this purpose.

The post-writing disks provided in The Writing Workshop and HBJ WRITER are quite different from the open shell programs in QUILL. HBJ WRITER and The Writing Workshop both offer an assortment of structured aids that analyze the drafted text and point out possible problems with usage (e.g., overused words such as *nice, good, very*; tricky words such as *accept/except, their/they're*), spelling, and punctuation.

In addition, HBJ WRITER has a component that checks organization: one program prompts the student to write a statement that summarizes the main points made in the paper, and it also creates an informal outline by printing out the first sentence (or other specified sentence) in each paragraph. Another program highlights all the transition words in the paper.

Both HBJ WRITER and The Writing Workshop include a program that enables another reviewer to add comments while critiquing the text. These comments are highlighted, or otherwise set off from the text, so the writer can easily find them, and then easily remove them from the text.

Data Base Programs

Data base programs that enable students to file and store information for easy retrieval can be useful for writing papers, especially reports that involve some amount of research. Here's how an electronic data base filing system can work for writers. When a writer collects information for a paper and plans to store it in a data bank (an accumulation of information that's been filed and stored, using a data base program), she starts by planning a format for organizing the information. It's rather like creating a file of paper index cards—she designs a uniform structure for sorting and labeling the file "cards," so that she can enter the units of information systematically on separate "cards." The advantage of the electronic filing system is that the "cards" can be instantly retrieved and/or regrouped, simply by using different keywords. Another advantage is that direct quotes that have been painstakingly entered on the electronic index cards can then be inserted into a report that's written on a compatible word processing program, without having to recopy them.

However, there are also disadvantages to relying on data base software for help in writing a paper. The value of an electronic system for taking notes dimishes if a computer isn't readily available when the researcher needs it. What's all too likely to happen in schools is that the writer will end up with a handful of handwritten index cards as well as a disk containing electronic index cards. This can be disconcerting. . . . Are writers then supposed to take the time to enter their handwritten notes on the computer, just so all their notes will be filed in the data base program? Another complication is that with most data base programs, a user must plan how to organize and label notes *before* they begin; otherwise the filing system will be chaotic, and thus unable to be of much use. In spite of these potential drawbacks, many students argue that electronic note cards can be handy, especially if their classmates also do research and store useful information in the classroom data bank for others to use.

The *Library* program included in the QUILL package, for example, is a data base filing program designed specifically for young writers. It works rather like a library's card filing system except that Library can file entire compositions, and it's electronic. A student writer creates a

Library card file entry by typing one or more paragraphs of information about a particular topic. When the entry is complete she types the title of the entry, her name, the entry number, and up to five keywords for cross-referencing the entry. The following is an example Library entry that was written as resource information for a science report on whales.

```
                        Killer Whales
Lilly
     There are two general types of whales; baleen whales
(like the blue whale) that have no teeth, and odontoceti
whales (like the sperm and killer whales) that do have teeth.
The toothed whales are smaller than the toothless whales. The
killer whale, which is the second largest of the toothed
whales (the sperm whale is the biggest) is typically over 30
feet long and weighs about 16,000 pounds.
     Male killer whales, called bulls, are larger than fe-
males, called cows. Killer whales eat fish, sea mammals, and
other whales. Killer whales often join together to hunt food;
in fact, in a group they can successfully hunt polar bears
and bigger blue whales. Killer whales don't chew their food;
they swallow it whole, in 50-pound hunks!
     Keywords: /Whales/Mammals/Sea Life/Ondontoceti Wha/
```

When the Library program is used in a classroom situation, the entries gradually accumulate so that students can potentially make use of the information that's been collected in the data bank. The purpose of this program is to provide students and teachers with a means of storing and sharing information reported by classmates. Whether such a system is actually used effectively as a means of distributing information depends upon the enthusiasm and support of the participants.

Data base software is a fundamental tool in the business world, so learning to use a data base program and becoming comfortable with it, is certainly an asset for students. Some sophisticated word processing programs, such as AppleWorks™ come with data base and spreadsheet programs that are all integrated into one package. The data base program in AppleWorks, for instance, which is fairly characteristic of professional data base programs, is in some ways quite different from the Library program in QUILL. The AppleWorks program empowers the user to create a customized format for each set of electronic file cards, and it provides a variety of ways to display the information within either a chart or list format. The AppleWorks program, however, is designed as a flexible filing system for specific, concise units of information; it's not intended to serve as a resource library of lengthy paragraphs or short reports, as is QUILL's Library program.

Figure 8.1 and 8.2 are portions of an AppleWorks data base file that was created for a research paper on Computers and Senior Citizens. Figure 8.1 shows how the file can be displayed and printed in the multiple-

```
File:   SENIORS                                                    Page  1
Report: Multiple-Records
Source           Title                Keyword           Keyword           Information
---------------  -------------------  ----------------  ---------------   ------------
Dodson, Marie    Participant in Hanso Motivation        Criticism         "The notion
Douglas, Mary    Administrator at Mar Motivation                          "You know th
General intervi  visit to the Marlo S Results                            One woman ha
Howard, Elsie    Member of Marlo Seni Motivation        Data base prog    "I wanted to
Jefferson, Tom   Co-director of the H Results           Teaching compu    Jefferson cl
Jones, Michael   Teacher at Marlo Sen Motivation        Teaching compu    Mr. Jones ha
Lewis, Mark      Computing teacher at Motivation/rati   Teaching compu    "A computer
Ludwig, Laura    Computing teacher    Hansonville Sci   Teaching compu    The Hansonvi
Smith, Louis     President of Compute Motivation        Teaching compu    "Two years a
```

Figure 8.1 A printout showing an example of the multiple-record layout from AppleWorks' data base program.

record format (the user can designate the number of columns and their width in the layout). Figure 8.2 shows how a single record (what would be contained on one index "card") looks when displayed on the screen in the single-record layout; it can also be printed in this format.

There are a whole range of data base programs on the market that could be useful for writing students. If you do decide to select one, be sure to look for one that will complement your particular curriculum and teaching methods.

Spreadsheet programs are designed primarily for users who need to organize and analyze financial information. The programs typically organize data into lists, tables, charts, and so on. Including a spreadsheet program in a word processing package is useful for writers who need to

```
File: SENIORS                   REVIEW/ADD/CHANGE           Escape: Main Menu

Selection: All records


Record 7 of 9
===============================================================================
Source: Lewis, Mark       (82 years old)
Title: Computing teacher at Marlo Senior Center
Keyword: Motivation/rationale
Keyword: Teaching computing
Information: "A computer forces you to be very logical and to think
(cont): consecutively.  It's good for the mind.  And it's especially
(cont): good for people getting older.  I think it actually helps
(cont): prevent senility.  In fact, several people have told me that
(cont): they've noticed their thinking process has improved since they
(cont): started computing."
(cont): -
(cont): -



-------------------------------------------------------------------------------
Type entry or use @ commands                              @-? for Help
```

Figure 8.2 A printout of a screen display that shows the single-record layout from AppleWorks' data base program.

insert financial data in written memos and reports. In the classroom, spreadsheet programs are currently being used in economics and business education courses. A few teachers are also introducing spreadsheets in elementary classrooms for manipulating data collected in various math, science, and even geography and history projects. Because spreadsheets deal more with handling numbers than words, we won't discuss them further.

Communication Systems

Local Area Communications

Classroom communication systems can be, in a sense, a school child's initiation into the vast world of electronic mail and computer networks. Some local communications software provides students with their own electronic mailing system for receiving and sending messages to other individuals or groups, and provides an electronic bulletin board for dispersing messages to everyone using the system. The purpose of including this kind of communication software in a school writing package is to encourage students to share their written work more widely and more frequently than they do in the traditional classroom.

The *Mailbag* program in QUILL is a characteristic example of local communications software that provides electronic mail services to students within a classroom. Here's how it works:

After loading the Mailbag program, a student may choose to read his mail or send messages. Let's say a student named Peter decides to read his mail. He types in his name and a screen message informs him that there are two personal messages waiting for him. One is from his teacher, who congratulates him for winning an art award in another class; the other is from his best friend, John, who wants to meet in the gym after school. Next, Peter looks for messages addressed to members of the radio club and learns that tomorrow's meeting has been cancelled. Finally, when he takes a look at the bulletin board, Peter discovers that Sue wants to trade her size 5 figure skates for a pair that's size 6, and Fred is looking for a good book about lizards for his next science report.

In order to send a message, Peter chooses the program's *send* option and then enters his message. When the message is completed he types the subject of the message, his name, and the name of the individual or group he wishes to receive the message; or, he can request it be posted on the bulletin board. For instance, we'll say he types this message: "Sure, I'll meet you at 3:00 in the gym." Then he enters the subject, "after school"; his name, "Peter"; and finally the name of the receiver, "John." His second message is slightly longer: "I've got some size 6 hockey skates that you can have, but if you want figure skates, ask my sister, Julie, who's in Mrs. Smith's homeroom. My mom says Julie's feet have grown like cucumbers since last winter." Then he enters "skates," "Peter," and "Susan H."

Telecommunications

Teachers who maintain that informal, regular written communication among classmates is essential, would probably adopt local communications software with great enthusiasm. However, a growing number of teachers are venturing even further with communications systems by installing telecommunications hardware and software so their students can send and receive electronic mail from all over the world. Special equipment (a modem and the related software), as well as a budget for covering telephone expenses and/or network services, are necessary to begin this kind of adventure. (See the Telecommunications subsection in the Newspaper section of Chapter 6, for a further explanation of Telecommunications.)

One of the obvious benefits of telecommunicating with other students in faraway places is that the speed with which written messages can be sent. In addition, telecommunication systems can provide a larger audience for writers and a greater variety of readers. Participating students can learn about different cultures and make new friends, too.

In most classroom environments, students generally write for the teacher and their classmates—they all know each other and they all live in the same local area. But, when they telecommunicate with students far away, two aspects of communication change. First, they discover that they need to write clearly and completely, because they can't have casual follow-up conversations to clarify confusing sentences or add missing information (which they can easily do with classmates they see every day). Second, students quickly discover that they cannot assume that peers from faraway places share the same knowledge about local fads, pastimes, popular expressions, and so forth. For instance, students from San Diego can't assume that correspondents from Wainwright, Alaska know about experiences such as boogie boarding or sitting in a jacuzzi. And the Eskimo children in northern Alaska can't assume that their peers from southern California know about Muktuk or walking on the ocean to catch fish. (If you want to know what a boogie board is, a jacuzzi, or Muktuk, check the glossary.) One time, the kids from California wrote a few words about the pet rats that they had in their classroom. Well, their north Alaskan counterparts, who had a different notion about rats, wrote back very concerned about the rats that had infested their friends' school.

When students write for a wider-than-classroom audience, whether it be for a school publication or a friendly letter to peers in another location, they tend to revise their work much more carefully, on both the surface level of mechanical corrections and the higher level of clarity of meaning. Kids take their writing more seriously when writing for an audience and they work harder at perfecting it.

The procedures for sending and receiving messages via modem are a bit more complicated than the procedures for using simple classroom communication systems, but the principle is the same—electronic communication systems provide students with a greater (and more immediate) audience for their written communication than they normally get when they just pass it in to the teacher.

In addition, electronic mail systems have the potential for helping students improve their writing simply by communicating in writing more often. If an electronic mail system successfully encourages them to communicate with one another frequently by writing message, kids will get more practice in writing, which in turn means more practice in structuring their ideas logically and coherently. A fair number of adults who use electronic mail systems regularly, claim that even their informal writing has become better organized and more lucid.

Specialized Composition Programs

Besides the pre- and post-writing programs designed to help a writer in the process of composing, there are also more specialized programs that guide writers by having them follow specific procedures within a given format. Story Tree™, Kidwriter™, and Story Maker: A Fact and Fiction Tool Kit™ are examples of this kind of specialized software. Kidwriter and Story Maker are designed for young, elementary-level writers. They both include story writing programs with limited text editing capabilities (rather than complete word processing programs), but they feature graphics capabilities that permit children to illustrate their stories by choosing pictures from a collection of graphic images already available on the disk. Story Maker also empowers kids to draw original pictures with a joystick or mouse; an electronic filing program is also included in the package. Figure 8.3 shows the beginning of a story that was written and illustrated using the Story Maker program.

Story Tree helps a writer create stories that have several possible middles and endings, patterned after the popular Twistaplot™ stories included in the disk magazine series, Microzine™. The writer begins a story and then periodically pauses to offer the reader choices concerning how the story will progress. The writer must invent different continuing dramas for each choice, and then provide further alternatives with separate plot developments at several points along the way. This process con-

Once upon a time there
was a boy named Jason
who wished he could
have a big silvery
motorcycle for his ?
birthday. He was going
to be ten years old.

On the morning of his
birthday he found a
note sitting beside his
plate at the breakfast
table.

Go out to the
back yard

Instead of a motorcycle
Jason found a golden
palomino pony tied to
the back fence.

To be
continued...

Figure 8.3 The beginning of a story written and illustrated
using Story Maker.

tinues until the end, or shall we say endings, since the writer must compose an ending for every "branch" that grows from the story "tree."

The following shows the contents of two screens from an example story, "The Magic Marigold Mine," on the Story Tree disk:

```
Bellowing, the warthog charges toward
you, eyes blazing with wrath.
Press the space bar to continue. . .
```

```
Suddenly, the frightening expression
disappears from the warthog's face.
He becomes quite friendly and invites
you to come see his collection of rare
kungaberry wood carvings.
You hesitate, unsure whether to trust
him or not.
The choices are:
          go see the wood carvings
          thank him politely and leave
Arrows move, RETURN selects, ESC exits.
```

Another example of a specialized program that teaches a particular type of writing is Writing With a Micro. This program is designed primarily for secondary and junior college level students. It prompts writers to compose poems using two specific poetry forms, the cinquain and the troilet. The disk also contains a blank page format that enables students to write short stories.

A *cinquain* is a specific poetry structure that can take either of two forms: a two syllable pattern form, or a metaphor form that's comprised of specified parts of speech. A *troilet* is a poetry structure that includes eight lines and requires that the first, fourth, and seventh lines be identical, and the second and eighth lines be identical. The lines must have the same rhyme or a two-rhyme pattern.

The following are two example cinquains from the disk as they would appear on the screen:

```
        THIS IS AN EXAMPLE OF THE CINQUAIN
            USING THE SYLLABLE FORM:
SCHOOL IS                         (2 SYLLABLES)
A CLOUD THAT WAITS                (4 SYLLABLES)
FOR A KEY FULL OF RAIN            (6 SYLLABLES)
TO SEED IT OPEN AND LET DREAMS    (8 SYLLABLES)
ESCAPE. . . . . . .               (2 SYLLABLES)
```

```
           THIS IS AN EXAMPLE OF THE CINQUAIN
              USING THE NOUN-TO-NOUN FORM:

DISCOVERY                          (NOUN)

INNOVATIVE, CREATIVE               (2 ADJECTIVES)

SEARCHING, LEARNING, SHARING       (3 VERBS)

WHAT TODAY WILL BRING, TOMORROW    (STATEMENT)
WILL ALWAYS REMEMBER.

STUDENT                            (NOUN)
```

These are just a few of the specialized prose and poetry software helpers on the market. None of the four packages mentioned above has full word processing capabilities. The specialized programs typcially have limited text editors which use unique editing commands that most likely are not consistent with the commands used in your classroom word processing program. Therefore, students would have to learn a different set of keyboard commands in order to write with each of these programs.

Courseware Programs for Writers

Tutorial software that is designed to help students learn specific skills (often called courseware) is available for writing students to use instead of, or in conjunction with, printed curriculum texts. Some language skills courseware includes lessons in spelling, grammar, standard usage, and mechanics. Some courseware tutors students in more general composition skills, such as paragraph organization, tense, or point of view. Courseware programs typically present an explanation of the particular skill being taught, accompanied by examples. This instruction is usually followed by practice exercises that may increase in level of difficulty

Many software publishers offer this kind of language skills courseware. Random House, for example, has a series of separate packages that provide students with rules and practice in basic writing skills such as punctuation, capitalization, and spelling (Fig. 8.4).

The Write Steps (Nystrom) offers a different tutorial approach. This five-disk courseware package is designed to help teach composition skills in conjunction with the Bank Street Writer word processing program. Each disk teaches several particular writing skills that fall within a general language skills category such as Sentences and Paragraphs, Everyday Writing, and Writing to Explain.

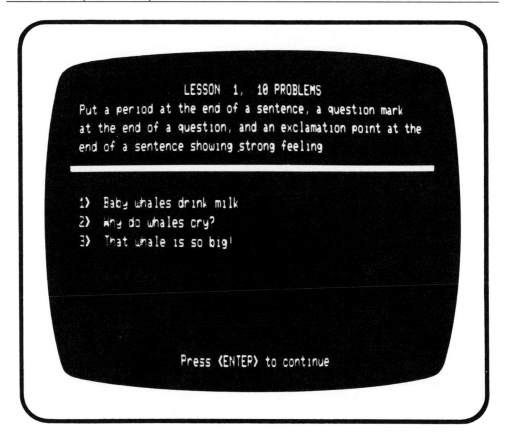

Figure 8.4 A screen shot from Fundamental Punctuation Practice. *(Courtesy of Random House, Inc.)*

The *Writing to Explain* disk, for example, includes six lessons on specific writing skills such as finding examples, using examples, writing comparisons, and explaining why. To learn the first skill, *finding examples,* the program first explains the purpose of using examples in a piece of writing, and provides an example with an analysis of its content. Each explanation that follows is accompanied by an interactive practice exercise the student does on the computer. Then, using Bank Street Writer, the program directs students to revise paragraphs already on the disk by deleting examples that do not belong in the paragraph and creating new examples that support the main idea. Following this, students select a topic from a list provided and compose their own paragraph, including examples. Then students write a paragraph—with examples—on a topic of their own choosing.

The following shows the content of two screens from the *finding examples* lesson:

```
Next you will see a paragraph with
several examples that help prove a
point.
One sentence does not belong.
Remember, all examples should
illustrate the main idea.
Press SPACEBAR to go on.
```

```
Everyone in Tony's family wears
sneakers. His father has fancy
running shoes. His older brother has
high-top leather sneakers. His
mother wears white canvas sneakers
around the house. Sneakers feel good
because they are so lightweight.
Even Tony's baby sister has a pair
of tiny pink sneakers.
In your notebook write the sentence
that doesn't fit.
00000000 Linda's Notebook 00000000

Use <-to erase.
Press RETURN when done.
```

```
    In the next screen, the sentence that does not belong is
highlighted within the paragraph, and the student is directed
to correct her sentence. ("Sneakers feel good because they
are so lightweight" is the sentence that's highlighted . . .
just in case you want to check.)
```

A Few General Remarks
Concerning Supplementary Software

Whatever you can imagine student writers might need to help them learn to write is available, or will be soon, so the software publishers claim. However, not only do these extra programs incur an additional expenditure for the school, but some of the software also ends up as a bitter disappointment to teachers who have not participated in purchasing decisions. A good deal of the commercial software that claims to assist students in the writing process never lives up to an individual writing teacher's expectations—either it's too specialized, too slow, too repetitive, or at the wrong academic level for a particular group of students.

Ideally, teachers should have the opportunity to examine supplementary software before it's bought for their classroom use. Even if school administrators do the actual software purchasing, individual teachers ought to be able to select which supplementary programs they want to use from the school's software library.

A few software tools, such as a flexible pre- and post-writing package, communications software, and an appropriate data base program, can be useful accompaniments to a powerful word processing program. But other, more specialized software choices are best left up to the discretion of individual classroom teachers, who must have the right to pick supplementary programs that work effectively with their personal teaching styles. Otherwise, the disks will simply collect chalk dust, instead of fingerprints.

The Word Processor and the Writing Teacher: Current and Continuing Trends

Software Trends

. . . an increasing emphasis on tool programs. . .

If you want to see a rather elaborate and sophisticated set of tools for writers, take a look at the UNIX™ WRITER'S WORKBENCH™ that's now being used at Carnegie Mellon University and Colorado State University. WRITER'S WORKBENCH runs only on a UNIX operating system, costs around two thousand dollars for schools (twice that for businesses), and includes more than twenty-five different programs that analyze text and assist the writer in the editing and proofreading stages of writing.

For example, there are programs that identify overly long and complex sentences in a piece of writing, programs that point out passive sentences, abstract words, spelling and punctuation errors; and programs that count the number of nouns, verbs, adjectives, adverbs, and prepositions. Other programs use this data to determine how the writing style of the entered text compares to pre-established standards for writing technical reports or training materials. Teachers can add other standards too, such as Dickens, Twain, or Updike, for instance.

The writer's work isn't finished after running through these programs, however, because the software doesn't revise the text automatically. At least not until the writer reviews the recommendations and decides which changes the program should make.

The WRITER'S WORKBENCH is a leader in the software trend that focuses on using the computer as a tool for analyzing text. Similar programs that are currently available for microcomputers at a more affordable price, such as HBJ WRITER and The Writing Workshop, have more limited text analysis programs, but do provide a variety of pre-writing aids that the WRITER'S WORKBENCH doesn't have.

Pre-writing programs that provide a format for writers to brainstorm ideas, group them, and develop an outline before writing a first draft, are now available and becoming a part of many a teacher's writing curriculum. Pre- and post-writing software will probably grow even more sophisticated and popular in the late 1980s.

Using the computer as a means to communicate is a second trend that is current and growing. The *Mailbag* program in the QUILL package is a forerunner in this area, at least for electronic communication within the classroom.

Many schools are already moving from operating local electronic mail systems that work within the classroom or school, to installing modems and telecommunication software in order to communicate with students in other cities, states, and in some case, other countries. The Intercultural Learning Network, based at the University of California at San Diego, initiated a telecommunication project in which news articles are passed back and forth between students of many different geographical environments and cultures. This project—The Computer Chronicles—has been so popular that the group is now developing content area activities that involve students from many sites in sharing research data and preparing joint reports on particular topics such as acid rain and migration patterns. These research projects rely heavily on sharing information that's been collected, indexed, and stored using a data base program—one more software tool that's increasingly being used effectively in schools.

Local electronic communication systems within classrooms, as well as far-reaching telecommunication systems, are a trend that's sure to grow in the next few years as telecommunication hardware and software become more common in schools.

Another major trend that's visible and growing more luminous, involves software programs that integrate text and graphics. For a couple of years now, educators have been experimenting with combining text and Logo designs, or text and drawings created on a graphics tablet. Story Maker is one of the first programs to actually provide the means to integrate text and pre-programmed or freehand graphics within the same program.

Considering the popularity of programs such as MacPaint™ and MousePaint™ for the Apple II, we can be certain that software that combines text and graphics will inevitably grow more sophisticated, and will very likely be well received by writers of all ages.

The integration of speech and text in a software program is one other major trend that seems to be growing stronger as the technology improves. Until recently, additional equipment (a speech synthesizer) was necessary in order to get a microcomputer to "speak" text that was entered on a keyboard. Now there are software programs that can do this without the use of a special speech board. KidTalk™ and SmoothTalker, for example, combine a word processing capability with a speech component. Text that's entered on the keyboard can be read aloud by the system's internal speaker, in either a male or female voice.

The vast potential for using talking text programs when helping young children learn to read and write is exciting to many elementary school teachers, as well as special education teachers who work with students with vision or communication handicaps.

The value of this kind of software is not limited to beginning writers, however. Writers at any level can use talking text word processing programs to assist with the editing phase of writing. For instance, one editing procedure that's recommended by many teachers is to read the written draft out loud in order to hear how the sentences "sound." Awkward sentences, weak transitions between paragraph, and problems with style and usage can often be detected immediately when the written work is read aloud. A word processing program that has the capability to speak the student's text with reasonable intonation, could help out in this process.

A few programs are now on the market that combine all three elements—text, sound, and graphics. Producer (being developed by First Byte), for example, is a software program that combines word processing, speech synthesis, graphics, music, and sound effects. Using this program a writer could enter a story, report, or poem, and also add graphic, music, or sound effects at any point. Then, the computer's internal speaker will read the text out loud, adding the sound and graphics just as they were orchestrated.

Software programs that have the capability to receive spoken text and convert it to printed text using voice recognition technology are still rather rare. The ones that are currently available can recognize a few words that serve as input commands, but they can't recognize all the sounds commonly included in a person's speech. However, the technology is rapidly becoming more sophisticated, and software developers claim that soon there will be programs that enable a user to dictate text that can be converted to printed words.

The future effects of integrating voice recognition with word processing software are somewhat alarming to some educators. . . . Will it eventually be common practice for students to dictate their compositions into a voice recognition device that will translate the spoken word into print? Will writers also be able to dictate corrections and revisions in the text—sort of a voice controlled word processor? Will this mean that there will be little or no distinction made between the spoken language and the more formal, carefully organized written language? Just the thought of how this might drastically lower traditional writing standards would horrify many educated adults today. Others claim that the new technology will have little or no affect on the standards of written language.

Educational Trends

> . . . an increasing integration of word processing into people's lives and a closer relationship between learning at school and learning at home. . .

One educational trend that already exists, and will certainly continue through the decade, is the increasing number of computers and word processing programs in schools and in students' homes. In the next few years writing students will have much more computer time available to them and will thus be able to use word processing as a regular, dependable writing tool for composing and revising school papers. This easy availability of computers ultimately means that becoming proficient on a word processor will be viewed as a fundamental skill, and using one regularly to complete school assignments will be common practice.

According to many computer-using educators, the increasing number of parents who are buying computers for their school-age children has brought on another trend—the reliance of parents on teachers to recommend educational software for their children to use at home. This practice is already common in many middle-class communities around the country where computers are prevalent in schools and homes. Does the fact that teachers are becoming influential in the purchasing of home software mean that they will have new power in the development and marketing of commercial software? And, if parents are frequently consulting with their children's teachers concerning appropriate educational software, does it mean that the relationship between learning in school and learning at home will become closer and more integrated?

If we look even further into the future we might see an electronic link between the home and the school. Perhaps it won't be too long before students, teachers, and parents can all communicate freely, using an electronic network that includes the entire community.

Another trend that is likely to emerge in schools that have fairly well-developed computer facilities is the addition of a second computer center used strictly as a writing lab. One advantage of this development is that if the computers are networked as single-purpose machines for word processing, a school would be able to provide students with easy access to computers for writing, at cheaper equipment costs.

The future of word processing as the customary tool for writing in almost any professional situation is inevitable. The word processor is replacing the typewriter as naturally as the electric typewriter replaced the manual typewriter. However, the use of word processing as an effective tool for teaching writing still lies in the hands of teachers. Writing teachers—and all teachers, for that matter—need to discover the value of word processing as a writing tool first, and then explore how they can improve their teaching of writing with this new tool. One of the greatest advantages of word processing is that it enables teachers to place a greater emphasis on the editing and revising stage of the writing process; yet, for many teachers, this means making significant changes in the traditional writing curriculum that treats writing as a one-step process. Many teachers are still skeptical, timid, or just plain too tired to change.

This leads us to another current trend that exists at the administrative level, in which the emphasis on large-scale purchasing of computer equipment is being replaced by an emphasis on teacher education. School administrators are finally realizing that owning computer equipment has little value in school if educators can't find ways to use the equipment to *improve* the educational process. Many educators are now moving beyond the goal of achieving ''computer literacy'' (a basic understanding of how to use a computer) toward a more critical examination of how computers can (and cannot) be used to improve the teaching of important skills, such as writing.

More specifically, it's important for individual teachers not only to teach themselves and their students how to use a word processing program, but also to examine how word processing can help them teach writing more effectively and help students become better writers. The fact remains, however, that no matter how powerful the word processing tool is, it can't teach a student how to write . . . that job still belongs to the classroom teacher. The teacher was, is, and probably always will be the most crucial force in the process of helping students learn to write.

Right now it's up to teachers who understand how to use word processing effectively to spread the word—share your ideas with colleagues so that they and their students can benefit, too.

This section was embellished by insights and suggestions from Jean Casey, LeRoy Finkel, Larry Frase, Jim Levin, Terry Rosegrant, Andee Rubin, Sue Talley, Ruth Von Blmu, and Dan and Molly Watt.

Appendix A
A LIST OF COMPANIES
MENTIONED IN THIS BOOK

Apple Computer, Inc.
20525 Mariani Avenue
Cupertino, CA 95014
(408) 996-1010

AT&T Bell Laboratories
190 River Road
Summit, NJ 07901
(201) 522-6107

Broderbund Software
1938 Fourth Street
San Rafael, CA 94901
(415) 456-6424

Corvus Systems, Inc.
2100 Corvus Drive
San Jose, CA 95124
(408) 599-7000

DCH Software/D.C. Heath and Company
125 Spring Street
Lexington, MA 02173
(617) 862-6650

EKEG Electronics Co., LTD.
P.O. Box 41699, Station 'G'
Vancouver, B.C. Canada V6R 4G5
(604) 685-7817

First Byte™
2845 Temple Avenue
Long Beach, CA 90806
(213) 595-7006

Gregg/McGraw-Hill Book Company
1221 Avenue of the Americas
New York, NY 10020
(800) 233-4180

Harcourt, Brace, Jovanovich Publishers
757 Third Avenue
New York, NY 10017
(212) 418-4100

InterLearn Inc.
P.O. Box 342
Cardiff by the Sea, CA 92007
(619) 452-2957

Josten's Printing and Publishing Division
5501 Norman Center Drive
Minneapolis, MN 55437
(612) 830-8424

Living Videotext, Inc.
2432 Charleston Road
Mt. View, CA 94043
(415) 964-6300

MicroPro International
33 San Pablo Avenue
San Rafael, CA 94903
(415) 489-1200

Microsoft Corporation
10700 Northup Way C97200
Bellevue, WA 98004
(206) 828-8088

Milliken Publishing Company
1100 Research Blvd.
St. Louis, MO 63132
(314) 991-4220

Nystrom
3333 Elston Avenue
Chicago, IL 60618
(312) 463-1144

Prentke Romich Company
8769 Township Road 513
Shreve, OH 44676-9421
(216) 567-2906

Raised Dot Computing
408 South Baldwin Street
Madison, WI 53703
(608) 257-9595

Random House, Inc.
201 East 50th Street
New York, NY 10022
(212) 751-2600

Scarborough Systems
25 North Broadway
Tarrytown, NY 10591
(914) 323-4545

Scholastic, Inc.
730 Broadway
New York, NY 10003
(212) 505-3800

Sierra On-Line, Inc.
Highway 41
Oakhurst, CA
(209) 683-6858

Sirius Software, Inc.
10364 Rockingham Drive
Sacramento, CA 95827
(916) 366-1195

South-Western Publishing Company
5101 Madison Road
Cincinnati, OH 45227
(513) 271-8811

Spinnaker Software Corporation
Kendall Square
Cambridge, MA
(617) 494-1200

Sterling Swift Publishing Co.
7901 South IH-35
Austin, TX 78744
(512) 282-6840

Sunburst Communications, Inc.
39 Washington Avenue
Pleasantville, NY 10570
(914) 769-5030

Telesensory Systems, Inc.
P.O. Box 7455
Mt. View, CA 94039
(415) 960-0920

Visualtek
1610 26th Street
Santa Monica, CA 90404
(213) 829-6841

VIVID Systems, Inc.
2440 Embarcadero Way
Palo Alto, CA 94303
(415) 424-1600

Appendix B

WRITING EXAMPLES FROM
CHAPTERS 4 AND 5

. . . . Sunday morning, when everybody over ten years old was still asleep, Mary decided to get her own breakfast. She climbed up on the kitchen counter and reached high for the cereal box. But, as she tried to pull it off the top shelf, out fell boxes of pretzels, Hershey bars, and marshmallows, instead.

Now, Mary, being a very well-behaved girl who naturally didn't want to cause a mess in the kitchen by pulling down any more boxes, decided to make do with what she had. Wearing a grin that made her ears wiggle, Mary munched a bowl of pretzels with chocolate chips and marshmallows on top. . . .

Dear Iggy,

My bicycle is the most special thing I own. You might not think that a bicycle could be so very special, but this bicycle is. You know why? Because it takes me far far away from my older sister. She's always yelling at me to pick up my stuff, or be quiet while she's talking on the phone, or something else. What a grouch! But, when I jump on my bicycle and ride far away, I don't have to hear her yelling.

Your friend,
Tim

Dad likes asparagus. He even bought five bunches of it today at the market. Next week I guess I'll go along with him and help him out with the shopping. This week we'll probably have to eat asparagus every night for supper—would you believe boiled asparagus, creamed asparagus, asparagus soup, and asparagus souffle? We'll probably even get asparagus pancakes on the last day, if we're unlucky. I wish Dad didn't like asparagus so much.

When Dad went food shopping today he brought home five bunches of asparagus. He didn't buy any other vegetable, so you can imagine what we'll be having for dinner every night until Sunday. I figure we'll have boiled asparagus tonight, creamed asparagus on Wednesday, asparagus souffle on Thursday, asparagus nut muffins on Friday, and asparagus soup on Saturday. And, if there's any left over, you can guess what's for breakfast on Sunday—asparagus pancakes. Next week I think I will go and help Dad with the shopping.

Informal, Personal Letter

(DATE:) April 11, 1985

(GREETING:)

Dear Steve,   **(MAIN BODY:)**

My mom told me that you're going to be in a play next month. Is it really true? She said you're going to be Captain Hook in the play, "Peter Pan." Boy, are you lucky! Captain Hook is my favorite character of all.

My mom also said that she would take me to see the play at your school and that I should find out from you how to get tickets. How much are the tickets and where can we buy them?

I can't wait until I see you in that play. Maybe you can come and stay overnight at my house afterwards. My mom says it's all right with her, so ask your mom, okay?

Write back soon.

(CLOSING:) Your cousin,
(SIGNATURE:)

John

Formal, Business Letter

111 Diamond Place
Scenic, CA 94043
September 25, 1985
Ms. Josephine Barry
Mayor of Scenic
City Hall
006 Main Street
Scenic, CA 94043

Dear Mayor Barry: **(MAIN BODY:)**

An article in this morning's *Town Tribune* stated that you support the recent proposal made by a realty company to close Baker Park and build a city office building there.

I can't understand why. The article says that a report made by the same realty company claims that Baker Park isn't used very much. Well, the people who wrote that report must be blind, or they've never been to the park. There are lots of kids (including myself) who play there every day after school.

If you close the park, where can we go after school? Should we play baseball in the City Hall parking area, or the vacant lot next to Luke's Lunch? Who knows, maybe we'll turn out to be juvenile delinquents if you take away our park.

Even though I'm not old enough to vote, I hope you will pay attention to these arguments. Besides, both my father and mother want you to keep the park too, and they are old enough to vote.

Please answer this letter.

(CLOSING:) Sincerely yours,
(SIGNATURE:) *Glenn Rudnick*

A new brown shoe with no foot wearing it is like a chocolate bar with no kid eating it. It's stiff and shiny, without a smudge of human contact. . . . You can even read the label. When you pick it up and bend it in the middle, a long dark wrinkle alters the shape permanently, making it look a bit older. It still smells like its ingredients, however, the shoe a little like leather, a little like glue, and a little like the box that contained it on the shelf.

The brand new object feels slick and slightly soft as fingers trace the sides, from top to bottom and right to left. Fluorescent light reflects off the polished surface and sharply distinguishes the rich, brown outer surface from the creamy beige inside. If you grasp it with a hand and tap the end on a wooden surface, the noise echoes softly in the classroom. Then, gently lick the smooth, chocolate-colored coating with your tongue, and you'll discover how silly it is to compare a shoe to a chocolate candy bar.

The air conditioner is always on. Business goes on all year round, but the summer weather brings crowds of people every day. A bell rings each time the door swings open and closed. White, spotless round tables rest in front of a long counter and a pink menu lies on each table. Four pink chairs patiently surround each one, waiting for a customer to sit down. On each side of the counter one can look through glass windows into icy freezers that hold 36 flavors of cool, creamy, and colorful ice cream. Nearby, dark brown hot fudge warms itself next to the golden butterscotch. A ladle stands in each container waiting to dribble its contents onto the flavor chosen by the eager eater. Chocolate, strawberry, and vanilla syrups sit until needed for shakes, sodas, and sundaes. Bananas, marshmallows, nuts, bits of pineapple, and cherries wait to be added to somebody's banana split.

The salesperson, dressed in white pants, pink shirt, and white smock, prepares whatever the customer desires. A few feet away, two children press their noses against the glass at the candy counter. Inside, jelly beans of all colors and flavors are lined up in little plastic bags with handwritten labels and pricetags on each one. Chocolates fill each beige paper dish, but the bright red and gold foil under the chocolate cherries gives them a special, classy look.

Just feasting my eyes on the creamy chocolates and the gooey caramel fudge ice cream makes me feel five pounds heavier.

I walk into the old farmhouse and see a ninety-four-year-old German lady sitting in a broken-down rocking chair in her dining room. She sits next to a table piled high with old newspapers and *Reader's Digests*. There are men's oxford brown shoes on her feet and heavy nylon stockings rolled to just under her knees. My grandmother has worn the exact same dress style for as long as I can remember. This one is a faded, wildly patterned print, and over it she wears a ratty, cream-colored, dress jacket. My family gives her new dresses and pretty sweaters and nightgowns, but they all reside in her dresser drawers, "too good to wear."

Her face has the vacant look of someone who is far away, and when I walk in her door, it takes several seconds for her to remember who I am, the oldest of seven grandchildren. Her hair is fluffed around her head, thin and soft as thistle-down. A face full of memories, and so many years of living, looks at me with a kind of absent-minded pleasure. Lines cobweb her worn face and masculine, bushy eyebrows bristle over her faded blue eyes. . . .

The Babysitter

While my parents were on a two-day vacation, a sixty-three-year-old crinkly-faced lady by the name of Mrs. Hunt stayed with my brother and me. Mrs. Hunt is not your everyday, run-of-the-mill babysitter, and this occasion was, in many ways, out of the ordinary.

We all went to the airport to send my parents off and Mrs. Hunt drove my brother and me home. She literally crawled along the highway at 20 mph in a 55 mph zone. Other drivers kept honking and screaming obscenities as they zoomed by. One man even pulled alongside of us and shouted, "Hey, lady, is your gas pedal broken?" I just hid myself from view until we got home.

For dinner that night, Mrs. Hunt prepared baked salmon, peas, brussel sprouts, and broccoli. Yeecccccchhh!! Obviously, the lady was big on green vegetables, and she sat down at the table making sure my brother and I ate every last bit. I pleaded with her not to make me eat them, but she was adamant. I even tried to squish the vegetables in my napkin when she turned her head, but she caught me, and I was forced to consume them until my plate was bare. As I rose from the table, a wave of nausea hit me and I threw up all over the place, including my brother and Mrs. Hunt. After I finished retching, she said coarsely, "You probably have the flu."

The next day, which was Sunday, I was feeling much better, and not waiting for Mrs. Hunt's permission, I snuck out of the house and headed for a carnival down the street, where I won a goldfish by throwing a ping-pong ball into its bowl. Winning the goldfish made me very happy because I'd been wanting to have pet fish for a long time. When I got home, I strolled into the kitchen with my goldfish and bowl, and there Mrs. Hunt stood, cooking more frozen vegetables, and giving me disapproving looks for sneaking out of the house while I was supposedly sick. After placing the bowl next to the sink, I raided the refrigerator for lunch, ignoring Mrs. Hunt's comments about children with poor manners.

Suddenly, I noticed that Mrs. Hunt was emptying the fish bowl into the sink. I was horrified! I raced over to her and screamed, "Stop!! What are you doing?!"

I'm cleaning out your fish bowl," she calmly replied. By then I was speechless because the fish had fallen into the garbage disposal, which was off, thank goodness. At that point, I decided to pull out the fish with the aid of two spoons, but before I could even get the spoons, Mrs. Hunt attempted to turn on a light, and instead, accidentally turned on the garbage disposal.

I cried—for about a day, and fortunately for me *and* Mrs. Hunt, my parents were only gone for two days. I can't imagine what would have happened had she stayed any longer.

THE KINGDOM

An old woman walked up to the park bench closest to the pond and plopped down with a sigh. Out from under her sweater she pulled a paper bag. With the rustle of the bag, fat pigeons flocked to her feet. The birds cooed while she threw crumbs to them.

From across the pond a young school girl rushed toward the woman. She threw her books on the end of the bench and glided shyly over to the old woman.

"Hi!"

"Oh, well hi there sweet thing."

"Whatcha doin?"

"Why, I'm feeding the birds, honey."

"Can I try?"

"Of course you can. Here."

The old woman handed the bag of crumbs to the anxious girl.

"Do you come to the park often?" asked the little girl.

"Oh, yes. I have a lot of friends here."

"Ya do? Who?"

"Well, the squirrels, the ducks, and of course these birds here."

"The animals are your friends?"

"Yes they are."

"Ah come on, you're foolin' me, huh?"

"No I am not fooling you."

"Yea, I bet they talk to ya too."

"Why, yes they do!"

"Ah, come on. Well, if they talk, tell me what they say."

"These birds tell me about their kingdom."

"Kingdom! No birds have a kingdom. Do they?"

"These birds have a kingdom. See that circle of trees over there?"

"Yea, what about it?"

"That's their kingdom. Inside the circle is a tall white porcelain castle where the birds live, and in the middle of that, there is a nice blue pool for the birds to bathe in."

"Have you been there?"

"Oh no, the birds just tell me about it. See that fat bird over there on top of that statue's head?"

"Yea."

"That is the king, King Charles. He changed his name a few years back, it was Bernie before."

"He still looks like a Bernie!"

"Yes, but don't tell him that, it would hurt his feelings. See that skinny bird hopping around below the statue? Well, that's the court jester.

227

The king always makes him entertain, with hardly ever a rest, not even to eat. That is why he is so skinny and why the king is so fat."

"What's the mark on the king's chest?"

"Oh that, that's an old battle wound from the War of the Pelicans. It's just a simple peck wound, but he proudly flaunts it."

"What a brat!"

"Look at that beautiful white bird sitting quietly at the edge of the pond. See her? Her name is Lily."

"She looks sad, or somethin'."

"Yes, she is very sad. You see, the king's son is very much in love with her and she with him. But the king disapproves of this, because she is the daughter of a beak cleaner, which the king considers to be very low, too low to be in love with his son anyway. There are plans for the marriage of the king's son with another bird from the kingdom across the pond."

"Oh no, that's awful. We should do somethin'."

"Yes we should, do you have any ideas?"

"Well, we could hmm . . . , well I guess we could, hmm . . ."

"We could switch brides at the wedding. Does that sound good?" the lady suggested.

"Yea, we could do that. But what do you mean?"

"The wedding is tomorrow afternoon. What we will do is kidnap the bride-to-be from the other kingdom and replace her with Lily. Then we can think of some way to get the bride and groom away from here after the wedding."

"Yea, that sounds good. We'll teach that old king!"

"All right, let's meet here at about this time tomorrow. That should give us enough time."

"Okay, I'll see you then."

As the little girl ran off across the park the old woman yelled out, "Bring some rice!"

A MOTORHOME

A motorhome is a vehicle that has all the necessities of a house built into the interior. Most motorhomes are two-axle motor vehicles that require a normal driver's license to operate. They are usually powered by big, V-8 engines, but sometimes smaller engines are installed to achieve better gas mileage. Ranging from 18 to 38 feet long, 10 to 13 feet high, and 8 to 9 feet in width, most motorhomes have hot and cold running water, electricity, ovens and cook tops with three or four burners, air conditioners, heaters, a separate toilet and shower, dining table, cupboards for storage, and a multitude of concealed beds. The motorhome is set apart from a camper or a trailer because the driver sits inside the living section—no walls separate the driver from the rest of the vehicle. They can travel anywhere a car or bus can go and are especially good for camping and long cross-country trips.

The motorhome first appeared in the mid-sixties. People needed a cheap, economical way to travel long distances on land. The first prototypes were rustic, oblong bodies, that looked like giant sausages. As the idea spread, more companies started building them. The shape became more aerodynamic and the prices dropped due to competition. When the oil shortages of the seventies appeared, people couldn't afford to pay for gas. The end seemed near, but now gas prices have dropped, and travelers are using the motorhomes more and more. It looks like the motorhome has moved into the lives of many Americans and is here to stay for a while.

WHAT'S WRONG WITH THE COMPUTER?

The Technological Revolution introduced computers to the civilized world and computers have introduced us to the Information Age. Since this has happened, the need for computer knowledge has become vital. However, there are many disadvantages of the computer, and the trend towards total dependency on the computer is frightening. Before we advance one step further towards computer dependency, we need to look closely at some of the nonbeneficial effects of computers.

As computers continue to replace humans in the work force, unemployment will also continue to rise. Computers and computer-operated robots are now doing a number of jobs. In the auto industry they paint and assemble cars. In the clothing industry they do the jobs of tailors. In business, the accountants are being replaced. In airplanes, the flight navigator is now a computer. In libraries, the computer catalogs and keeps track of books. In classrooms, teachers' aides are being replaced by computers. In the medical field, symptoms are entered into a computer which calculates diagnosis, thus replacing the physician as diagnostician. In hotels, making reservations and many of the other services are being done by computers. The goal of these "advances" is to get more work done by fewer people. The final outcome is fewer people working and greater unemployment.

With computers taking over jobs previously done by people, the problem of dehumanization grows. As businesses and schools replace people with computers, it becomes apparent that there is a disregard for the large group of people who need the gratification received from work. Human qualities are exchanged for machine performance; for example, when a teacher's aide is replaced by a machine, the student will not experience humanness—facial expression, eye contact, and the effects of voice inflection. In this situation, the students don't receive the human interaction that is vital to wholesome learning.

Loss of human interaction is probably one of the most detrimental long-range disadvantages of the computer. Those who work alone with their computers will lose the opportunity for social stimulation. Children who organize their lives around computers for play and learning will fail to learn how to socialize. One well-known psychologist at Stanford University, Dr. Zimbaro, has already seen this development and calls it "hacker syndrome." These kids would prefer to communicate to the person sitting next to them via computer terminal. Some fear that their vast experience of computer games and simulations, and their limited experience interacting with other human beings will greatly distort their view of reality.

Purchasing and maintaining a computer requires a sizable amount of money. Thus, there is a concern that computers can widen the gap between the rich and the poor. It is already evident that white, middle class children are by far the majority of young personal computer users. It's becoming evident that those who don't learn computer skills will face an obstacle to future employment, and schools in poor areas cannot afford computers and teacher training.

Even when businesses or individuals purchase computers and become dependent on them, they face problems. If the computer is accidentally unplugged, or the electricity goes off for even an instant, everything that was in the computer's internal memory is lost. In addition, if the operator makes any mistake when giving an instruction, such as typing a dash instead of a comma, the program won't work. For example, several years ago all long distance telephone service was cut off to Greece because of such an error. It took months to correct the program and restore the phone service.

A new area of crime is also emerging with the increased use of computers. Tampering with data is easy once a person gets access to the program, and embezzlement is rising.

The tremendous amount of knowledge that computers can store and rapidly display makes information about every citizen in the country accessible to the government. Financial records, personal records, school and job records—there may be no escape from the past. How far this invasion of privacy will go, remains to be seen.

In conclusion, there is no doubt that the computer is the machine of the present and future. It will create more spare time for the worker *who has a job.* In some ways it will do a better job than the people it replaces, but at what cost to human qualities and the human race? The wise will keep in mind the dangers of growing computer dependency and will work to avert the social and economic difficulties that the computer age will bring.

SHABBY ANDY'S ENDS SEARCH FOR LARGER SERVINGS

One of the more irritating things that the restaurant diner experiences is without a doubt the "micro-steak syndrome." The hungry eater transports himself somewhere on the classier side of the restaurant world, only to be dismayed by the steak (or lack thereof) that is placed before him. He has spent up to $30 on a hunk of beef that he has a difficult time locating on the plate.

But, remember, nice restaurants don't necessarily focus on quantity—quality is job one. So the eater gets a tiny portion, but is treated to an elegant environment. "Big deal!" the serious eater would retort. Fortunately for his kind, a restaurant does exist that goes against the grain.

Located in Campton on Campton Avenue just before the Route 221 overpass, one finds Andy's. Upon absorbing your first view of this place, discouragement may overcome the prospective porker. The parking lot is composed of gravel, and by the looks of his establishment, Andy doesn't attach much importance to appearances. But you mustn't be misled by looks—even when you're inside. The door opens up into a semi-sleazy bar inhabited by some varied individuals. It usually isn't too crowded. Another doorway leads into the dining room, which is no spectacular sight either. Very humble table settings are spread around the room with the barbecue in a corner. The barbecue—that's the star of the show.

Andy's barbecue is the site of the creation of a limited number of simple but choice meals. All of the menu items (steak, chicken, and ribs) share one particular quality: they're large and engrossingly tasty. The steaks are unusually hefty, about 24 cubic inches, and call for a relentless jaw and a well-developed slicing motion.

Accompanying the steaks on the grill are Andy's renowned ribs. Basking in luscious barbecue sauce, they too are sizable and are delivered in large quantities to the customer.

Chicken is also a tasty possibility. The diner may choose a half or a whole fowl which is barbecued precisely for maximum flavor.

All dinners come with a baked potato that resembles an oval softball. The potato is smothered in melted American cheese, if the eater so desires, or else just butter. As a special treat, garlic French bread is served after being smoked on the barbecue.

The total meal costs from about $10 to $20. This includes the added attraction of watching the cook prepare the food, deftly wielding a butcher knife and adjusting the barbecues so as to acquire the best possible quality. It's something to do if the table conversation is boring. Service is rather fast—about fifteen minutes—and the servers are polite but informal.

So, if you're sick of being a victim of the "micro-steak syndrome," enjoy a healthy dinner at Andy's. It might not be the most glamorous place around, but it's satisfying and relaxing.

Dear Class,

Has it been three months already? This summer has whizzed by so fast I've hardly had time to do my favorite activity—nothing, nothing but sleeping in the sun, dreaming up poems in my head.

By the way, my name is Debbie Smith. Original, huh? There were three other Debbie Smiths in my high school. The kids called one Debbie, one Deb, and one Deborah. They called me Debbie Smith. The Smith was always attached, just like the Brown in Charlie Brown.

I was born in Hong Kong and spent the first ten years of my life living in various places in the Orient. My father was an American writer in Taiwan and my mother was a young Chinese girl looking for a job as a secretary. Just like in old Susie Wong movies, East met West and here I am. I've lived in Sealand, California, for almost nine years. As a freshman in college I attended U.C. San Diego, but got sick on cafeteria food and dorm living, so I am now a sophomore at Sealand College Business School.

So much for my exciting life. As I was saying, the summer was much too short. I spent most of my time working and playing at Johnson's swim school and club pool. For eight hours a day, five days a week, I lived in a small 95 degree indoor pool teaching kids how to blow bubbles, doggie paddle, and do big arms. My skin dried out like a peach pit and my hair was killed by chlorine poisoning. I had crying kids, screaming kid, kids that splashed, sneezed and spit in my face, and kids that peed in the pool. I'd just smile through it all and think to myself how lovely it would be to punch their little faces in. Then they'd smile back so innocently or bring me crayoned pictures or cookies the next day, and I couldn't help loving the stinkers.

On the weekends, I worked as the Social Director for the swim club, organizing such activities as barbecues, beach parties, over-nights, and treasure hunts. Being the kind of person who rarely plans or organizes anything, I found this job to be extremely challenging and a pain in the neck.

I should have been rich by the end of the summer but most of my paychecks went to my parents for school, and the rest went for dozens of swim suits, record albums, parties, crazy hats, and ice cream cones. I've been a spendaholic since I was ten, and collect all kinds of things from wine bottles to apple seeds. I save almost everything except my money

I spent my last summer weekend in Santa Cruz with three friends of mine. For three days we played in the sun like six-year-old kids— making sand-people, throwing frisbees, pretending to be fish. We swam in the cold, chlorine-free ocean, catching rides on the backs of waves. I love the ocean. I could watch it forever, rising and falling, pounding in the bones of my ears and sucking my feet down into the sand. Actually, I was born in the ocean but I climbed out onto the land where my fins grew into arms and legs. If I die, I want to be buried at the bottom of the sea so I can start all over again.

Before we left Santa Cruz we watched the sun sink into the ocean one last time, blew the last of our money on popcorn, cotton candy, souvenir trinkets, and rides at the Boardwalk. We got drunk on Mateus and wandered around the town like gypsies, listening to and singing with the sidewalk musicians.

Then I was back at Sealand, standing in a line to get my name checked off so I could stand in another line. I finally got through the line to see my advisor . . . Computer Science, Business Law, Organizational Theory, Finance I, Managerial Communications, and Creative Writing. I guess it's back to business.

Yours truly,

Being kicked repeatedly by unsatisfied customers gets very irritating after a while. I break down occasionally; but give me a chance, nothing is perfect! Give me thirty-five cents and I will return your offering with any one of six flavored sodas. But there are certain signals you must read before you proceed. Above all, be friendly, and chances are I will be friendly in return. If all of my lights are on, don't press the issue or you may be sorely disappointed, not to mention that you won't get your money back. If there is a little white piece of paper on my chest that says OUT OF ORDER, just leave me alone, or you will really be sorry. Just remember these little signals and we will get along fine.

I am a chipmunk. I have fluffy red hair which can be spotted from far away. I love to nibble constantly and use my small, sharp teeth to help me gnaw what I eat. My steady diet consists of nuts, nuts, and more nuts. Peanuts, hazelnuts, walnuts, almonds, you name it, I eat it.

When I am not nibbling, I am probably sleeping. I sleep quite often, usually when there is something that needs to be done. Admittedly, I am lazy. I am also incurably curious, constantly sticking my nose in where it doesn't belong. One day I'm going to get it bitten off, I know, but so far I've been lucky.

I also have a dreadful habit of hoarding things, or so Ma and Pa Chipmunk tell me. Really useless things. . . . Ma and Pa say it's just a phase and hope that I'll grow out of it soon. So do I! Ma and Pa put everything I bring home in my room and some of those tin can lids are darned uncomfortable to sleep on.

white as a sheet
chip off the old block
sharp as a tack
fast as lightning
agree to disagree
avoid like the plague
face the music
in the same boat
short and sweet
sell like hotcakes
walking on air
swear like a trooper
wrong side of the tracks
twinkling of an eye

apple of one's eye
play with fire
dyed in the wool
head over heels
stars in her eyes
raining cats and dogs
cute as a button
life is a bowl of cherries
peaches and cream complexion
water over the dam
don't count your chickens
flat as a pancake
it was a dream come true
speaking of the devil

Traces of age, hours of smiles are like deltas reaching out from sea-green mirrors surrounded by forests of lashes. These rivers run along to feed golden rushes of waterfalls, flowing freely down my cheek and shoulder. My nose becomes a cave, protruding from some porous rock, maybe lava, shimmering with minerals. My vision is like a cliff dweller's as I move down to my lips, wrinkled and full of lines as an old Indian's smile would crinkle his face. There are soft, rolling hills down to the jutting cliff of my chin, and a drop into sheer nothingness. Then I move back to those green eyes . . . the center of life in a face, and begin again.

There is a face in the mirror in front of me. Do I ever, truly, look at this face, except as a canvas for my make-up? Why is that face so pale and drawn, with lines finely etched around each eye? There is no sparkle today, and each eye is shot through with traceries of blood across the white. Deep within each eye—there is no personality reflected, just colors—blue, green, and amber, melt one into the other. Dark circles are unsuccessfully hidden by make-up under each eye. Eyebrows are brushed up like a collapsed wooden fence in the snow. Wispy, reddish-brown hair surrounds my rounded face, punctuated with a slightly lopsided chin. There are hints of grey at the temples trying to hide under the rest of the hair. Corners of my mouth are drawn down with memories of past laughter carved on each side. One lip is thinner than the other, with even, closely spaced lines running along each lip. Wedge-shaped shadows on each side of my nose draw my face downward. When I look at this face, I see answers to questions I didn't know I needed to ask.

. . . The mouth is partly open. The corners droop lifelessly. The lips are parched and pale only partially revealing the slightly yellowed teeth. The lower portion of the face bears a darkened look starting in front of the ears just below the hairline and continuing down the sides to eventually meet at the chin. . . .

. . . Immediately, one is drawn to her eyes, which glow like those of a Siamese cat in pitch blackness. They are almost hypnotic, as if you are standing along the beach on a bright day, and the sea's perpetual greenish blue waves are rolling in.
Next are her teeth, white as caps on the waves of the sea and perfectly aligned like rows of chairs in an auditorium. . . .

When he smiles, his thick nose points down like a perfect equilateral triangle, while the lines around his mouth bend as large parentheses.

The most distinguishing feature of his face that immediately intrigues most people is his magnificent, aquamarine eyes. The indigo outer circles melt into a rich and mesmerizing deep sea of glass. As his skin is so brown, these placid pools resemble small inlets of a turquoise Caribbean Sea surrounded by a dark tan beach.

GRANDPA

As we walked down the magnolia-lined dirt road, it was as if the sun was lighting a candle on every treetop. In one hand, Grandpa would carry the fishing poles, the tackle box, and the plastic bucket to keep the fish in. I'd carry the small wicker basket filled with peanut butter sandwiches, potato chips, oranges, and the brownies that Grandma would bake fresh that morning and sneak into our basket.

The sun would rise higher as we slowly walked down the road. When I looked up, it seemed to form a halo on Grandpa's cloud-white head. I remember how tiny my hand would feel in his. Those hands, warm and calloused, would gently cup over mine.

The road would take us to our secret place—a pond, hidden by Eucalyptus trees and hip-high jungle grass. Actually, it was more like a large mud puddle than a pond. I was never quite sure if there were any fish living there, but it never mattered. We'd hook the squiggly worms, cast our lines out into the muddy water, and wait.

When the sun had climbed to the top of the sky, we'd rest our fishing poles by the log at the edge of the pond and eat our lunch, if there was any left by then. Then Grandpa would lean back against his favorite tree, close his eyes, and tell me stories about his boyhood. I'd lie on my belly with my chin resting in my palms, listening to the music of his voice and watching his hands act out the lyrics. I'd try to picture him as a little boy and would giggle because Grandpa's head and Grandpa's hands looked so funny on the body of a six-year-old.

He taught me how to whistle "Yankee Doodle" and I remember how he clapped his hands when for the first time, I tied my own shoes. What a feat it was to whistle and to tie my own shoes.

I'd tell him how we could build a boat out of magnolia trees and sail around the world. How I'd have a farm just like Grandpa's when I grew up. How there would be at least ten ponies on that farm. There was no dream too trite to share with Grandpa. He'd hold them all in his hands, nourish them, caress them with his fingertips.

Always too soon, the sun would turn into a pink-orange haze and we'd know then that the day was over. We'd gather our things—the wicker basket, the fishing poles, the tackle box, and the empty plastic bucket. As we stalked back through the jungle grass, I'd feel for Grandpa's hand. We'd walk and whistle down the road to home.

Joe took $2.00 from his sister's bureau drawer and spent it on candy for himself. When his sister found her money missing, Joe said he saw her friend, Sara, take it.

MOTHER

She lives in a four-bedroom, two-and-a-half bath townhouse on the west side of a big city. Not many people enter her domain except for the maid who comes in once a week. Two college degrees hang framed on the wall above her bed, yet she doesn't work. Whenever they hang the least bit crooked, she immediately straightens them.

During the day, she busies herself with errands. She drives through the city in a sparkling clean, copper-colored Mark V that has a mere two thousand miles on the speedometer. Usually, her errands take her to the bank, or to the stockbroker's office, or to the grocery store. Her days are functional and for the most part cheerful; but when the sun departs, it takes with it the brightness of her day.

As darkness fills the house, she goes to the liquor cabinet, opens it, and takes out a fifth of Scotch. Within an hour, the contents of the bottle are nearly gone. She sits on a couch, with an ashtray very near, overflowing with cigarette butts. There isn't any light present in the room, yet a shadow is cast on the space by light from other rooms. The stereo plays low classical music. She hasn't had dinner yet. The bottle sitting on the table next to the cigarette butts is dinner.

As she puffs on a cigarette, she carefully caresses the gold medallion hanging around her neck and fondly thinks of Greece, the place where she purchased the treasure. Her long, slim fingers house many gold objects as do her arms. She rarely takes these prized possessions off, not even when she sleeps. She says she wants to be buried with them.

She sits almost stonelike on the orange couch. Long, slim legs are crossed, and her feet are bare, with toenails painted orange like her fingernails and lips. An untucked shirt reveals rolling flesh. All parts of the woman's body are long and thin except for her protruding middle which has nurtured four children and much alcohol. Her face is streaked with the make-up that she has forgotten to remove. Purplish bags lie beneath brown, fawnlike eyes, and framing them, her auburn hair is cropped short and caked with the remains of that morning's hair spray.

With midnight approaching, she gets up from the sanctuary to refill her glass once more and to empty the ashtray. As she makes her way to the kitchen, she stumbles and the five-foot seven-inch body tumbles to the ground. Cigarette butts scatter and the glass explodes into many tiny pieces. As she lies there, cheek pressed to the cold floor, tears fall out of the dark, glossy pools. She thinks of her children and her possessions and her life. Many minutes pass, and her thoughts turn to the future. As she drifts off into oblivion, she dreams of the new day and how bright it will be.

Last year Susan won every college math competition in the country. The kid can even remember major characters in novels she read years ago in junior high school. Once I saw her complete the Times crossword puzzle in thirty-two minutes flat!

Hands clenched to the chain wall of the tennis court, Sid watched him play with the sharp eye of a hawk, waiting for his prey to falter. Every day Sid studied the serve, stance, footwork, and swing of his rival. When the stalked player gained a point, Sid's brows slammed together; then, his teeth glistened when the player missed a ball and lost the point.

GRANDFATHER'S PIZZA PARLOR

It is 7:30 on Friday night and Grandfather's pizza parlor has reached its normal level of hysteria. Behind the counter the staff bustle back and forth like ants after their hill has been trampled. There are seven of them pounding dough, cutting vegetables, filling pitchers of beer, and bussing tables. Each is wearing the brown short-sleeved shirt which bears the name of the establishment in yellow writing. Occupying the larger tables in the center are three or four groups of men in their late twenties. Each group is dressed the same. These are softball teams; they've come here to eat a little pizza, drink a lot of beer, and make as much noise as they possibly can. Around the sides of the room sit the couples who've come for dinner. They are watching the people in the middle. Some of them are amused, but most appear somewhat annoyed.

Over in the far corner are the video games. Surrounding the machines are all types, ages, and sizes. At this hour the bunch consists mainly of kids in their early or mid teens. Each of the machines is humming, clicking, buzzing, or beeping away under the control of one while the others look on. At the top of each machine is a neat row of shiny silver quarters belonging to those awaiting their turn. This method of waiting in line is a courtesy among avid video fans, and a violation of this system is looked on with extreme distaste. A strong smell of cigarettes pervades this portion of the room. The pay phone in the corner rings frequently; each time it is answered by the nearest free hand, and the name of the person being called is shouted above the confusion. Some of the video players turn occasionally to glare in disgust at the noisy jocks who are pounding on their tables and yelling constantly. A collective groan arises each time one of them stumbles to the juke box and replays the same song over and over again.

SMALL TRAGEDY

He peeked through the window of the motor home and noticed the shredded sun visors, and the chewed-apart dashboard. The thought of vandalism tore through his mind until he noticed the door was still locked. When he inserted the key and turned it to the right, a shiny aluminum door flew open, and the stagnant smell of a dog kennel rushed out of the gap. The one plush brown carpet was covered with chunks of foam rubber that had escaped from the cushions on the couch. Sections of hard black plastic had been gnawed until only the metal frame shown on the steering wheel.

The room looked as if someone had a raging party. But there were no empty beer cans thrown in the corner or cigarette butts smoldering in the carpet. Only foam rubber, shredded cloth, and torn screens remained.

The battle for survival was over. There were no longer the sounds of cloth tearing or screens ripping, only the mournful whimpering of a young boy could be heard.

The silver door handle on the inside of this death chamber was gouged and scarred, but it didn't give way. Curtains which had hung so elegantly over the windows were torn in uneven strips on the floor.

The boy made his way past the veneer-covered dining table and headed toward the compact bathroom. A voice rose over the cries of the boy and told him not to go any further. The boy was oblivious to the warning and he entered the tan colored bathroom. In the fiberglass tub lay his dog, cold and finally at rest.

There is a place where crisp dresses hang in rainbow assortment. Below them are red and white saddle shoes and black Mary Janes, pushed up into a patent leather mound. In the corner a little girls sits and plays with her dolls, in silence.

A bright yellow bedroom, with a four-poster canopy bed and a handmade lace bedspread, stand in constant display. The little girl can only sleep there. Along with the four-poster canopy bed is a chestnut vanity that has a matching roll-top desk. Everything in the room matches perfectly.

Behind the closet door, the little girl has built her dolls a house out of old shoe boxes. On her hands and knees, she peeks her head into the box and tucks the tissue tightly around her sleeping dolls. The little girl giggles at the sound of her mother's voice calling her name. Her mother doesn't know about her new hiding place.

While she waits for her dolls to wake up, she fixes them a meal of blueberry jam and bread. She didn't have time to steal a knife from the kitchen, so she spreads the gooey jam with her finger. Her mother's footsteps pound down the hallway. The little girl pulls the closet door shut and tells her dolls to be very still if they happen to awake. She loses her balance while shutting the door, falls against it, and stains her dress with sticky jam. In darkness and in tears she hopes her mother won't find out about the only place she can play. Footsteps thump into her bedroom.

Quickly, the little girl hides the jam and bread underneath the hill of patent leather shoes. Silently, she leans down and kisses her sleeping dolls. Angrily, her mother looks under the four-poster canopy bed. The little girl's heart pounds against her dress that has been stained with jam and fear. She hears her mother's fingernails scratch the closet door open.

TRUCKERS' DELIGHT

It was gettin' on about three a.m. in Rosalee's Good Eats Cafe off I-80 some-wheres in Nevada with Tammy Wynette cranked up fierce on the jukebox and a couple o' lonesome Jakes filterin' Sanka black through their guts when I walked in all stiff-like from a long haul up from Virginie way. Now, these dudes were truckers clear through—I could tell by the way they sat on the swivel counter stools with cigarette melt-holes in the red vinyl cushions of 'em, with their legs all spread out—they was just drownin' their lonesome highway blues. They all had them trucker's wallets too; you know the kind with a chain attached? Yeah, those chains ain't no good iffen somebody gets it in mind to take your dough, but they sure lets you know in time to get out your Barlow an' let some blood. Sure gets 'em thinkin' when that blade flashes. Yeah, oh . . . sorry. Any-how, I come in all sore from haulin' straight through from Kansas an' kinda pissed-off on account of my log-book being way behind, so I ordered up some brews and kicked back at the bar, hopin' to get some re-laxs.

Then up outa nowhere comes this broad with a set of hallelujah headlights like Dolly Parton or Miss goddam America. Truth is, though, she was ugly. Mug face, you know? You woulda had to tie meat around her neck just to get the dogs to look at her, but I had some Bud in my brain.

"Hi there, Mister," she says. Yecch.

"Ma'am," I says, trying to keep my eyes offa them jugs she was totin'.

"What brings you to the Eats so early in this lonesome part of the country?"

Now I've seen all this before, and once you hear the ol' "lonesome parts," you better take off, or look out. So all I said was, "My Kenworth . . . Ma'am."

"Would y'all be planning on resting here a spell?"

"Not likely, Ma'am, see I gotta make my run, and I gotta get caught up on my schedule."

"Why surely you aren't in any hurry, oh, and my name is Bessie Mae. Bessie Mae Moocho."

"Billy Bob." I tipped my Stetson.

Now right about then I wanted to get about a hundred-thousand miles between me and ol' Bessie Mae Moocho, so I scused myself and made off for the pisser. It was a nasty ol' truck-stop john with them long wall fixtures with soggy cigarette butts in 'em and Skoal and Red Man spat on the wall and those urinal mints tos-sed in but as don't do any good. Cracked yellow tiles on the floor and a cracked mirror over the rusty sink looked like somebody sneezed on it. Real high-class head, though. Had music piped in from the juke and it was playing "Bony Fin-gers."

Then in comes this dude all sore-like, bloodshot eyes looking for me—gonna break my face for messin' with his dame. Just figures.

Don't ever try to reason with a drunk kicker—they just get meaner. He comes up to me with, "You been messin' with my sweet patootie!"

"Your *what?*"

"My gal." Now he's lookin' at me all squinty.

"Look fella, I'm just here to be off the road, I'm not lookin' for trouble and my own girl somewhere else. Better lookin' too."

"I saw you makin' eyes at her!"

"Now hold on one single minute, there guy. That broad rolled up to *me* and gave *me* the time of day."

That's when he swung. Connected too, right in the jaw. I guess I got mad and we went at it. At the end, I got in a couple of good ones and he fell into the stall and onto the turlet, out for the count, real natural-like. I came outa there quick, laid a five on the counter and made ready to split when a chair hits me right on the back. Sonovabitch!

I grabbed that sucker and rang his chimes and tapped his head real friendly-like up against the bar there. Then I ran him out the door into a post, and I was kinda upset, so I was fixin' to stomp on his miserable face with my Tony Lamas when, well, that's when you came up to me, officer.

A CASE OF MISTAKEN IDENTITY?

"Moonlight, wine, and roses" I croon along with the love song playing on the transistor radio. Going about my pre-date ablutions, milky bath, powder, make-up, and perfume, I like to talk to the cat and daydream. "This is the night that will change our lives, Kittycat. No more tuna for you, it will be trout on a silver platter from now on. No more thrift shop clothes for me. Goodbye one-room apartments, ratty furniture, and complaining neighbors. Goodbye bounced checks and GOODBYE to you, single life!"

Everything must go right tonight. I've been eyeing this beauty for months. Linen suits, gold watches, and Jerry Brown haircuts. Funny . . . somehow I just can't picture his face. . . .

I'll open the door. His long, lingering gaze will travel slowly up and down my svelte body, his will tense with longing; he'll bring me roses. A bundle of 'em. Probably twenty-four. He'll bring champagne which we'll drink in his Rolls out of long-stemmed crystal glasses. We'll go to a secluded French restaurant, the kind with candles and white linen tablecloths. We will hold hands and gaze with longing at each other over the tabletop. It will be so sweetly sad and romantic—just like a Harlequin romance!

I slide into silk stockings and my brand new, bought-for-this-occasion blue silk shantung dress. A touch more lipstick . . . and there's the doorbell!

I open the door slowly, majestically.

There he stands . . . frozen pizza in one hand, a six-pack of beer dangling from the other. "Didn't I tell you? The fights are on tonight. Ali against Norton. Where's the tube?"

Two dogs, who happen to be out for a walk in the park with their respective owners, get into a fray. The owners, who don't know each other, begin fiercely arguing over whose dog started the fight. Eventually, the argument evolves into a conversation and the two discover a common love for Mozart. They decide to go to a concert together that evening, without the dogs.

"When I was a senior in high school I performed in the school play, *Finian's Rainbow,* as one of the singing and dancing chorus girls. . ."

(The teacher continued the tale by describing particular tension-building details and events that preceded opening night. She described the costumes—hers was a floor-length evening gown that draped casually over one shoulder. Then she described the dance routines and a few other details that came to mind at the time.)

". . . .Eight o'clock arrived on opening night; all the seats in the theatre were filled, and pretty soon the show began. . . . . The first act was just fine. The actors were pleased with their performance and so was the audience."

"The curtain went up for the second act and it continued with the same intensity as the first. Toward the end of the second act the chorus did a dance that required the girls to leap-frog over the guys, and then the guys pulled the girls through their legs and up to a standing position for the second act finale. . . . I leap-frogged over my partner and he pulled me through and up, right on cue." (The storyteller demonstrated this leap frog routine with a student in the class.)

"However, my partner was standing on my dress, and as he pulled me up, the dress stayed down. I stood in the center of the stage facing 200 people in my underwear.

"When the show was over, the director asked if I'd be willing to do it again, tomorrow."

FAIRY FABLE

Once upon a time in Fairy Land there was a beautiful princess named Alexandra. Her flowing brown hair and soft shy smile, combined with soothing blue eyes and a 37C bust, made her the sight of the land. Here she stood in her five-foot seven-inch curved frame waiting, just waiting to be whisked away by some gallant prince. But alas, there were no gallant princes. Every gallant prince that she knew of was already reserved for a later story, or he was married, living in California and playing a lot of tennis. So Fairy Land was definitely short of gallant princes. There were a few princes, but nothing gallant.

The beautiful princess was heartbroken, all this virgin talent unused. Finally she got an idea! Fairy Princess Alexandra sent a telegram to other countries asking for gallant princes to come to Fairy Land and make an appointment for a personal interview. Well, they came by the thousands, by the hundreds of thousands! There were dragon slayers, war heroes, knights of bold, knights of gallant, princes of poet, even the King of Wall Street was there! Nowhere else could she find such a better selection of gallant men. After two years of interviewing she finally narrowed her selection down to two; Sir Henry Ganse of Tulipesville and Sire Walter Yuddle of the well-known Yuddle Lillies (a very renowned family).

Princess Alexandra was in a jam. First, no gallant princes and now too many gallants. "What's a beautiful and rich princess to do?"she uttered. Once again an idea came to her. She would have these two meet for the first time at a clearing in the forest. Dressed in full combat gear, a battle would be fought to the death. Left in the clearing would be the princess' vast fortune and a single horse enabling the winner to ride out a rich gallant hero, and whisk the beautiful princess off her feet.

Battle day was set and the gallant princes trained very hard. The day came. The two tramped into the thick forest and met. They eyed the priceless treasure and then each other behind walls of steel. With swords drawn the battle began; grunting and yelling and blows of steel could be heard throughout the land. Sir Ganse was struck in the head by a swift blow; he then crashed to the ground. All the metal encaging his body acted as a weighted death trap. Sir Ganse lay on the ground—helpless, knowing that death was about to conquer him. Sire Yuddle, standing over him with the heavy sword raised above his head said, "You know this must be." The reply was a courageous, "Yes, but before I die remove thy mask to let me see better the victor." This Sire Yuddle could not refuse. Taking off his mask, he then reached down and removed Sir Ganse's helmet. The two had never seen another perfect man before. Handsome, muscular, tall, and most important of all gallant, they were without a doubt, the cream of all the countries. Silent, the two stared—and stared. They were in love! How could Yuddle possibly kill someone he loved as much as himself! The two, hand in hand, picked up the vast riches and mounted the horse, leaving the beautiful Fairy Princess Alexandra waiting to be whisked away.

About a year later the Princess received a candy-gram from her two gallant men thanking her for the riches (most of her vast riches anyway) and for her part in getting them together.

As of this date, the beautiful Fairy Princess has sagged a little, but is still a sight to see. As for Sire Henry and Sire Walter, they are now a gallant company, "Ganse and Yuddle," abbreviated G-A-Y and are living in California, working hard for gay rights and playing a lot of tennis.

Moral of the Story: It is sometimes hard to distinguish gallant men from fairy princes.

GRATITUDE AND SPAGHETTI

The room is dark except for the dim light of the table lamp beside me. I sit in the deep, cushioned armchair, waiting for him to come home. I have always waited. Again I look around the small, neat house. The coffee table has been polished well. The long white couch has not a speck of dust on it. The old wooden floor has lost its shine but it is clean. Every corner, every crack has been carefully swept. All the windows have been washed twice today. I can see my reflection through the glass. No, the windows could not be cleaner. He likes our house to be neat and clean. It has always been neat and clean.

I hear the old grandfather clock chime in the next room. It is six o'clock. I wait and listen. Soon, I hear the sound of his shoes clicking against the cement pathway to our door. I count the footsteps, six of them altogether, then I push myself up from the chair and try to smooth the fine wrinkles of my dress. It is his favorite dress. There are two shuffles against the bristly welcome mat, silence, then the screen door opens and shuts with a metal clang. A shadow fills the doorway and moves into the darkened light. He is home.

I go to him and take his hat and coat. He bends down to kiss my cheek. He is a tall man, almost six foot six, with a lean but muscular build. His hair is thick and black and just slightly touched with grey. He is very handsome. He has always been handsome.

I hang the hat and coat in the closet and go to the kitchen. When I return he is seated at the far end of the supper table, reading the evening paper. On the table there are two porcelain coffee cups and a large bottle of Chianti. In the center there is a tiny glass vase with one red rose which I picked from our garden this morning.

I place a plate of steaming spaghetti in front of him and spoon out a mound of thick, lumpy red sauce. He puts down the paper and tastes the spaghetti. He looks up at me as he chews and smiles. I pour some of the dark Chianti into his cup and place it before him. Again he tastes, again he smiles. Everything is just right. He is pleased.

I sit down at the other end of the table and quickly eat my spaghetti. When I finish, I drink my Chianti and watch him over the rim of my cup. He puts a large forkful of spaghetti in his mouth and slowly chews. Then he places the fork down, wipes his lips with a napkin and takes a sip of Chianti. I love to watch him eat for he savors each bite, first with his eyes and then with his mouth. I pour Chianti in my cup and wait.

He pushes the empty plate aside, wipes his lips again and places the soiled napkin on the table. I quickly get up and shuffle back to the kitchen and bring out the cake I have baked for him. It is chocolate, his favorite. Three layers of rich, creamy chocolate cake. He smiles but shakes his head and rises from the table. He comes to me and again I point to the cake. He pats my arm and brushes a kiss to thank me. Yes, he has always thanked me.

I get up from the table and carry the dirty dishes to the kitchen. Then I hear the screen door cry open and shut again. I listen to the six hollow footsteps on the pavement and then, once more there is silence. I wash each dish carefully by hand and put them neatly away in the cupboard. I go back to the dining room to get the cake and carry it back to the kitchen. Such a beautiful cake. It will spoil if no one eats it. I take a clean knife from the drawer and slice a large piece for myself. As I eat my cake, I lean on the counter and stare at my reflection in the newly cleaned windows. I am old and fat.

THE FIRST TIME

I was walking down the hall to my history class when I saw it. That crooked metallic smile. I pretended not to notice, turned quickly around, and headed in the other direction.

"Hey, Julie!"

"Oh Alex, hi."

"You haven't forgotten about this afternoon, have you?"

"This afternoon? Oh yeah, this afternoon. Listen Alex, I . . . ."

"You're chickening out huh?"

"No. No, I'll be there."

"Good."

"Alex?"

"Yeah?"

"Do you think we should?"

"Sure, you'll really like it."

"But what if someone sees us?"

"Stop worrying. Just remember—behind the Texaco station in the grove at 3:15."

It was impossible to concentrate through my last two classes. "Sure, you'll really like it," he had said. Most of the girls in my class had tried it and liked it. I hated being the odd-ball, the weirdo.

When the 3:00 bell rang, I walked slowly down the hall to the bathroom. I carefully combed out an imaginary tangle in my hair and stared in the mirror. It was now or never.

I waited in the grove, watching the red and black Texaco sign spin around and around. Maybe he wasn't coming. Maybe he forgot.

"Are you ready?" I saw the crooked smile again as he stepped out around the station.

"Sure. . . . Alex?"

"Yeah?"

"I—uh—I've never done this before."

"You're joking."

"No. Will it hurt?"

"Nah. I'll be careful."

"I don't know, I. . ." He reached out to hug me. I felt his clammy hands grip my bare arms. And then his spongy lips were on mine. He had lied— it did hurt. His braces scratched my lips. Thank God he couldn't get his tongue through the rubber bands on his braces. Thank God I didn't have braces or we might have been stuck there forever.

"Let's go sit down over there."

"Let's just go, Alex."

"What's the matter, didn't you like it?"

"Loved it, but let's not overdo it."

"O.K., I'll see you tomorrow, same place, same time."

"Alex, I. . ."

"See ya." He started walking off toward the station, then turned around so I could see his crooked metallic smile one more time.

NO SMOKING, PLEASE

CHARACTERS: **Older Woman**—a middle-aged non-smoker
Woman—a smoker in her mid-twenties
Friend—a woman who is eating with the Woman in the restaurant
Young Woman—a non-smoker in her early twenties
Two Men—Neither has any lines of script. One accompanies the Older Woman and the other accompanies the Young Woman.

SETTING: The play is set in a small restaurant at lunchtime. The Woman and her friend are seated at a table. They have finished their meal and are talking over coffee. One of the women reaches into her purse and pulls out a pack of cigarettes. She takes one out and lights it with a gold lighter. The Older Woman, sitting at a nearby table with her husband, turns to the two women.

Older Woman: Excuse me, but do you think you could extinguish your cigarette? It really irritates me while I'm eating.

Woman: *(turning to the older woman)* Oh, I'm sorry. *(She puts her cigarette out in the ashtray, then looks at her friend curiously, then back to the older woman.)* Wait a minute. Isn't this the smoking section?

Older Woman: Yes, it is, but it's the only seat we could get. The non-smoking section is full.

Woman: Well, the smoking section is for people who want to smoke. You should have waited for an available table in the other section. *(She takes out another cigarette and lights it.)*

Older Woman: Please put your cigarette out. It really bothers me.

Woman: I enjoy having a cigarette after a meal. I have the right to smoke in this section of the restaurant. If it bothers you, move.

Friend: Joan, maybe we should go if it bothers these people.

Woman: *(voice raises)* No. I'm sick and tired of all this nonsense about smoking. They should have known people would smoke in this section. Time after time, I'm asked to put out my cigarette. I have the right here—they don't. *(She blows smoke in their direction.)*

Older Woman: *(fanning the smoke with irritation)* We would have waited for another table, but we have to be somewhere in a half an hour, and we didn't have time to wait. *(to husband)* It's just the principle of the whole thing. She can't even wait to smoke until she gets outside. Some people just have no will power. Oh, Harold, I feel sick. I can't even finish my meal.

Woman: Okay, then leave. You aren't making me feel guilty. *(She looks directly at the older woman.)* That is what you are trying to do, isn't it?

Older Woman: I just thought you could be considerate enough to wait until we had left or until you were outside. I guess you like being obstinate and rude.

Woman: *(She puts out her cigarette, takes out another and lights it.)* I feel you are the one being rude. It's the principle of the matter. I have the right to smoke here and you are violating my right by asking me not to smoke.

Older Woman: Oh, this is ridiculous.

Woman: Isn't it.

Older Woman: Let's go, Harold. *(They get up.)*

Woman: Toodles. *(As they pass, she blows smoke in the older woman's direction. The older woman glares and storms past.)*

Friend: Joan, don't you think you were overdoing it a little?

Woman: Hell no. I do have the right to smoke here. I swear it's a never-ending battle with all this smoking business, and I'm sick of being so polite all the time. I have just as much right to smoke as they have to tell me not to. *(A waitress seats a young couple next to them. Joan takes a puff of her cigarette and blows out the smoke.)*

Young Woman: Excuse me, but do you think you could put out your cigarette? I'm allergic to smoke. . . .

Lights fade . . . Curtain closes. . .

Sometimes
    When it's raining
    The sun still shines
    In your eyes
        And wishes
          Slide down rainbows
Releasing thoughts
Of time,
When happiness
Was walking through
Mud puddles.

I spit out anger
Like watermelon seeds
A juicy mouthful stored—
Then blasted rapid fire.
When the battle is finished
I wait a long while
For the next childish feast.

Cool calm breezes rustle
Through hanging trees, burdened
With polluted sorrows
Carelessly created.

RISING IN THE MORNING

Suddenly alerted—mind blinks, eyes flutter, jump up. . .
Like toast pops and abruptly cools, as it
    leaves the warm place into a fast-food world

Anger broods inside
Caged,
Like a trained wild beast
That sits within
When the door is
Open.

THE KEYBOARD

Over its rectangular back
lie rows of shiny scales
with letters.

Bright yellow words on the chalkboard
whisper
to foul phrases that
shriek
from the wall outside.

Computer mirror at my desk
Who writes better than the rest?

The smell of a burning 100 watt bulb
Is mildly chemical
As the smell of a cellophane-wrapped pie
Is mildly apple.

Holds together thoughts of brilliant men
A simple paper clip.

That first kiss;
A thousand avenues open.

California Fall
Like a birthday child waiting
For presents of rain drops.

My daughter is like a door that says
"Private Do Not Enter"
My soul is closed
To you.

Too much to do
Urgent deadlines to meet.
I feel
Like a blender whirling
Still ridiculously twirling
Though the substance has
Clogged.

A love affair is like a piece of chocolate
So sweet, yet quite
Unnecessary.

As I ate the strawberries I felt a
Shimmering tingle go down to my toes.
They were rich   red   fat   and juicy
Squishing through my teeth
Making my glands water
And slowly
        sliding
            down
                to my
                    stomach.

Bored
Sipping coffee
Sucking candies
'Till I'm bloating
Mad.

LAST MINUTE OF CLASS

Tense bodies edge forward
Waiting for teacher's nod.

WHEAT HEADS

Clusters of fluffy wheat heads—
Coquettes—
toss yellow locks
in the morning breeze.
But
soon they sit still and
bake brown by a desert sun.
A sudden dust storm
ages blonde curls with gray dust.
And
terrified, they cling
to cracked soil while
wind blasts threaten to uproot them.

HOUSEWIVES

Every morning
I wheel up the long avenue of
palms and sprinklers and housewives
in bandanas and gardening gloves.
They never once look
up from their weeds.

They live in the walls
of small houses, sealed in
dust-free carpets.

Their hearts vacuumed,
dreams thrown out with the garbage,
their eyes are as empty
as sucked eggs.

I watch them,
line by line, like clothes
strung out in winter.
Then I go home
and chase rainbows.

SOUVENIR

Bent iron and twisted steel
grow like a vine
around the telephone pole
as thousands of sparkling glass diamonds
peer wickedly
from the calloused pavement.

People, crowding close
to see the blood,
make their awkward, foolish comments,
push nearer to see
the most interesting thing in life—
Death.

The burnt rubber tires askew on their axles
like dilated eyes, spin
unfocused.
Plush leather seats are streaked with red—
lips kiss the dashboard.

A small boy pushes out from the crowd
and looks at the blond hair
tangled in the jagged window.
He stops to pick up a splinter of glass—
as a souvenir.

PAST AND FUTURE LAWS FOR MINORS

Crimes such as vandalism, shoplifting, reckless or drunken driving, and drug use, are committed every day by people of all ages. The punishments given for these offenses depends on the age of the lawbreaker and the severity of the crime. Punishments for offenders under 18 years of age is now typically so lenient that the convicted teenager does not hesitate to repeat the crime.

In California, a proposal has recently been drawn up to deal with young lawbreakers. The underlying assumption of the proposal is that if minors feel they can get away with committing petty crimes, they will advance to more severe and serious offenses as they get older. The following paragraphs present the current laws for minors and the new, recommended laws for minors, concerning acts of vandalism, shoplifting, drug use, and reckless or drunken driving.

Ripped-up lawns, spray paint on the sidewalks, broken windows, and egged fences are just a few ways that people vandalize public or private property. In the current laws, vandals are given a choice of punishment: they must repair the damage, pay to have it repaired, or be assigned to community service. Doing community service work involves working up to thirty hours in activities such as caring for the elderly, cleaning the streets, and working in the police station.

The new proposal forces vandals under 18 to either pay or fix the damage. If the minor is not capable of personally making repairs, he must supply the money that is necessary to have the repairs done professionally. If the offender cannot supply the money, his/her parents will be held responsible. The vandal will also be assigned up to forty hours of community service work. This proposal not only provides definite punishment, it also involves the vandal's family, who should be fully aware of the crime their child has committed.

The current law states that shoplifters over 18 are automatically fined and/or taken to jail. However, the punishment for a minor who is caught shoplifting depends on the police, the parents, and the store involved. Shoplifters' parents are called right away, but many times the punishment ends there. The police who are called into the store to handle the situation can decide whether the minor needs to be taken to court. The parents also help decide on the punishment. If they insist that their child has never had any problems in the past, and that they will be able to straighten everything out themselves, the police will typically let the child go, possibly with community work assigned. If the parents refuse to take responsibility and if the child has already been involved in other crimes, the police can take the child to Hillcrest, a temporary juvenile jail that keeps and counsels lawbreakers under 18. The latter of these punishments is very rare. Most often, the store drops the charges and the shoplifter walks out of the store feeling a bit nervous, but frequently not nervous enough to refrain from trying again.

The new proposal for shoplifters under 18 warrants that every criminal be sentenced to a specific type of punishment. The first offense will result in thirty to forty hours of community work. The second offense results in double the amount of community work and the shoplifter is put on probation for three months. The third offense will automatically put the minor in Hillcrest for as many as thirty days, regardless of the value of the stolen object.

The use of illegal drugs is fairly common among teenagers. According to today's law, it is impossible to lock up a person of any age for the possession of marijuana. If caught with this drug, the minor is usually put on probation and/or assigned up to thirty hours of community service. If the minor does not fulfill this obligation, he/she still cannot be put in jail. However, the possession of any other narcotics causes immediate arrest. Possession of cocaine, for example, means three to four years of imprisonment at Camp Glenwood, a ranch that has a special school for problem children. The ratio of students to teacher is 15:1, thus giving the lawbreakers the extra attention they normally don't receive in public school.

The new proposal for lawbreakers under 18, who are caught with any type of narcotics is as follows: the offender must attend a weekly drug abuse class, is put on probation, and must attend special counseling sessions at Glenwood every weekend for one year. A second arrest means the offender will be sentenced to four years at Glenwood.

Reckless driving is a major cause of automobile accidents, but the punishment does not give the driver any reason to stop speeding or driving through flashing red lights at 2:00 in the morning, for example. Depending on the mood of the police officer present, a ticket may be given, the driver may be taken to jail, or just a simple warning may be issued. If the reckless driver injures a pedestrian, the driver is taken to jail, the parents are called in, and a date is set for a court appearance.

The new proposal for dealing with reckless drivers suggests that these lawbreakers be automatically sentenced to a three-month probation with one full weekend of traffic school. They will also be fined $50 and receive a ticket that will go on his/her driving record. If a reckless driver injures another person, the driver will lose his/her license for six months and will spend two weeks at Hillcrest.

Reckless driving is often caused by alcoholic beverages. When a minor is pulled over and accused of driving "under the influence," the police officer can make an arrest, or just extend a warning. If arrested, the minor is taken to juvenile court and assigned community service and alcohol abuse counseling. The driver's license is often suspended, although if a drunken driver is caught with an already suspended license, he/she can be sentenced up to six months at Glenwood.

The major change in the new proposal for drunken driving insures that every minor who is pulled over is brought to court. The police will not have the choice of deciding whether or not to arrest the suspect. If proven guilty, the driver will have to attend driving and alcohol abuse classes. When a drunk driver injures another person, he/she must pay for the damage, plus pay a fine of up to $1,000. The driver's license will be suspended for up to a year and he/she must attend alcohol abuse classes.

These new proposed laws are designed to make potential offenders think at least twice before going ahead with an unlawful act. Many of the current laws do not put enough pressure on soon-to-be criminals. A warning, or telephone call to parents is not enough. The specific punishments outlined in the proposed laws will hopefully stop many minors from committing any sort of crime now, or ever.

Cross-country skiing and downhill skiing are two winter sports that are extremely popular with Americans. However, just because they both involve skis and poles worn by people who travel across snow-covered terrain, it doesn't mean they are the same. [*thesis statement:*] In fact, they are strikingly different.

[*Thesis statement:*] There's a social war going on at Greendale High School between the downhill skiers and the cross-country enthusiasts. Every day at lunch, from November 'til March, the two armies sit at opposite ends of the cafeteria, firing comments about the virtues of their preferred sport, or the deficiencies of the other.

After six months of surviving in the scorching flatlands of southern Malawi, I tried to recall my original reasons for joining the Peace Corps.

If when you say whiskey you mean the devil's brew, the poison scourge, the bloody monster, that defiles innocence, dethrones reason, destroys the home, creates misery and poverty, yea, literally takes the bread from the mouths of little children; if you mean the evil drink that topples the Christian man and woman from the pinnacle of righteous, gracious living into the bottomless pit of degradation and despair, and shame, and helplessness, and hopelessness, then certainly I am against it.

But if when you say whiskey you mean the oil of conversation, the philosophic wine, the ale that puts a song in their hearts and laughter on their lips, and the warm glow of contentment in their eyes; if you mean Christmas cheer; if you mean the stimulating drink that puts the spring into the old gentleman's step on a frosty crispy morning; if you mean the drink which enables a man to magnify his joy, and his happiness, and to forget, if only for a little while, life's great tragedies, and heartaches, and sorrows; if you mean that drink, the sale of which pours into our treasuries untold millions of dollars, which are used to provide tender care for our little crippled children, our blind, our deaf, our dumb, our pitiful aged and infirm; to build highways and hospitals and schools, then certainly I am for it.

This is my stand, I will not retreat from it. I will not compromise.*

A PROPOSED HIGH SCHOOL EDUCATIONAL SYSTEM

When you think about the most memorable times of your life, chances are you'll remember your high school years. After all, during that time you may have met some lifelong friends, enemies, sweethearts, and possibly your spouse. You may have enjoyed brief fame as a basketball player, President of the Student Council, or Junior Prom Queen. The recollections of the school dances, football games, and other events further enhance these memories. But when you come right down to it, did you learn anything during your four-year stay at Metropolis High? Well, if you're not too sure whether you did or not, you might be in favor of a more academically oriented high school experience for your children. The paragraphs that follow propose a new high school eductional system that will both teach kids academics and enable them to enjoy their time at school.

As we have all heard, many of the high school systems are now beginning to revert back to emphasizing the 3 R's—reading, 'riting, and 'rithmetic. This is due to major studies done a few years ago that showed many college freshmen are deficient in basic skills.

The proposed required classes for a new high school system would put a great deal of emphasis on these needed skills. It would include a minimum of four years of English, which includes essay writing, world literature, spelling and grammar, business writing, and speech. The proposed system emphasizes the importance of being able to express oneself verbally as well as on paper; these required English skills are designed to help sutdents learn to communicate better with peers in the working world. Math is also emphasized in the new system. Students will be required to take two and a half years of mathematics. A half year of basic math, a half year of business math, and the other year and a half of upper division math (e.g. Algebra, Geometry, Trigonometry). This will help the student later in life when he/she will be required to fill out tax forms, balance checkbooks, etc. History is also of prime concern in the new system. Students will have to take three years of history. This includes one year of U.S. History, one year of state and local history, half a year of U.S. Government, and half a year of Psychology. Computer Science is also of prime concern. Since computers are now being widely used by businesses and individuals, we feel that there should be a class to teach the basics of computing. Upper division courses would also be offered. Students should take a minimum of two years of Science, including one year of Introductory Biology and the other year in an upper division class like Biology II, Chemistry, Physics, or Computer Science.

The last required course is Physical Education. Students would take two years of P.E., or one year, if he/she participates in a competitive sport such as football, baseball, tennis, or swimming. Students need to be educated physically, of course, but not to the extent that they have been recently. The proposed system does not discourage physical fitness by any means, but it does put a greater emphasis on academics.

The grading system in the proposed high school system will set "C" as the passing grade for all courses. However, there will be various levels of most courses offered, so that students will be able to enroll in the courses that suit them best. There will be Math, English, and Science "lab times" so that students can obtain extra help whenever they need it. The labs will be run by college students who are majoring in the subject they will be tutoring. Tutoring by the subject teachers will also be available when the students request it.

The requirements for graduation are basically that all the mandatory courses must be passed with a grade of "C" or better. Also, students must pass competency tests in reading, writing, and mathematics before graduation. The tests will by no means be easy; therefore, classes to help students pass these tests will also be available.

Class size is another issue addressed in this proposal. No class may exceed twenty-five students. When necessary, another section of the class will be added to accommodate the overflow. Every required class will also have lab sessions for students to attend in order to get extra help. The labs will be open one hour before school and two hours after school. The school will make every effort to insure that students get the help they need.

Other regulations include a strict set of rules designed to maintain order in the school at all times. The purpose is to keep kids out of trouble, while giving them all fair treatment. The length of the school day will be seven hours, from 8:00 to 3:00. The classes will be 55 minutes long, with a ten-minute passing time between classes. A fifteen-minute break will be held between second and third period and lunch will be one hour long. Freshmen, sophomores, and juniors will be required to take six periods, while the seniors, who are holding jobs or taking classes at a community college, will be required to take two classes. Seniors who hold jobs will also be required to take a Work Experience class. The campus will be open during lunch and closed at other times of the day.

Attendance is also an important element of this proposal. Students are allowed two tardies per class during a semester. Every two tardies after that will result in the reduction of the student's grade by half a grade. However, the tardies may be worked off by doing chores around the school (e.g., painting, clean-up work, etc.). Cutting a class will be considered equal to two tardies. If a student is caught loitering off campus, two hours of work will be issued to the student and a cut will also be recorded in the teacher's records. When students are sick or otherwise absent with a parent's permission, the student must bring a note from a parent within two days, or the absence will be recorded as a cut. The school will enforce these rules without exception.

Two final regulations that pertain directly to students are a dress code and rules about the possession of illegal drugs. No shorts (mid-thigh) will be allowed at school and no other revealing attire will be tolerated. Hair length will be left up to the students' discretion. No illegal drugs are allowed on campus; if any student is caught possessing illegal drugs, he/she will be immediately suspended from school. The same rules apply for weapons. The school will enforce these rules without exception.

All teachers that are hired after this new system is adopted, will be certified by the state and will have majored in the subject they are assigned to teach. Teachers will have to be on campus from 7:30 to 3:30 every school day, except on the days when they are scheduled to be in the lab—on those days they will be at school longer. Teachers will have to submit weekly attendance records, as well as reports of the curriculum material covered and the assignments given during the week. These will be filed in the administration office. One of the anticipated benefits of this procedure is that students who have been absent and need to catch up on past lessons and assignments, can get this information for all their classes at the office.

This proposed high school educational system is one that we could adopt without huge expense to the taxpayers—no new buildings or expensive equipment are being proposed, only a new way of operating the already existing facility. The proposed system is tougher and stricter than the present one because it stresses academics more and maintains a higher degree of discipline. But after all, high school is supposed to be primarily a place to learn academics—having a good time is something that will happen quite naturally in the process.

STUDIO UNION 54

Last night I was sitting in my room thinking about the Student Union. This is not something I do all the time, but I began falling asleep while I thought about it. Admit it, "Let's go and hang out at the Student Union for a while," is seldom heard at Marlow. There must be a reason for this, and I think I know why.

Basically, the Student Union needs *pizazz*. It really has no excitement or appeal; my apologies to the architect and the decorator (if there was one). Right now there are very few uses for the Student Union, and I, for one, go over there only when necessary.

Now, when I say pizazz, I don't mean turning it into Studio Union 54. God, can you imagine that? Pulsating lights, Donna Summer moaning, and big lines at the door with a bouncer turning away people because "They just wouldn't fit in with the crowd?" For some reason, I wouldn't want to see that.

The Student Union needs good, good, good, music, and a nice atmosphere. Now I actually feel guilty when I buy something at the Snack Bar because it's exacly the same as the cafeteria food I'm already paying for. Wouldn't it be great for once to be able to order a really good avocado sandwich? I wouldn't feel a bit guilty about that. There should be a snack bar with a varied menu of "homemade" food. Let's hear it for hot pastrami and a beer.

Music, if nothing else, draws people together and the Student Union has lots of room for it. I can see the headlines of the Marlow Press now. . . "The Rolling Stones Appear at the Student Union—One Night Only." Hey, come on, don't be a skeptic—you never know what can happen.

I am constantly overhearing people say, "I wish there were a place where I could go to meet people and just sit and talk." The Student Union could be the answer, if it were designed correctly. Pinball machines, interesting guest speakers, a juke box, backgammon tournaments, performances by Marlow musicians, and countless other ideas could be put into use for the betterment of the Student Union. Another thing that should be changed is that dull name: Student Union. It conjures up boring thoughts right away. But for now, let's just think of ways to fix it up.

Some day, I hope one will be able to hear a group of people driving down Main Street saying, "Oh, wow, I wish I went to Marlow College. They've got the most terrific student union—every other weekend they host a band concert and informal dance."

Oh hell, I guess I'll go and get an Eskimo Pie before I go to sleep.

SPORTS ARE NOT EVERYTHING

Once again the Olympic Games are about to take place, and once again political controversy is prevalent. The Olympics only represent one example of how sports affect everything and everyone. We have all been led to believe that sports, either through participating or spectating, are not only healthy, but also a positive force in our society.

Sports have provided recognition for Blacks, whose exposure through media has speeded up integration in this country (or so we are told). But for every Black sports hero, like O.J. Simpson, Kareem Abdul-Jabbar, or Reggie Jackson, there are thousands, and maybe millions, of Black youngsters who devoted their energies to sports when they should have been directed toward careers in other areas. Because the success of several athletes was publicized, many more kids spend their time on the playground until it was too late for them to qualify for anything above marginal work.

Our society has distorted sports to the point where the winner is more important than the game. Athletics are structured around certain values, such as hard work, honesty, and extreme dedication—these are the steps to success. Obviously, these values are not limited to the sports realm exclusively, for they are also prevalent in our everyday dosage of America's way of life. Unfortunately, these values are but a definition of manhood, and not necessarily a proven solution to the task of being successful.

A New York sportswriter summed it aptly when he stated: "Here in America, sports' insidious power is imposed upon athletics by the banks that decide which arenas and recreational facilities shall be built, by the television networks that decide which sports shall be sponsored and viewed, by the press that decides which individuals and teams shall be celebrated, by the municipal governments, which have, through favorable tax rulings and exemptions from law, allowed sports entertainment to grow until it has become the most influential form of mass culture in America."

JOHNNY WILL LEARN

First, Johnny's mother told him enthusiastically, "You're going to go to school today!"

"Why?" Johnny asked quite curiously.

"So you can meet lots of people and make lots of friends and have lots of fun," she answered, straightening her dress that looked rather like the kind the First Lady liked to wear.

"Why?"

"So you can get an education. And I wish you wouldn't say 'why' all the time, Johnny." Johnny was always asking why, and it annoyed everyone. Johnny's mother had to admit that although she loved Johnny very much, he was becoming a bit of a nuisance, and she would be glad to have him out of the house while school was in session. "Besides, it's only for a few hours a day," she thought.

"What's education?" Johnny asked. She didn't know the answer, so she said, "You'll get to learn about arithmetic and—"

"What's arith . . . arith—"

"—and the alphabet, and—"

"But I already know the alphabet. A, B, C, D, E, F . . ."

"Johnny, please!" She rolled her eyes and sighed. Johnny looked down at his red and white canvas tennis shoes. "It's very good that you already know the alphabet, because now school won't be as hard for you. Don't worry, you're going to like school. I promise."

Later, when Johnny saw the ugly buildings and all the crying children and the frowning parents, he said, "Mommy, I don't like school."

"Nonsense!" she said abruptly. "You're *going* to like it. You'll see."

Holding Johnny by the hand, his mother marched him up to the little beige bungalow that said KINDERGARTEN on a piece of construction paper taped to the door. A name tag on a woman's dress said, "Virginia Brooks, Kindergarten." The woman's hair looked like the First Lady's.

"Hello, Mrs. Brooks," Johnny's mother said. "I'm Loretta Jenkins."

"How do you do, Mrs. Jenkins. And, oh, this must be John."

"Johnny!" the little boy blurted out. A bit embarrassed by her son's correction, the boy's mother smiled at the teacher and said, "Johnny, say 'how do you do,' to Mrs. Brooks."

"How do you do, Mrs. Books."

"My name is Mrs. Brooks, John, and it's very nice to meet you. I'm going to be your teacher."

"My name's Johnny," the boy said. "are you my new mommy?"

Johnny did not want his mommy to leave him there, and he told her so, but she left him anyway. Still, he wasn't as upset as some of the children. He had come to trust his mommy, even if he did not know exactly what a mommy was.

Besides, when he looked around the classroom, he liked what he saw. He saw colorful building blocks and lots of paints and "millions and millions" of crayons. He liked to draw with crayons and he had never seen so many before. On the wall of the classroom were several crayon drawings that he knew had been drawn by children. He wondered if he would get to draw with crayons. He looked around for some paper to draw on, but something caught his eye. There in front of him was a slate with his name on it: "John Jenkins." Best of all, the slate was resting on a chair, a chair that Johnny thought was the most beautiful chair he had ever seen, for this was the first chair Johnny had ever seen that was just his size!

He began to sit down in the chair when something else commanded his attention. On one wall, above the chalkboard, was written the alphabet on a long piece of paper. Johnny recognized all the upper-case letters; he even knew how to write them. But he did not recognize the lower-case ones. Just as he thought he would use the slate with his name on it to try to copy the letters he didn't know, the teacher called out to him, "John, pick up the slate in front of you and sit down in the chair."

He wondered if he had done something wrong. The woman's voice, to Johnny, seemed a bit mean, but he did what she told him. He felt embarrassed. It hadn't occurred to him that, because all the other boys and girls were sitting down, he should sit down too. He would remember to follow them from now on.

The teacher had each of the children tell his name to the class, and, covering their slates with a sheet of paper, asked if they could write their names. Almost all of them could, including Johnny.

For the next fifteen minutes, the teacher had them play with the building blocks. Then she made them stop. Then she had them paint for half an hour. Then she made them stop. Then she told them it was recess. "Time for milk and cookies!" she announced with fake enthusiasm.

She gave everyone two cookies and a tiny carton of milk. Johnny was not hungry, and he told her so, but she made him eat the cookies and drink the milk anyway. "They're good for you!" she said.

After recess, the teacher told the class that it was "nap time." She had the boys in the class stack the little chairs and cover most of the floor with the padded, brown mats they were to sleep on. Johnny wasn't tired, and he wanted to tell her so, but he did not want to be embarrassed again, so, following the rest of the class, he lay down and closed his eyes, pretending to be asleep.

After the fifteen minutes, the teacher made them put the mats away and get their chairs, and for twenty minutes she had them draw with crayons. Then she made them stop. Then she had them copy the alphabet on their slates. Then began fifteen or twenty years of repeat-after-me's.

The next year Johnny would learn about grades. The year after that he would learn how to take an exam. Then he would learn about cheating. Then he would learn about truancy. Then he would learn about drugs. Then he would learn about sex. Then he would learn about college. Then he would learn about Skinner.

CO-ED HOUSING AT LAST!

The Board of Trustees approved a proposal March 12 for co-ed housing options to be offered in the fall. The plan will put men in suites of Howell and Mitchell halls and women in a wing of Collins Hall, a floor of Krause Hall, and eventually one side of Peterson Hall.

Although the Trustees and Administration have long disapproved of the idea, the proposal went through because, said President Robert Riley, "Marlow is finally ready for it."

A year ago, a group of students, headed by now-alumna Sandra Atkins, drew up an extensive plan for the establishment of co-ed housing at Marlow College. The proposal included a campus poll which showed that an overwhelming majority of students were in favor of co-ed options.

According to the sponsor of the final proposal, Dean of Students, Richard Thompson, "A great deal of the information in the proposal that went to the Trustees was taken from Sandra's study, and the most persuasive part of the proposal was the fact that students had made such a good case." The Dean added that the idea did not become a reality years ago probably because the Trustees "were not convinced that students were serious about the change."

In the fall, students may still elect to live in a single-sex dorm, and participation in the co-ed program will be based on selectivity in the screening of student co-ed housing applicants.

President Riley stated: "I think the co-ed housing option will provide a more serious academic environment."

WOMEN'S VOLLEYBALL BEGINS

"We have a lot of young and inexperienced players, some of which have never played on a varsity team before. But they really do have a desire to play and they've improved 100 percent since the beginning," said the Assistant Coach for the women's volleyball team, Susan Hill. There are thirteen women on the team, all trying to do their best.

Sue is a physical education major and her position as Assistant Coach gives her the practical experience she needs for certification. She remarked, "I really like working with Judy (the head coach) and the girls on the team." Sue was also As-

VANCE'S UPHILL CLIMB

"It helps my studying, it puts me in a disciplined mood, it gives me lots of exercise, and most importantly, I enjoy it," said Marlow freshman Vance Moorley. Vance is a bike racer; he has ridden in approximately twenty races and leads a regular training schedule, riding an average of 275 miles per week.

Vance started riding only two years ago; three months later he was riding his first race. "Someday I'd like to take it as far as I can. In three years I want to ride the Red Zinger, where the top Olympic racers are invited. It'll take me six years before I should reach my peak. I'd like to try to make it to the 1988 Olympics, if possible."

As an Interim project . . . well, you guessed it . . . he rode. He kept a regular schedule for training; during the weekdays he rode about thirty to forty miles a day, and on Sundays he rode eighty miles, usually over to Half Moon Bay. Towards the end of the month he broke his arm, but that didn't stop him. He had his cast fitted to the handle bars. Also added to his schedule is a diet of well-balanced meals and relaxing nights; no late parties. Due to his schedule and his seriousness about racing, he does have to sacrifice most activities on campus such as joining any clubs. "It will pay off," he said.

When asked how he got started in racing, he replied, "In 1976 I saw the Red Zinger Bicycle Classic. These racers were held next door to me in Denver, Colorado. A year later I was able to ride with these same racers."

Vance's decision to come to Marlow . . .

DEPARTING DEANS DISCUSS GOALS FOR MARLOW

Though many students aren't aware of it, Marlow will lose two deans effective at the end of this semester. Both Dean of Students Richard Thompson and Business School Dean John Dennis have decided to pursue other directions. Richard Thompson is retiring, while John Dennis will move on to Metro University as Associate Dean of the School of Education. Both men expressed their reservations in leaving Marlow, and discussed their hopes for the future of the college.

Richard Thompson told the Press, "I would like to see the students raise their standard of priorities more towards studying and also show some intellectual curiosity." S.B.A. Dean Dennis would like to see "increased use of cases, instead of lectures or textbook approaches, and more courses stressing quantitative and qualitative approaches simultaneously." He also felt that "Business students are spending a lot more time studying and there is increased seriousness, but the level of business writing could be improved." Dennis added that there should be a full-time business writing staff.

When asked about his replacement, the Dean of Students replied, "He or she should be interested in students, forthright, and consistent in his or her judgments." Thompson's responsibilities included those of the Director of Athletics, but, he felt, "It is not necessary for [my replacement] to take on both responsibilities as long as separate Deans cooperate with each other."

Both Deans agreed they will miss the contact with students that they enjoyed at Marlow.

Richard Thompson, in his ninth year here, spent 29 years in the U.S. Marine Corps as an aviator, and was a commanding officer in the Naval R.O.T.C. He also spent three "controversial" years during the Vietnam Era as the Professor of Naval Science at Stanford University.

John Dennis, who became the Dean of the Business School four years ago, received his Master's Degree in Business at the Harvard Business School and his Doctorate of Education at Stanford University.

Selections for the two Dean positions are to be made prior to the end of the Spring semester.

"HARDBODIES" FLASHES 90 MINUTES OF TASTELESS TRASH

The ads promise that *Hardbodies* is "more hilarious than *Gandhi*." Well it is, at least a little bit. But then, *Gandhi* is not comedy. And to put it simply, neither is *Hardbodies*.

Hardbodies is likely to be the most tasteless movie of the year. The plot is almost nonexistent, the characters are ridiculously exaggerated stereotypes, and the acting is revoltingly inept.

The movie deals with three wealthy, sex-starved businessmen, played by Garth Wood, Michael Rapport, and Sorrels Puckard, who lease the best house on the beach and try to meet girls.

Of course, they are hopeless—until they meet Scotty Palmer (Grant Cramer), the "hunk" of the town. Scotty generously agrees to teach the men to get "hardbodies" ("the foxy little things on the beach," Scotty explains) for a mere $600 a month plus full use of the house.

Scotty teaches them "dialogue" and explains how to offer girls a "B.B.D." or "Bigger and Better Deal." Predictably, all three are hopeless at first. But they improve with practice, as well as haircuts and completely new wardrobes, all chosen by Scotty.

The three then decide to have a party, with all the hardbodies invited. The party is a smashing success, as are the three now-capable men, who each gets a girl. They continue having more of these parties, and therefore, more of the girls.

The movie continues in this moronic fashion until one man, Hunter, becomes a bit over-zealous in his pursuit of the opposite sex. Scotty sides with the object of Hunter's lust, so Hunter promptly fires him. In addition, Hunter gets Scotty's girlfriend, Kristy, to break up with Scotty.

Eventually, but not soon enough for anyone watching the movie, Kristy realizes that Scotty is the only man that she (along with just about every other girl in the town) truly loves. So she returns to him and decides to go back to college and to live with Scotty.

The ostensible stars of the movie are the four men. But the real star is *skin*, because that's almost all that anyone wears throughout the movie. It seems that the girls of this town enjoy nothing more than tearing off their clothes at any given time or place and jumping into bed with the nearest male. And when they do have clothes on, they generally limit themselves to bathing suits that leave almost nothing to the imagination.

I think I laughed about three times throughout this hour and a half of mindless drivel. *Hardbodies* is about four cuts below the last major teen sex flick, *Porky's*, if that level of trash can be imagined.

In short, *Hardbodies* is probably the worst way to spend five dollars available. For a "B.B.D.," watch the break-dancers in the parking lot. They're free.

FINAL JOURNAL ENTRY

Go back and re-read your whole journal from beginning to end. List approximately four to six subjects that you wrote about most frequently—things that kept "popping up" over and over again. For example, you might have repeatedly mentioned certain people, a concern about grades, parties, values, sports, animals, jealousies, physical health, appearance, school, politics, your future, love, death, the weather. . . .

Then, take each of these "themes" and explain fully how you feel about each one now, and whether you have developed or altered your views since you began your journal.

This final journal entry is to be shared with me, so if there are certain sentences or paragraphs that you wish to keep completely private, be sure to delete them (temporarily) just before you print a copy to hand in. Your journal entry will never be read by anyone but me, unless you choose to share it.

GLOSSARY

applications program: *see* tool program.

block of text: in a word processing progam a section of text can be marked (typically by inserting a specific symbol at the beginning and end of the section, or highlighting it) and then moved, deleted, or manipulated in some other way. The specific section of text is called a block of text.

boogie board: a small surfboard; also called a belly board.

boot: to load a program into the computer's memory. This must be done before the computer can follow any instructions.

branching story: a story that periodically offers the reader choices concerning what will happen next. Each time the reader makes a choice, the story follows that particular story line, or "branch," of the story "tree." A story thus has many possible branches and many possible endings.

buffer: a place in the computer's memory where data may be temporarily stored.

bulletin board: an electronic bulletin board is like a traditional bulletin board in that it is available for people to post or read messages. However, to use an electronic bulletin board, a person has to "call up" the board (using a modem or otherwise connecting electronically) so that the bulletin board appears on the computer screen. Then the user can read messages, or post messages by entering them on the keyboard.

camera-ready: copy that's in its final form for photo printing.

central processing unit (CPU): the part of the computer that controls the operations. It receives instructions, decodes them, executes them, and prepares them for delivery back to the user.

character: in computer language, a character is a letter, number, or symbol that can be entered into the computer by an input device, typically the keyboard.

cinquain: a particular type of poetry form. The software program mentioned in this book that teaches the cinquain, introduces two types: the syllable pattern form and the metaphor form that's created by specific parts of speech.

compatible: *hardware compatible* means that the components can be used with the particular computer system. *Software compatible* means that information can be passed freely between the two programs.

component: the units or separate devices that connect to make a computer system. System components include the Central Processing Unit (CPU), display screen, keyboard, disk drive, printer, etc.

computer center: a room designated as the place where several computers will be housed, and often where they must be used. Secondary schools and colleges typically place computers in computer centers, also called computer labs.

computer lab: *see* computer center.

computer language: the programming language that consists of machine codes which the computer understands, such as machine language and assembly language (*see* programming language).

computer literacy: there are many levels of definitions for this term. Some educators believe it means an introductory understanding of how computers work, what they can and cannot do, and how to operate a microcomputer system. Some educators believe that learning to program a computer is part of becoming computer literate. Others feel that learning to use a variety of applications programs, such as word processing, data base, and spreadsheet programs, is more appropriate for attaining computer literacy.

copy: the text and graphics being prepared for publication.

courseware: tutorial software that is designed to help students learn specific skills.

CPU: *see* central processing unit.

cursor: a small marker on the sceen that indicates where information may be entered. In a word processor the cursor marks where the next character will be entered and it moves from left to right as the user types. When editing text, the cursor can be moved freely around the text to the position where changes will be made.

data: a collection of letters, numbers, and/or symbols.

data bank: an accumulation of information that's been filed and stored using a data base program.

data base: a set of related data organized into a format that enables the user to sort and/or retrieve the data by a variety of index labels. Users can usually add data and revise it freely, as well as use the data base information for a variety of different purposes.

disk drive: a device that stores information on a disk and retrieves it when needed. It sends the data to and from the computer to which it is connected. Floppy disk drives have slots in front for inserting the floppy disks. Hard disk drives seal the permanent hard disks, which then cannot be removed.

Dvorak: the newer keyboard layout that was designed so that the most frequently used letters and letter combinations are on the home row keys. The Dvorak home row keys are: AOEUHTNS (*see* QWERTY).

electronic mail: messages, letters, files, etc., that are sent electronically from one computer to another (*see* telecommunications/network).

electronic network: *see* network.

embedded format commands: some word processing programs enable the user to give format commands in the middle of a document; these are called embedded format commands. For example, if a user wants to underline a word in the text, he or she would insert a command before and after the word to be underlined. The rest of the text would not be affected by this format command (*see* format).

error message: When there is something wrong with the program, or the user has made a mistake, an error message that attempts to describe the problem usually appears on the screen.

external memory: (*see* memory).

file: information to be stored in a computer needs to be divided into blocks, called *files*. Users generally organize this information into logical units, similar to files stored in a file drawer. The user gives each file a heading, and each file includes information that pertains to the subject heading.

floppy disk: a thin, flat, round, flexible piece of Mylar that's coated with a film of magnetic material on which data can be recorded. Floppy disks are commonly 8″, 5 ½″, or 3 ¼″ in diameter. When inserted into a floppy disk drive they can be used to store and retrieve mass amounts of information externally. Floppy disks are also called floppies, flexible disks, diskettes, etc.

format: when writing and printing with a word processor, the *format* is the way the information is arranged on the page. Elements of formatting include margins, line spacing, type font, boldface, underline, etc. Format commands in a word processing program are the instructions a user gives (via keyboard or mouse) concerning the format of a document.

graphics tablet: a flat device connected to the computer that is used with a pen-like object to draw graphics which will appear on the display screen (*see* input device).

hairlines: very thin, straight lines that may be added to a page layout to separate blocks of copy.

half-tone: the process of preparing photographic prints of photos and artwork for publication. The half-toned prints consist of minute dots that can be altered to produce a gradation of dark and light tones.

head, or **headline:** the title, or caption of a printed article, section, chapter, etc., typically printed in large, boldface letters.

Subheads are smaller headlines that separate and label sections of the article.

help display: short messages that remind users of keyboard commands, or otherwise try to help users proceed when they are having trouble. Help menus present a selection of the types of help messages available.

help menu: *see* help display.

icon: In computer language an icon is a small graphic symbol that appears on the screen display and indicates a particular function or command the user may select. Icons are sometimes presented with, or instead of, words in the menu.

information: a collection of letters, numbers, and/or symbols that is meaningful to a person.

input: (1) the data entered into the computer by a user for processing; (2) the data received by a computer from a connected input device; (3) to enter commands or information into the computer via keyboard, mouse, or other input device.

input device: a device connected to the computer that's used to enter data, such as a keyboard, mouse, joystick, graphics tablet, lightpen, etc.

integrated: integrated software is fully compatible, which means that information can be passed freely and quickly between the programs with no additional translation or aid needed. Integrated programs are often located on the same disk.

internal memory: *see* memory.

jacuzzi: a pump that throws hot water in and around a large tub of water. It originated as a device for hydrotherapy, but became popularized as a means of relaxing in a hot tub. Used loosely, the term means both a pump and a hot tub.

joystick: a lever mounted on a box that can be manually tilted in many directions in order to move the cursor around the computer screen (*see* input device).

justify: to arrange text so that the first and/or last characters in every line are at the edge of the margin. Text is commonly left justified with ragged right margins, or right and left justified so that both sides of the printed page have straight margins.

keyboard: an input device connected to the computer that looks somewhat like a typewriter keyboard. When pressed, a key sends a signal to the computer that represents a particular letter, number, or other symbol (*see* input device).

keyboarding skills: learning to use the alphabetic, numeric, symbol, and function keys on a computer and/or typewriter keyboard.

ladder: in publishing, a ladder is a page-by-page list of what will appear on each page of a publication. A ladder is often used to keep track of yearbook pages.

lay out: to arrange text and graphics on its designated page.

layout: the arrangement of text and graphics on a page.

lightpen: a pen-like device connected to the computer that can be used to draw graphics on the display screen (*see* input device).

load: (1) to insert a disk into a disk drive (or cassette into a tape recorder, etc.); (2) to transfer information from mass storage (e.g., a disk) to the computer's internal memory.

memory: the components of the computer system that hold data. The system's *internal*, or *volatile*, memory is inside the computer and will disappear when the computer is turned off. The *external* memory is the information stored on disks (cassettes, etc.) that will not disappear when the system is turned off. The data in external memory may be loaded into the computer's internal memory for immediate use. The amount of information a computer's internal memory can hold is measured in kilobytes (1,024 bytes). Computers differ in their internal memory capacity, but the ones most commonly used in schools and homes have anywhere from 48K to 512K of internal memory.

menu: similar to the menu offered at a restaurant, a program menu offers the computer user a list of choices. These selections are displayed on the screen and they include various functions the software program can instruct the computer to perform.

micro: an abbreviated term for microcomputer (*see* microcomputer).

microcomputer: the smallest kind of computer (minicomputers and mainframe computers are larger). Microcomputers were originally distinguished from the larger computers because the microcomputer's CPU was all on one chip, called a microprocessor. Now some larger computers also use microprocessors.

mnemonic: a word that is easy to remember. Users sometimes think up mnemonics to help them remember keyboard commands. For example, if Control-B is the keyboard command in a word processing program used to reformat a paragraph after it has been edited, the mnemonic for the command could be "Beautify," meaning beautify the paragraph.

mode: a method or category of operation. A word processing program may have several modes of operation, such as *write* mode (for entering text) and *edit* mode (for adding and deleting text).

modem: an acronym for MOdulator–DEModulator. It's a device that transforms digital data from a computer into analog data that can be transmitted over communication lines to another modem, which transforms the analog data back to digital data so the receiving computer can process it.

mouse: a device connected to the computer that is manually rolled around a flat surface in order to control the cursor on the screen. It also has buttons for selecting menu items or giving commands (*see* input device).

muktuk: whale skin; Eskimo villagers chew it like gum.

network: a computer network is a communication system comprised of more than one computer (or one computer plus terminals) that are connected for the purpose of sharing software programs and/or information.

package: in computer language it usually refers to a software program or set of programs and support materials (e.g., user's

manual, tutorial, warranty card, etc.) that are marketed together.

productivity tool: *see* tool program.

program: *see* software program.

programming language: a set of code words and rules that determine the way instructions must be written to create a program that will run on the computer. High level languages, such as BASIC, Pascal, and Logo contain English words and syntax rules. However, a low level language such as machine language, which contains binary codes the computer understands, and a component that translates the high level language into a low level language, are also needed for the program to run.

QWERTY: the traditional standard keyboard layout. QWERTY stands for the keys that are located on the third row from the bottom, left-hand side. The QWERTY layout was designed to slow down fast typists, so they wouldn't jam the old manual typewriter keys. The home row keys are: ASDFJKL;.

 search and replace: the word processing feature that enables a user to search through a file for a specific word or set of characters and then replace it with a new word or set of characters.

shell program: a loosely structured program that provides the user with a format. The user must then fill the shell with useable material, such as exercises, activities, etc.

sized: printed text or graphics that have been enlarged or shrunk by a photo process in order to make them fit the page layout.

software: computer systems need both hardware and software to operate. The software is the program instructions and data that tells the hardware what to do and also contains the resulting information (*see* software program).

software program: a set of instructions that directs a computer to perform certain operations. The program is usually written in a programming language (such as BASIC, Pascal, or Logo which also has a translator component that can translate the language into machine language that the computer understands.

speech synthesizer: a device that converts numerical code that the computer understands into speech that a person can understand. Formerly a special speaker was needed; however, currently the internal speakers in some computers can be used, so that the speech synthesizer is actually a software program.

spelling checker: a software program that loads a dictionary into the computer's memory and then compares every word of a text file with the dictionary. It then indicates the words from the text that were not recognized by the dictionary and provides a format for the user to change or ignore the unrecognized words. Unrecognized words may include misspelled words, typos, or correctly spelled words with prefixes, suffixes, tense forms, etc., that the dictionary doesn't list. Some spelling checkers can also offer a choice of correctly spelled words that appear similar to the unrecognized word.

split-screen editing: some word processing programs enable the user to get two files on the screen simultaneously. One method for displaying the text of the two files is to split the screen in half, displaying one file on top and the other on the bottom portion of the screen. The user can then edit either file as well as move parts of one file to the other.

telecommunications: the process of transmitting data over distances electronically. Computer files can be sent and received via telephone lines or satellite relay.

text: the words of something written or printed (*see* text file).

text editor: a capability that enables the user to enter text and then edit it. The text editor in a full word processing program typically includes many kinds of editing functions. A very simple text editor only provides minimum editing functions.

text file: a computer file is labeled according to what kind of data it includes; a text file is generally a word processing file that contains primarily sentences and paragraphs (*see* file).

tool program: a software program designed to serve many purposes; it is intended to be a general purpose aid that can help with a variety of jobs. Some example tool software: word processing programs, data base programs, spreadsheet programs, graphics programs.

troilet: a particular type of poetry form. The software program mentioned in this book that teaches the troilet describes it as a French poetic form with a refrain. It includes eight lines and requires that the first, fourth, and seventh lines are identical, and the second and eighth lines are identical. The lines must have the same rhyme or a two-rhyme pattern.

typewriting skills: the development of speed and accuracy at the keyboard as well as the application of those skills in a production mode.

user: the person who is operating the computer system. *Users* also refers to individuals who frequently operate computers.

waxed: when laying out a page of a publication, the text, photos, and graphics that have been sized to fit the page are then *waxed* on the back so they'll stick on the layout sheets.

word wrap: the feature in most word processing programs that automatically continues a line of characters down to the next line on the screen. The return key is generally used to indicate a new paragraph.

yankback: a feature in some word processing programs that enables the user to retrieve text that has just been deleted. When the user deletes text it goes into a temporary storage buffer so that it can be called back immediately (if the length of the text doesn't exceed the buffer limit, and if there haven't been other commands following the deletion).